A joint produ[...]
agencies of th[...]

C000234100

Motoring Info[...]

Distance Chart - Motorway Information   B

Motorway Schemata   C-G

Legend to National Maps   H

National Maps   1

City Maps   71

71 Dublin   81 Limerick
73 Belfast   82 Lisburn
75 Cork   83 Newry
77 Londonderry   84 Waterford
78 Armagh
79 Galway
80 Kilkenny

Golf Information   85

Gazetteer   87

Motoring Information Republic of Ireland

	EXAMPLES
Regulatory Traffic signs Generally circular with a red border and black symbol or letters on a white background. These signs must be obeyed they show a course a driver must follow and an action they are required to take or forbidden to take. Mandatory Regulatory signs are blue and white These signs indicate the direction traffic must take at junctions.	Pass Either Side Traffic May Not Proceed in the Direction of the Arrow STOP YIELD
Warning traffic signs These signs are diamond or rectangular in shape and have a black border symbol or letters on a yellow background. These signs warn road users of hazards ahead. These signs will have an orange backgroud for roadworks.	Sharp Corner Ahead Roundabout Ahead Series of Bends Ahead T Junction with Dual Carriageway Advance Warning of a Major Road Ahead Junction Ahead With Roads of Less Importance Junction Ahead with Road or Roads of Equal Importance T Slippery Stretch of Road Ahead Sharp Rise Ahead Road Works Ahead
Direction/Information signs These signs show directions and the location of services or places of tourist interest. Blue background motorway. Green background national road. White background Regional road Brown background Tourist information.	4 km 2 km  Slí na Bóinne BOYNE DRIVE Eolas do Thurasóirí TOURIST INFORMATION
General Speed limits Motorways 120km/h National primary and secondary 100km/h Regional and local roads 80km/h Built up areas 50km/h You must obey speed limit signs at all times. Speed limits can vary for different vehicle types.	120 100 80 60 50 30 km/h Maximum speed limit

Motoring Information Northern Ireland

Traffic signs: Signs giving orders Signs with red circles are mostly prohibitive. Signs with blue circles but no red border mostly give positive instruction.	Give priority to vehicles from the opposite direction No left turn Motor vehicles prohibited No U-turns No right turn Turn left (right if symbol reversed)
Traffic signs: Warning signs Mostly triangular.	Crossroads Double bend, first to the left (may be reversed) Two-way traffic Road narrows on both sides Staggered junction STOP 100 yds Distance to "Stop" line ahead
Traffic signs: Direction signs Mostly rectangular. Signs on motorways - blue backgrounds. Signs on primary routes - green backgrounds. Signs on non-primary and local routes - black borders	Craigavon A3 Dungannon A29 Newry A28 Roundabout ahead at junction of two primary routes Cullybackey B93 Rasharkin B64 Junction ahead of two non-primary routes M1 Start of motorway End of motorwa
General Speed limits Motorways 70mls/h Elsewhere 60/70mls/h Built up areas 30mls/h You must obey speed limit signs at all times. Speed limits can vary for different vehicle types.	70 60 50 30 Maximum speed limit National speed limits apply

Distance Chart / Motorway Information

Scála 1:210 000 / Scale 1:210 000

Scale bar: 5 · 0 Kilometres · 5 · 10 · 15 · 20
3 · 0 Miles · 3 · 6 · 9 · 12

Kilometres in black - 100
Miles in blue - 62

Distances — Kilometres (black)

	Athlone	Armagh	Belfast	Cork	Londonderry	Donegal	Dublin	Dundalk	Lisburn	Galway	Kilkenny	Killarney	Larne	Limerick	Newry	Portlaoise	Roscommon	Rosslare Harbour	Shannon Airport	Sligo	Waterford	Wexford
Armagh	158																					
Belfast	60	227																				
Cork	424	383	219																			
Londonderry	428	117	109	209																		
Donegal	69	402	180	127	183																	
Dublin	222	237	257	167	129	126																
Dundalk	85	158	156	325	84	145	145															
Lisburn	69	154	174	129	409	14	51	212														
Galway	294	238	219	204	272	209	306	237	93													
Kilkenny	172	278	198	117	309	335	148	284	264	126												
Killarney	198	193	457	652	309	407	441	87	436	389	232											
Larne	470	319	330	50	116	204	228	114	451	34	93	261										
Limerick	357	111	113	105	349	241	198	296	328	105	323	278	121									
Newry	265	95	402	219	264	47	21	105	158	140	351	61	29	163								
Portlaoise	190	114	285	225	51	150	237	151	84	257	282	174	253	212	74							
Roscommon	106	171	151	249	264	158	82	217	151	146	151	211	251	224	156	32						
Rosslare Harbour	241	135	259	211	364	275	100	274	309	246	163	391	297	208	330	285	209					
Shannon Airport	235	154	138	286	24	381	135	137	92	370	265	222	283	351	129	346	264	134				
Sligo	219	327	85	191	177	232	240	343	245	138	188	167	217	66	135	336	206	157	117			
Waterford	293	153	85	208	100	267	129	367	193	48	220	319	243	158	357	383	126	333	293	174		
Wexford	63	307	214	19	222	114	240	190	346	254	80	253	294	227	142	372	378	178	309	264	188	
Wicklow	90	141	261	251	116	198	124	158	227	243	335	124	270	203	137	51	275	288	267	219	177	177

Distances — Miles (blue)

	Athlone	Armagh	Belfast	Cork	Londonderry	Donegal	Dublin	Dundalk	Lisburn	Galway	Kilkenny	Killarney	Larne	Limerick	Newry	Portlaoise	Roscommon	Rosslare Harbour	Shannon Airport	Sligo	Waterford	Wexford
Armagh	98																					
Belfast	37	141																				
Cork	264	238	136																			
Londonderry	266	73	68	130																		
Donegal	43	250	112	79	114																	
Dublin	138	147	160	104	80	78																
Dundalk	53	98	97	202	52	90	90															
Lisburn	43	96	108	80	254	9	32	132														
Galway	183	148	136	127	169	130	190	147	58													
Kilkenny	107	173	123	73	192	208	92	177	164	78												
Killarney	123	120	284	219	192	253	274	54	271	242	144											
Larne	292	198	205	31	72	127	142	71	280	21	58	162										
Limerick	222	69	70	65	217	150	123	184	204	65	201	173	75									
Newry	165	59	250	136	164	29	13	65	98	87	218	38	18	101								
Portlaoise	118	71	177	140	32	93	147	94	52	160	175	108	157	132	46							
Roscommon	66	106	94	155	164	98	51	135	94	91	94	131	156	139	97	20						
Rosslare Harbour	150	84	161	131	226	171	62	170	192	153	101	243	247	129	205	177	130					
Shannon Airport	146	96	86	178	15	237	84	85	57	230	165	138	176	218	80	215	164	83				
Sligo	136	203	53	119	110	144	149	213	152	86	117	104	135	41	84	209	128	93	73			
Waterford	182	95	51	129	62	166	80	228	120	30	137	198	151	98	222	238	78	207	185	108		
Wexford	39	191	133	12	138	71	149	118	215	158	50	157	183	141	88	231	235	116	192	164	117	
Wicklow	56	88	162	156	72	123	77	98	141	151	208	77	168	126	85	32	171	179	166	136	110	110

Key to Motorway Schemas

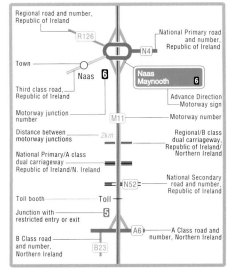

- Regional road and number, Republic of Ireland — R126
- National Primary road and number, Republic of Ireland — N4
- Town
- Naas
- Naas / Maynooth — Advance Direction Motorway sign — 6
- Third class road, Republic of Ireland
- Motorway junction number
- Motorway number — M11
- Distance between motorway junctions — 2km
- Regional/B class dual carriageway, Republic of Ireland/Northern Ireland
- National Primary/A class dual carriageway, Republic of Ireland/N. Ireland
- National Secondary road and number, Republic of Ireland — N52
- Toll booth — Toll
- Junction with restricted entry or exit — 5
- B Class road and number, Northern Ireland — B23
- A Class road and number, Northern Ireland — A6

The following Motorway Schemas show the major motorway routes and junctions for Ireland.

These maps are for route planning only indicating to drivers the junction numbers showing the exit and entry sliproads complete with relevant signage.

The schemas are not to scale and therefore do not indicate the length of the road.

Motoring Schemata

M11 Bray Bypass

North

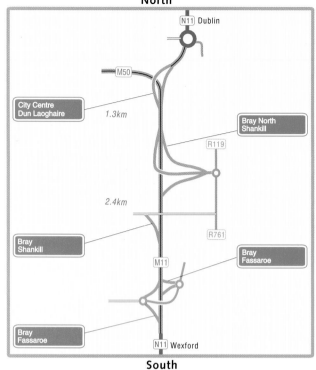

South

M4 Leixlip to Kinnegad

West

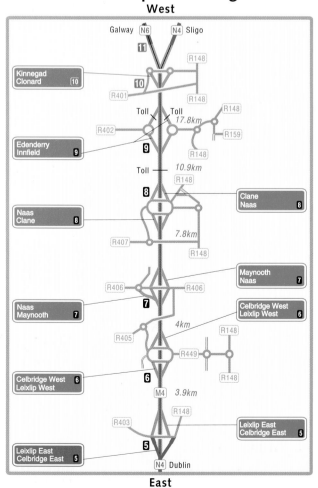

East

M8 Kilworth to Dunkettle

North

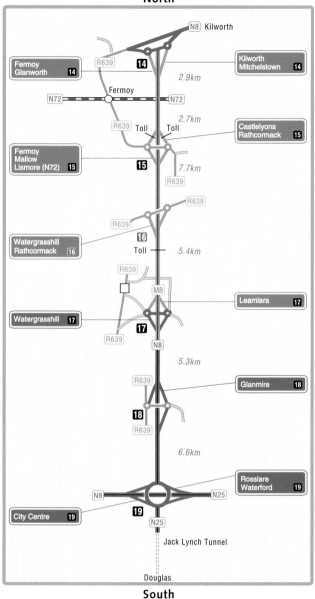

South

M1 Dublin to Drogheda
North

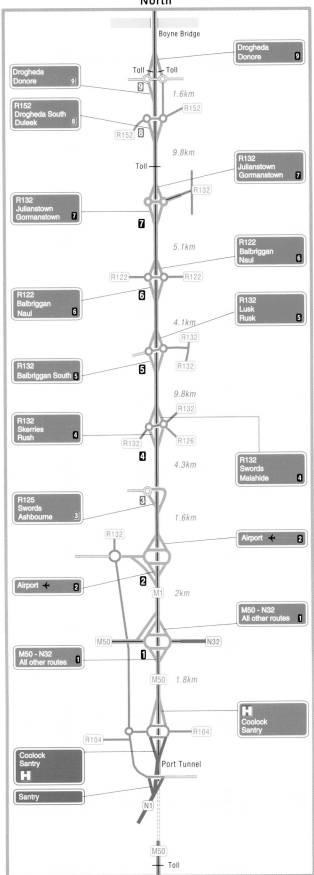

M1 Drogheda to Belfast
North

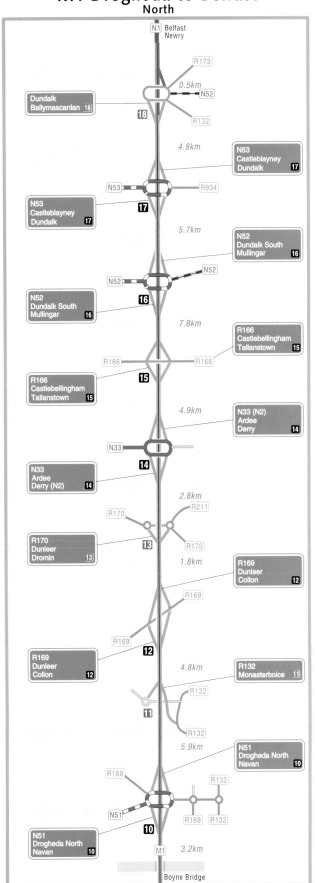

South

Motoring Schemata

M50 Bray to Ballymount

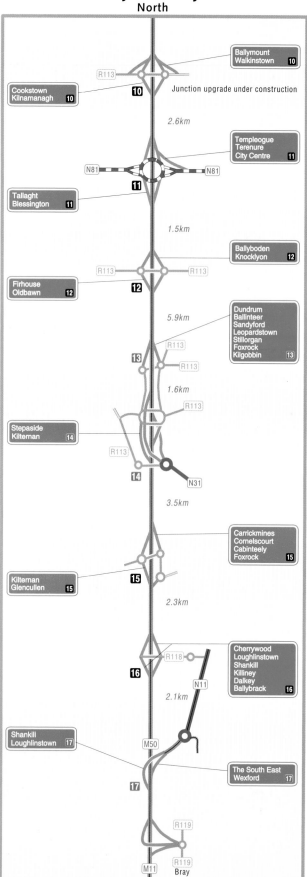

North

Ballymount
Walkinstown 10

Cookstown
Kilnamanagh 10

10

Junction upgrade under construction

2.6km

R113

Templeogue
Terenure
City Centre 11

N81 — N81

Tallaght
Blessington 11

11

1.5km

Ballyboden
Knocklyon 12

R113 — R113

Firhouse
Oldbawn 12

12

5.9km

Dundrum
Ballinteer
Sandyford
Leopardstown
Stillorgan
Foxrock
Kilgobbin 13

R113

13

R113

1.6km

R113

Stepaside
Kilternan 14

R113

14

N31

3.5km

Carrickmines
Cornelscourt
Cabinteely
Foxrock 15

Kilternan
Glencullen 15

15

2.3km

Cherrywood
Loughlinstown
Shankill
Killiney
Dalkey
Ballybrack 16

R118

16

N11

2.1km

Shankill
Loughlinstown 17

M50

The South East
Wexford 17

17

R119

R119
Bray

South

M50 Ballymount to East Wall

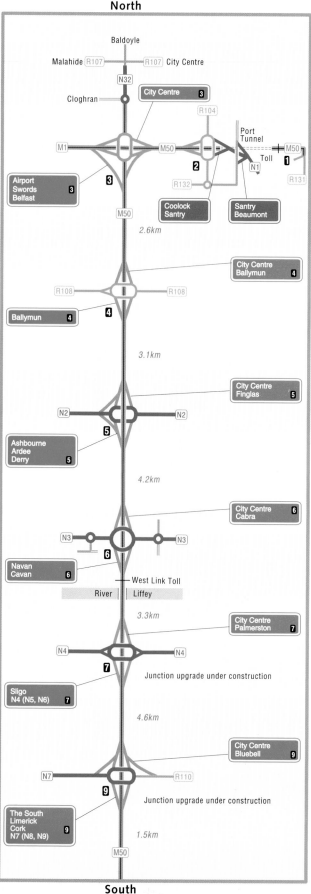

North

Baldoyle

Malahide R107 — R107 City Centre

N32

Cloghran

City Centre 3

R104

Port
Tunnel

M1 — M50 — Toll

2

M50

N1 — M50

R132

R131

Airport
Swords
Belfast 3

3

Coolock
Santry

Santry
Beaumont

2.6km

City Centre
Ballymun 4

R108 — R108

Ballymun 4

4

3.1km

City Centre
Finglas 5

N2 — N2

Ashbourne
Ardee
Derry 5

5

4.2km

City Centre
Cabra 6

N3 — N3

Navan
Cavan 6

6

West Link Toll

River | Liffey

3.3km

City Centre
Palmerston 7

N4 — N4

7

Junction upgrade under construction

Sligo
N4 (N5, N6) 7

4.6km

City Centre
Bluebell 9

N7 — R110

9

Junction upgrade under construction

The South
Limerick
Cork
N7 (N8, N9) 9

1.5km

M50

South

Motorway Schemata

M7 Naas to Portlaoise

West

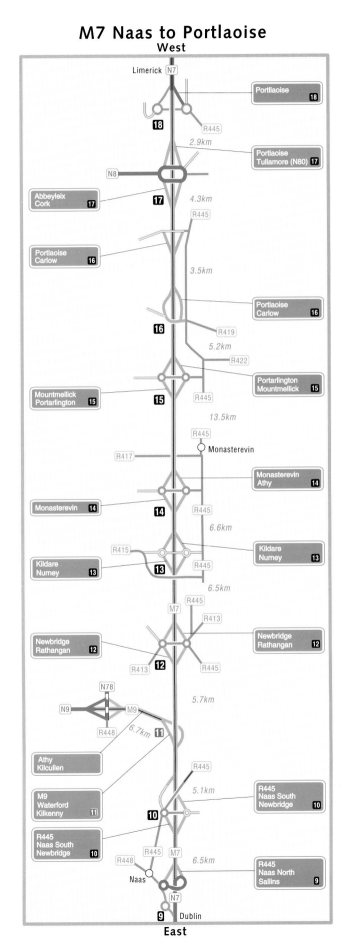

Limerick [N7]

Portllaoise [18]

[18]

[R445]

2.9km

Portlaoise
Tullamore (N80) [17]

[N8]

[17]

Abbeyleix
Cork [17]

4.3km

[R445]

Portlaoise
Carlow [16]

3.5km

Portlaoise
Carlow [16]

[16]

[R419]

5.2km

[R422]

Portarlington
Mountmellick [15]

Mountmellick
Portarlington [15]

[15]

[R445]

13.5km

[R445]

[R417]

○ Monasterevin

Monasterevin
Athy [14]

Monasterevin [14]

[14]

[R445]

6.6km

Kildare
Nurney [13]

Kildare
Nurney [13]

[13]

[R445]

6.5km

[R445]

[M7]

[R413]

Newbridge
Rathangan [12]

Newbridge
Rathangan [12]

[R413] [12]

[R445]

5.7km

[N78]

[N9] [M9]

[R448] 6.7km [11]

Athy
Kilcullen

M9
Waterford
Kilkenny [11]

[R445]

5.1km

R445
Naas South
Newbridge [10]

R445
Naas South
Newbridge [10]

[10]

[R445] [M7]

[R448] 6.5km

Naas ○

R445
Naas North
Sallins [9]

[N7]

[9] Dublin

East

M1 Belfast to Maghery

West

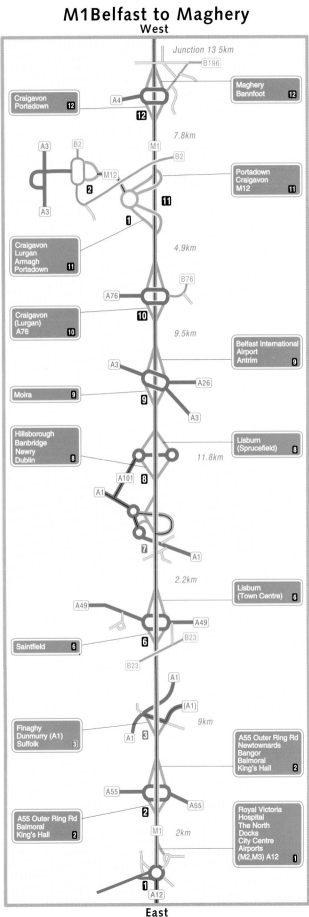

Junction 13 5km

[B196]

Craigavon
Portadown [12]

[A4]

[12]

Maghery
Bannfoot [12]

[A3] [B2] [M1]

[B2]

[M12]

2

[A3]

Portadown
Craigavon
M12 [11]

1

[11]

Craigavon
Lurgan
Armagh
Portadown [11]

4.9km

[A76] [B76]

Craigavon
(Lurgan)
A76 [10]

10

9.5km

Belfast International
Airport
Antrim [9]

[A3]

Moira [9]

9

[A26]

[A3]

Hillsborough
Banbridge
Newry
Dublin [8]

Lisburn
(Sprucefield) [8]

[A101]

8

11.8km

[A1]

[A1]

7

[A1]

2.2km

Lisburn
(Town Centre) [6]

[A49]

[A49]

Saintfield [6]

6

[B23]

[B23]

[A1]

(A1)

Finaghy
Dunmurry (A1)
Suffolk [3]

9km

[A1]

3

A55 Outer Ring Rd
Newtownards
Bangor
Balmoral
King's Hall [2]

[A55]

[A55]

A55 Outer Ring Rd
Balmoral
King's Hall [2]

2

[M1]

Royal Victoria
Hospital
The North
Docks
City Centre
Airports
(M2,M3) A12 [1]

2km

1

[A12]

East

Motoring Schemata

M1 Maghery to Dungannon

West

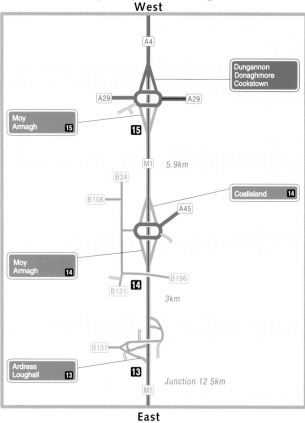

A4

Dungannon
Donaghmore
Cookstown

A29 | A29

Moy
Armagh **15**

15

M1 | 5.9km

B34

B106

Coalisland **14**

A45

Moy
Armagh **14**

14 | B196

B131

3km

B131

Ardress
Loughall **13**

13

Junction 12 5km

M1

East

M2 Ballymena Bypass

North

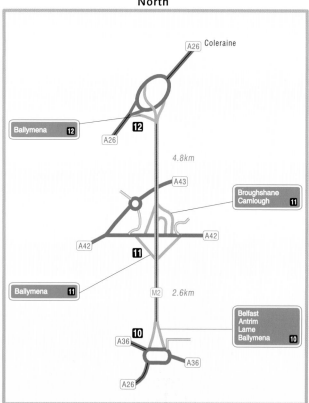

A26 Coleraine

Ballymena **12**

12

A26

4.8km

A43

Broughshane
Carnlough **11**

A42 | A42

11

Ballymena **11**

M2 | 2.6km

Belfast
Antrim
Larne
Ballymena **10**

10

A36 | A36

A26

South

M2, M22 Belfast to Randalstown

West

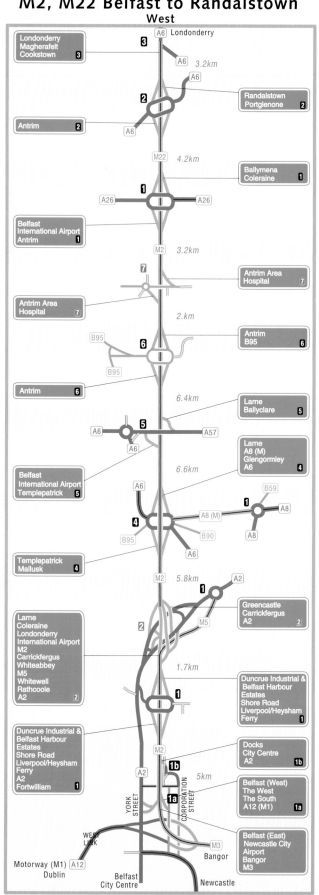

A6 Londonderry

Londonderry
Magherafelt
Cookstown **3**

3

A6 | 3.2km

A6

Randalstown
Portglenone **2**

2

Antrim **2**

A6

M22 | 4.2km

Ballymena
Coleraine **1**

A26 | **1** | A26

Belfast
International Airport
Antrim **1**

M2 | 3.2km

7

Antrim Area
Hospital **7**

Antrim Area
Hospital **7**

2.km

B95

Antrim
B95 **6**

6

B95

Antrim **6**

6.4km

Larne
Ballyclare **5**

A6 | **5** | A57

A6

Larne
A8 (M)
Glengormley
A6 **4**

Belfast
International Airport
Templepatrick **5**

A6

6.6km

B59

1

A8 (M) | A8

4

B90 | A8

Templepatrick
Mallusk **4**

B95

A6

M2 | 5.8km | A2

1

Larne
Coleraine
Londonderry
International Airport
M2
Carrickfergus
Whiteabbey
M5
Whitewell
Rathcoole
A2 **2**

Greencastle
Carrickfergus
A2 **2**

M5

2

1.7km

Duncrue Industrial &
Belfast Harbour
Estates
Shore Road
Liverpool/Heysham
Ferry **1**

Duncrue Industrial &
Belfast Harbour
Estates
Shore Road
Liverpool/Heysham
Ferry
A2
Fortwilliam **1**

M2

1

Docks
City Centre
A2 **1b**

1b

YORK STREET

CORPORATION STREET

5km

A2

1a

Belfast (West)
The West
The South
A12 (M1) **1a**

WEST
LINK

M3

Belfast (East)
Newcastle City
Airport
Bangor
M3

Motorway (M1) A12
Dublin

Belfast
City Centre

Bangor

Newcastle

East

Legend To National Maps

	Gaeilge	English	Français	Deutsch
M 1 ... 1	Mótarbhealach (Uimhreacha ceangail)	Motorway (Junction number)	Autoroute (Numero de l'échangeur)	Schnellstraße (Nummer der Anschlussstelle)
N 11 / A 11	Bóthar príomha náisiúnta	National Primary Road	Route nationale principale	Nationalstraße erster Ordnung
N 71	Bóthar tánaisteach náisiúnta	National Secondary Road	Route nationale secondaire	Nationalstraße zweiter Ordnung
	Bóthar á dhéanamh	Road under construction	Route en construction	Straße im Bau
R 574 / B 202	Bóthar Réigiúnach	Regional Road	Route Régionale	Landstraße
	Bóthar den tríú grád	Third Class Road	Route de troisieme classe	Straße dritter Ordnung
7	Achair bhóthair (I gciliméadair)	Road Distances (in kilometres)	Distances routières (en kilomètres)	Entfernung (in Straßenkilometern)

In Northern Ireland roads are designated by the letter A, B or M.

In the Republic of Ireland roads are designated by the Letter N, R or M.

The representation on these maps of a Road, Track or Path is no evidence of a right of way.

	Gaeilge	English	Français	Deutsch
	Láithreán (idrthurais carbhán)	Caravan site (transit)	Terrain de camping (pour caravanes)	Campingplatz für Wohnwagen
	Láithreán campála	Camping site	Terrain de camping	Campingplatz
	Brú de chuid (An Óige)	Youth Hostel (An Óige)	Auberge de Jeunesse (An Óige)	Jugendherberge (An Óige)
	Brú saoire Neamhspleách	Independent Holiday Hostel	Auberge de vacances Internationale	Unterknuftsmöglichkeit
P	Ionad pairceála	Parking	Parking	Parkplatz
	Láithreán picnicí	Picnic site	Áire de Pique-nique	Picknickplatz
	Ionad dearctha	Viewpoint	Point de vue	Aussichtspunkt
Northern Ireland	Ionad eolais turasóireachta (ar oscailt ar feadh na bliana)	Tourist Information (regular opening)	Information Touristique (ouverture régulière)	Touristeninformation (regeimäßig geöffnet)
Northern Ireland	Ionad eolais turasóireachta (ar oscailt le linn an tséasúir)	Tourist Information centre (restricted opening)	Information Touristique (ouverture limitée)	Touristeninformation (beschränkte Öffnungszeiten)
	Tearmann Dúlra	Nature Reserve	Réserve naturelle	Natureschutzgebiet
A T Republic of Ireland	An Taisce ar oscailtar feadh na bliana	An Taisce always open	Propriété du An Taisce ouverte toute l'année	An Taisce Immer geöffnet
N T Northern Ireland	National Trust ar oscailtar feadh na bliana	National Trust always open	Propriété du National Trust ouverte toute l'année	National Trust Immer geöffnet
N T Northern Ireland	National Trust ar oscailt le linn an tséasúir	National Trust opening restricted	Propriété du National Trust ouverte en saison	National Trust nur während der saison geöffnet

	Gaeilge	English	Français	Deutsch
	Cathair/Baile mór	City/large town	Grande ville/ville	Großstadt/Stadt
○	Baile eile	Other towns	Autres villes	Andere Städte
⊕	Aerfort	Airport	Aéroport	Flughafen
	Aerpháirc	Airfield	Aerodrome	Flugzeuglandeplatz
	Galfchúrsa, machaire gailf	Golf Course or Links	Terrain de Golf	Golfplatz oder Golfbahnen

	Gaeilge	English	Français	Deutsch
⸸	Ardeaglais	Cathedral	Cathédrale	Kathedrale
○	Stáisiún cumhachta (uisce)	Power Station (Hydro)	Centrale électrique (hydraulique)	Kraftwerk (Wasser)
◉	Stáisiún cumhachta (breosla iontaiseach)	Power Station (Fossil)	Centrale électrique (fossile)	Kraftwerk (fossile Brennstoffe)
CH •	Séadchomhartha Ainmnithe	Named Antiquities	Monuments mentionnes	Namentlich aufgeführte altetümer
(1798)	Láthair Chatha (le dáta)	Battlefield (with date)	Champ de bataille (avec date)	Schlachtfeld (datiert)
■	Ionaid eile spéisiúla	Other Place of interest	Autre cuiosité Sonstige	Sehenswüdigkeit
	Ráschúrsa	Race Course	Hippodrome	Rennplatz
	Loch	Lake	Lac	See
	Canáil, canáil (thirim)	Canal, Canal (dry)	Canal, Canal á sec	Kanal, Kanalbecken (trocken)
	Abhainn nó sruthán	River or Stream	Rivière ou Ruisseau	Fluß oder Bach
	Teach Solais in úsáid/as úsáid	Lighthouse in use/disuse	Phare que fonctionne/ désaffecté	Leuchtturm benutzt/ unbenutzt
	Líne bharr láin	High Water Mark	Marque des hautes eaux	Hochwasserstand
shingle, mud sand or loose rock	Line lag trá	Low Water Mark	Marque des basses eaux	Niedrigwasserstand
	Cuan/Cladach	Marina/Mooring	Marina/Amarrage	Marina/Verankern
	Trá (Bratach Gorm 2003)	Beach (Blue Flag 2003)	Plage (Drapeau blue 2003)	Strand (Blaue Markierungsfahne
Ferry V	Bád fartha (feithiclí)	Ferry (Vehicle)	Bac (véhicules)	2003)
Ferry P	Bád fartha (paisinéirí)	Ferry (Passenger)	Bac (Passager)	Fähre (Fahrzeuge)

	Gaeilge	English	Français	Deutsch
Disused Railway	Iarnróid	Railways	Chemins de fer	Bahnlinie
	Staisiún traenach	Station	Gare	Bahnhof
	Tollán	Tunnel	Tunnel	Tunnel
LC	Crosaire comhréidh level	Crossing	Passage á niveau	Bahnübergang
	Teorainn idirnáisiúnta	International Boundary	Frontières internationales	Landergrenze
••••••••	Teorainn chontae	County boundary	Limite du Comté	Grafschaftsgrenze
	Páirc Náisiúnta	National Park	Parc National	Nationaler Park

	Gaeilge	English	Français	Deutsch
	Relíf	Relief	Relief	Relief
	>550m	250-550m	150-250m	0-150m
△ 647	Cuaille triantánachta	Triangulation Pillar	Pilier de Triangulation	Trigometrische Säule
123 •	Spota airde	Spot Height	Point Cuminant	Höhenpunkt

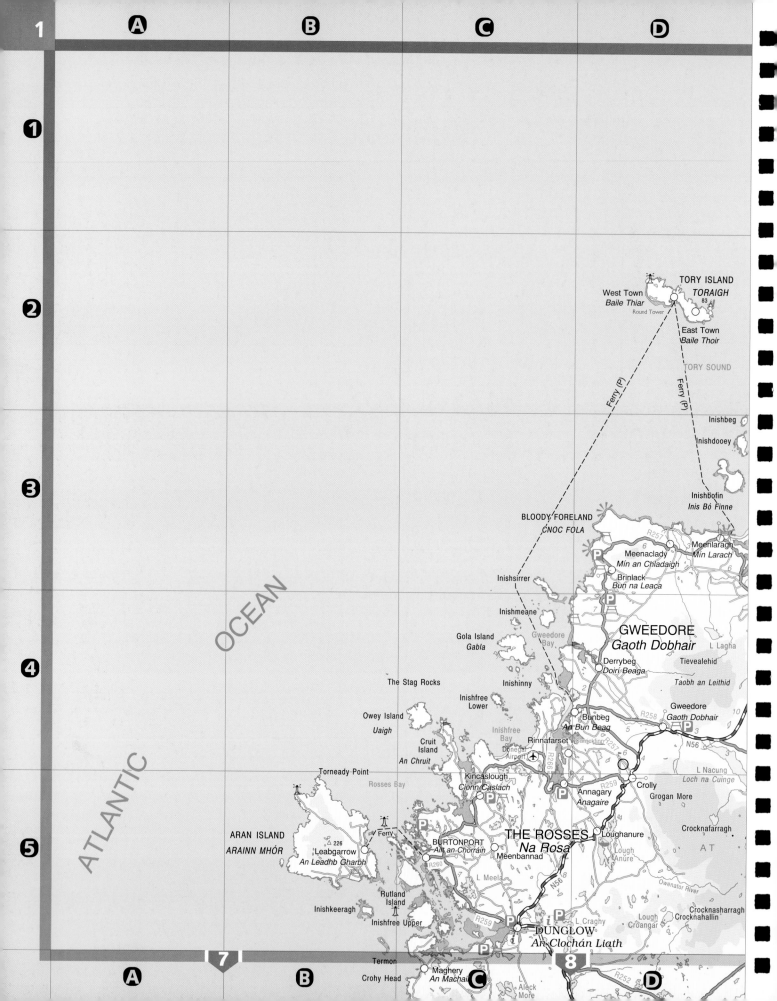

Ⓐ Ⓑ Ⓒ Ⓓ

❶

❷

❸

❹

❺

OCEAN

ATLANTIC

TORY ISLAND
TORAIGH

West Town
Baile Thiar
Round Tower
83

East Town
Baile Thoir

TORY SOUND

Ferry (P)

Ferry (P)

Inishbeg

Inishdooey

Inishbofin
Inis Bó Finne

BLOODY FORELAND
CNOC FOLA

R257

Meenlaragh
Mín Larach

Ⓟ

Meenaclady
Mín an Chladaigh

6

Brinlack
Bun na Leaca

Inishsirrer

Ⓟ 7

Inishmeane

Gweedore
Bay

GWEEDORE
Gaoth Dobhair

L Lagha

Gola Island
Gabla

Derrybeg
Doirí Beaga

Tievealehid

The Stag Rocks

Inishinny

Taobh an Leithid

Inishfree
Lower

2

Gweedore
Gaoth Dobhair

R258

10

Owey Island

Uaigh

Bunbeg
An Bun Beag

Ⓟ

3

Cruit
Island

Inishfree
Bay

Rinnafarset

Crannckfinn

R257

5

N56

An Chruit

Donegal
Airport

R262

L Nacung

Torneady Point

Kincaslough
Cionn Caslach

4

Loch na Cuinge

Rosses Bay

R259

Crolly

Grogan More

ARAN ISLAND
ARAINN MHÓR

△ 226

Ferry

Ⓟ

Annagary
Anagaire

Crocknafarragh

Leabgarrow
An Leadhb Gharbh

Ⓟ

BURTONPORT
Ailt an Chorráin

THE ROSSES
Na Rosa

Loughanure

Lough
Anure

A T

R260

Meenbannad

84

Inishkeeragh

L Meela

N56

Crocknasharragh
Crocknahallin

Rutland
Island

R259

Ⓟ

Ⓟ

L Craghy

Lough
Croangar

Owenator River

Inishfree Upper

Ⓟ ℹ **DUNGLOW**
An Clochán Liath

ℹ

Termon

Maghery
An Machair

Ⓟ

L
Aleck
More

R252

Ⓐ Ⓑ Ⓒ **8** Ⓓ

Crohy Head

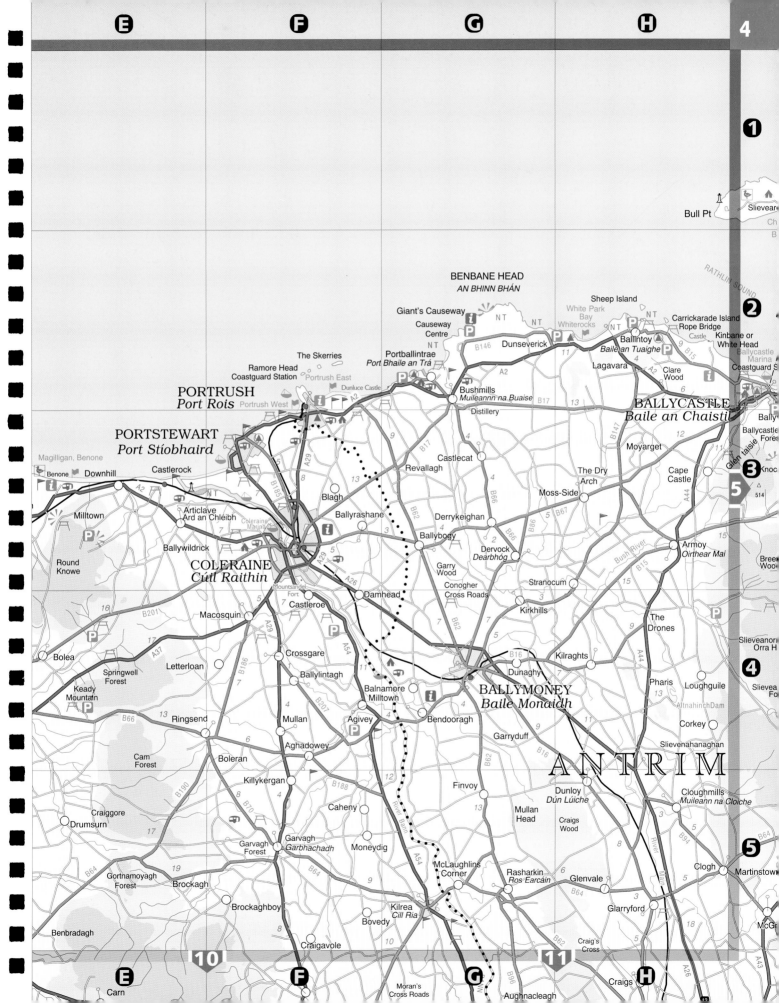

BENBANE HEAD
AN BHINN BHÁN

Bull Pt
Slievear

RATHLIM SOUND

Sheep Island

Giant's Causeway
Causeway
Centre
White Park
Bay
Whiterocks
Carrickarade Island
Rope Bridge
Kinbane or
White Head

The Skerries
Portballintrae
Port Bhaile an Trá
Ramore Head
Coastguard Station
Portrush East

Dunseverick
B146
A2
Ballintoy
Baile an Tuaighe
Lagavara
Clare
Wood
Castle
Ballycastle
Marina
Coastguard S

Bushmills
Muileannn na Buaise
Distillery
B17
13
BALLYCASTLE
Baile an Chaistil
Bally
Ballycastle
Fores

PORTRUSH
Port Rois
Portrush West
Dunluce Castle

Castlecat
Revallagh
B17
Moyarget
Glen taisie
12

PORTSTEWART
Port Stíobhaird
Magilligan, Benone
Benone
Downhill
Castlerock
Coleraine
Marina
Blagh
9
13
Ballyrashane
B62
Ballybogy
Derrykeighan
B66
The Dry
Arch
Moss-Side
B66
B67
Cape
Castle
A44
Knoc
514
Knoc

Milltown
Articlave
Ard an Chléibh
NT
Coleraine
Marina
4
4
Dervock
Dearbhóg
Armoy
Oirthear Mai
15
Bree
Woo

Round
Knowe
Ballywildrick
COLERAINE
Cúil Raithin
A29
Garry
Wood
Conogher
Cross Roads
Stranocum
Bush River
B15
15

Bolea
B201
16
Macosquin
A29
Mountsandel
Fort
Damhead
A26
B62
Kirkhills
The
Drones

Springwell
Forest
17
Crossgare
A54
Ballylintagh
11
Dunaghy
Kilraghts
A44
Slieveanor
Orra H

Keady
Mountain
B186
Letterloan
B207
Balnamore
Milltown
4
BALLYMONEY
Baile Monaidh
Bendoorragh
Pharis
13
Loughguile
Slievea
Fo

Ringsend
B66
13
Mullan
Agivey
Garryduff
B62
B16

Cam
Forest
Aghadowey
Boleran
B62

Craiggore
Drumsurn
17
Killykergan
B190
Caheny
B188
12
River Bann
Finvoy
13
Mullan
Head
Craigs
Wood
Dunloy
Dún Lúiche
Cloughmills
Muileann na Cloiche
B94

Gortnamoyagh
Forest
Brockagh
B70
B64
Garvagh
Forest
Garvagh
Garbhachadh
Moneydig
A54

Benbradagh
B64
19
Brockaghboy
9
Kilrea
Cill Ria
Bovedy
10
McLaughlins
Corner
Rasharkin
Ros Earcáin
6
Glenvale
B64
Glarryford
18
Clogh
Martinstow
B94
McG

ANTRIM

Carn
Craigavole
Moran's
Cross Roads
Aughnacleagh
B96
Craig's
Cross
Craigs
A26
A43

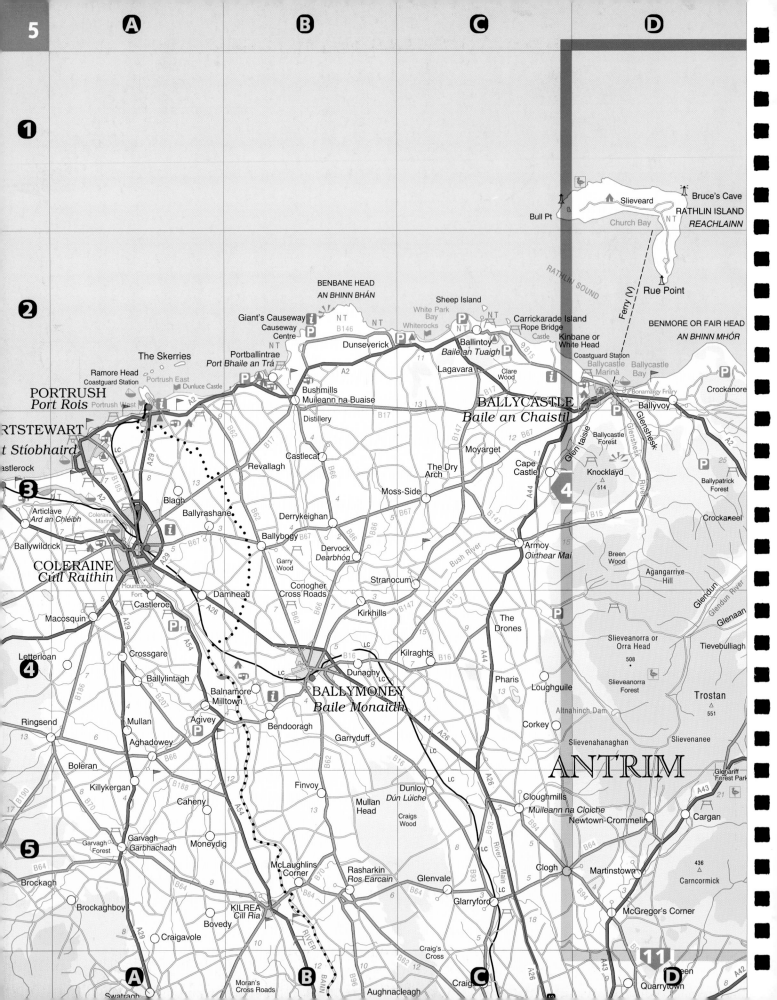

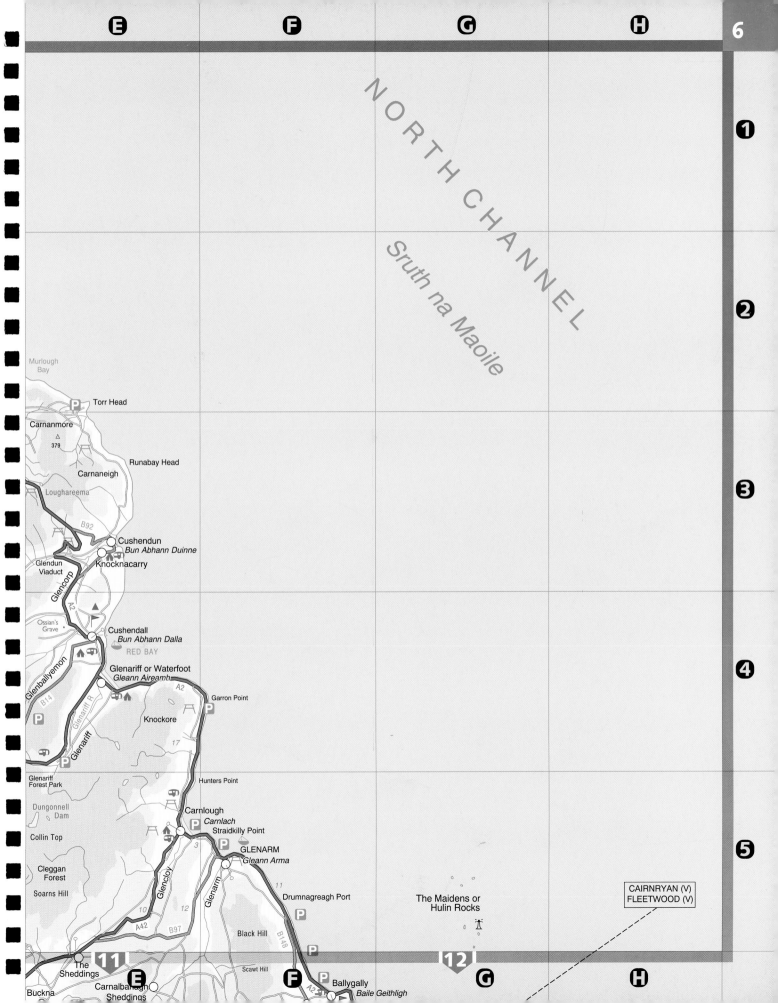

1

2

NORTH CHANNEL

Sruth na Maoile

Murlough
Bay

Torr Head

Carnanmore

△
379

Runabay Head

Carnaneigh

Loughareema

3

B92

Cushendun
Bun Abhann Duinne

Glendun
Viaduct   Knocknacarry

Glencorp

A2

Ossian's
Grave

Cushendall
Bun Abhann Dalla

RED BAY

Glenballyemon

Glenariff or Waterfoot
Gleann Aireamh

Glenariff R.

A2

Garron Point

B14

Knockore

P

4

Glenariff

17

P

Glenariff
Forest Park

Hunters Point

Dungonnell
Dam

Carnlough
Carnlach
P   Straidkilly Point

Collin Top

Glencloy

3

P

GLENARM
Gleann Arma

Cleggan
Forest

Glenarm

11

Drumnagreagh Port

Soarns Hill

The Maidens or
Hulin Rocks

CAIRNRYAN (V)
FLEETWOOD (V)

5

10

12

A42   B97

Black Hill

B148

P

The
Sheddings

11

Scawt Hill

P

12

Buckna   Carnalbanagh
Sheddings

E

F   P   Ballygally
Baile Geithligh

G

H

Inishkeeragh

Termon

Roaninish

Narin

Dunmore Head

Portnoo
Port Nua

Dawros Head

Rossbeg
Ros Beag
Lough
Kiltooris

Inishbarnog

Sheskinmore
Lough

LOUGHROS MORE BAY

Loughros Point

Loughros Beg
Bay

Crannogeboy

Tormore Island

Slievetooey

• 511

Port Hill

Glengesh
Hill

Glengesh Pass
Forest

Sturall

Crockuna

Lough
Nalugraman

Croaghacullion

Meenacross

Glen
Head

Crocknamurrin

Glencolumbkille

R230

Crocknapeast

497

Rossan
Point

Malin More

Glencolumbkille
Gleann Cholm Cille

Meenaneary

Mulnanaff

R263

8

Cloghanmore

9

Malin Bay

L
Inna

Malin Beg
Málainn Bhig

Carrick
An Charraig

Clonasillagh
Forest

Rathlin O'Birne
Island

Slieve

△
595

League

5

Crownarad

Teelin
Tieleann

Kilcar
Cill Charthaigh

12

Largy

Carrigan Head

R263

Fintra

Muckros
Head

Fintragh
Bay

Drumanoo
Head

Inishduff

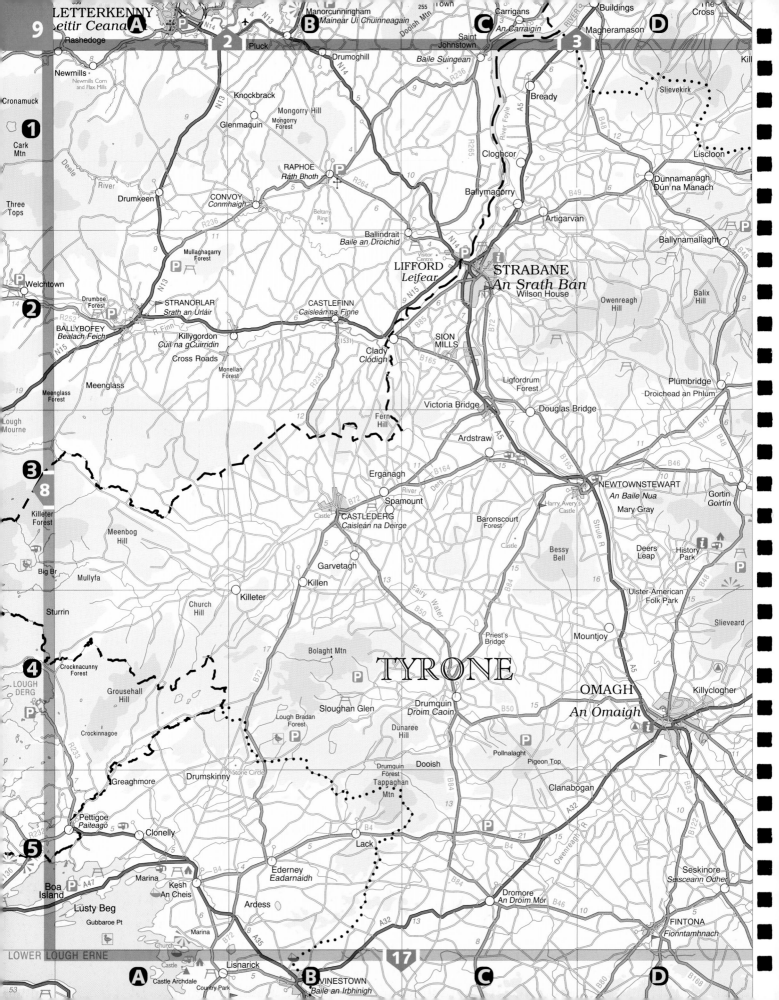

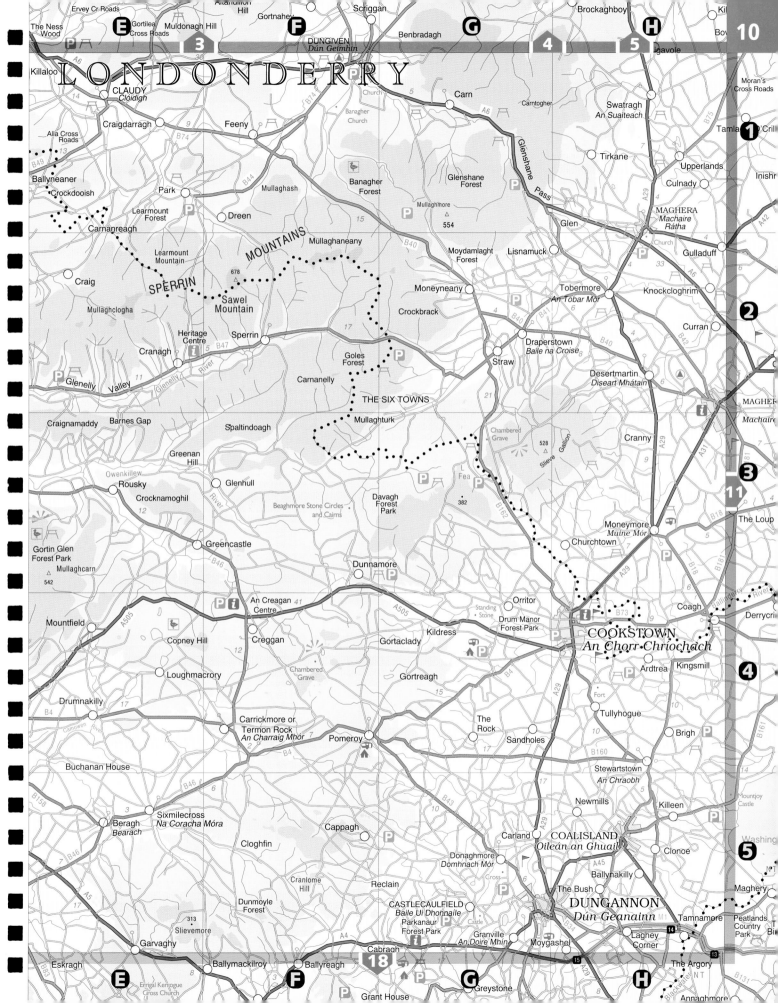

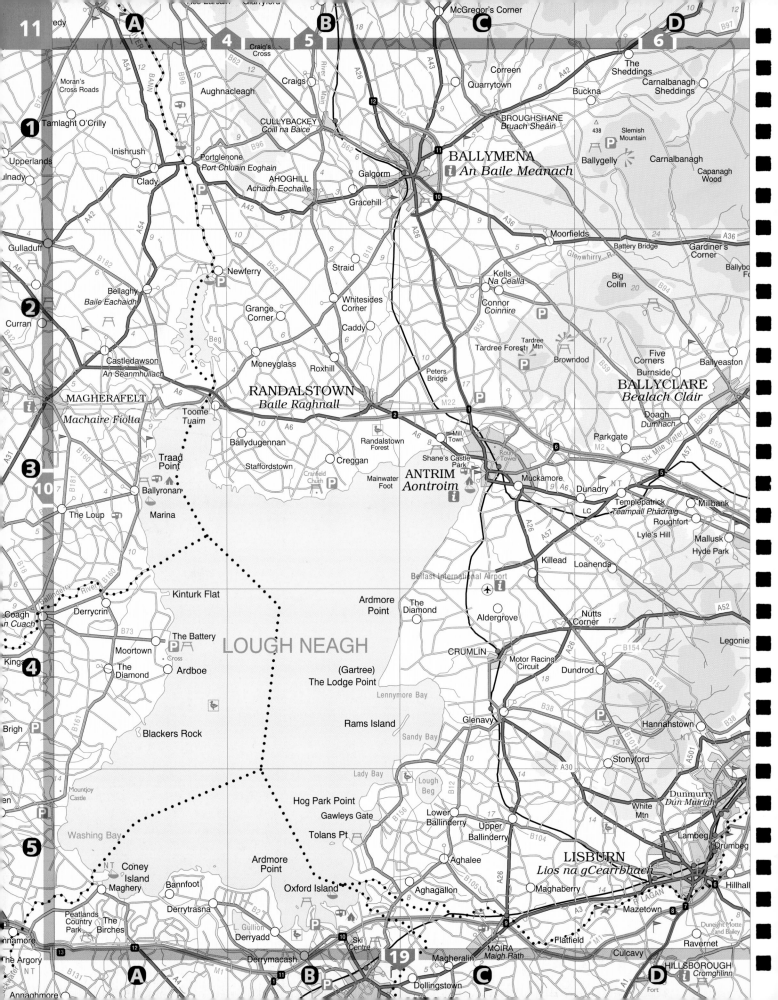

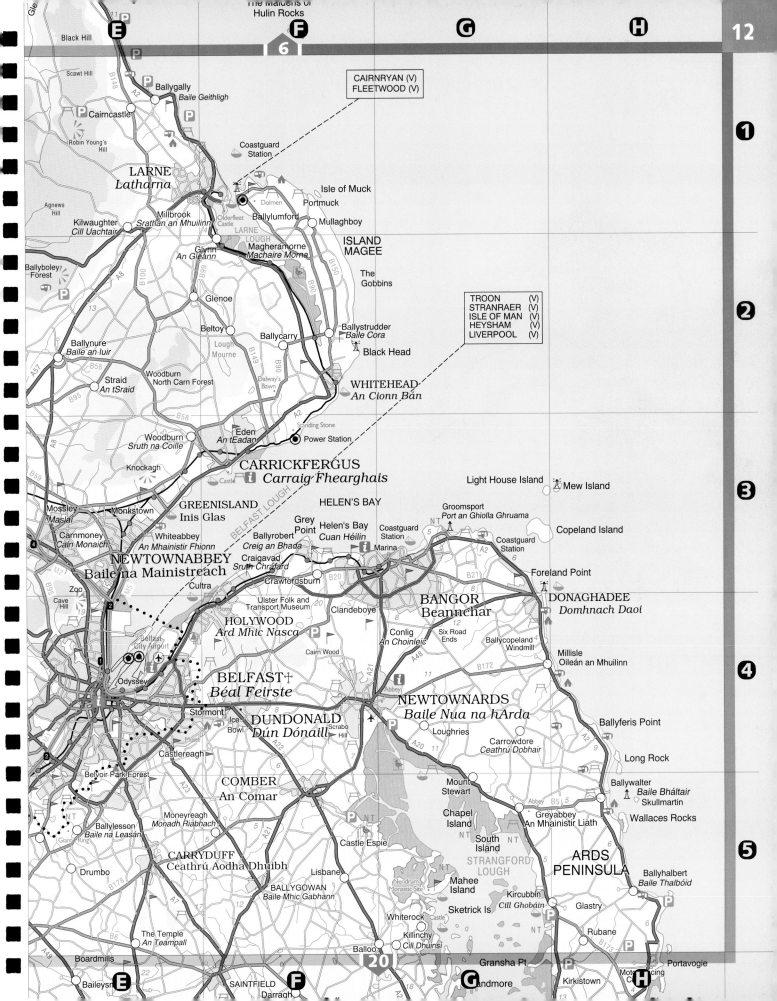

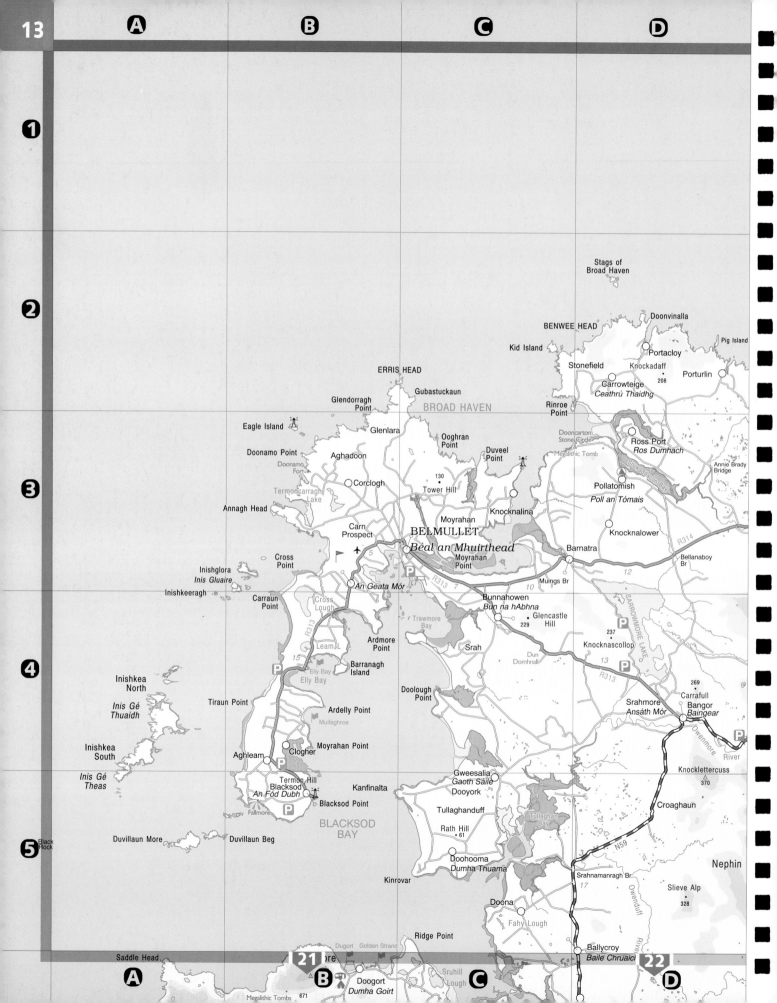

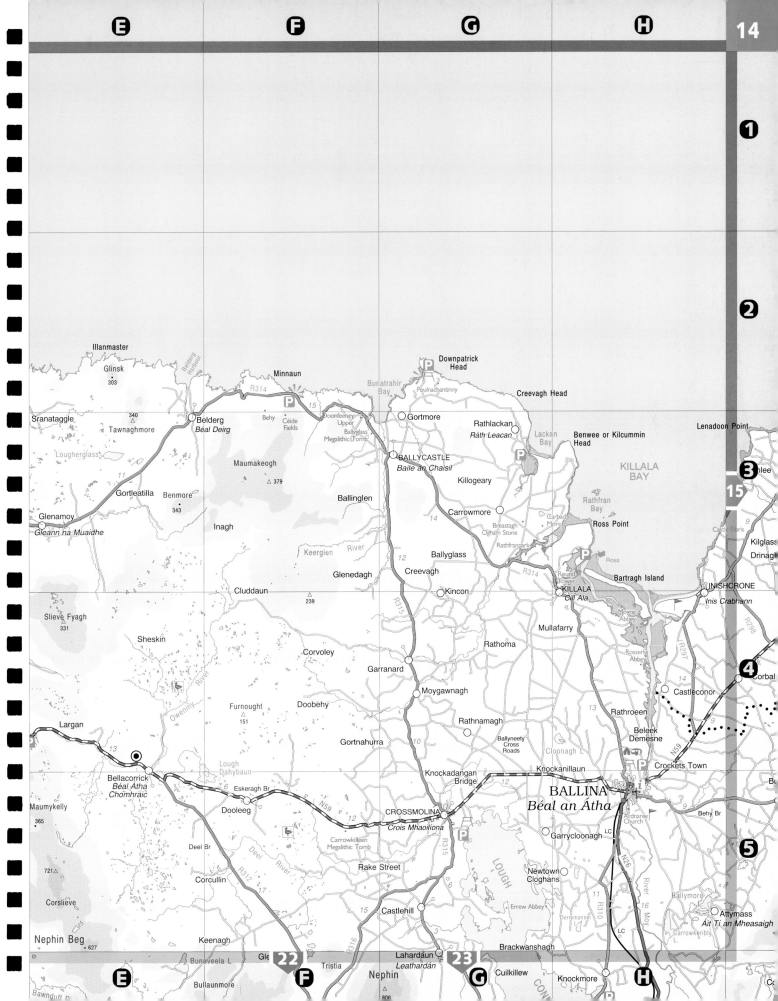

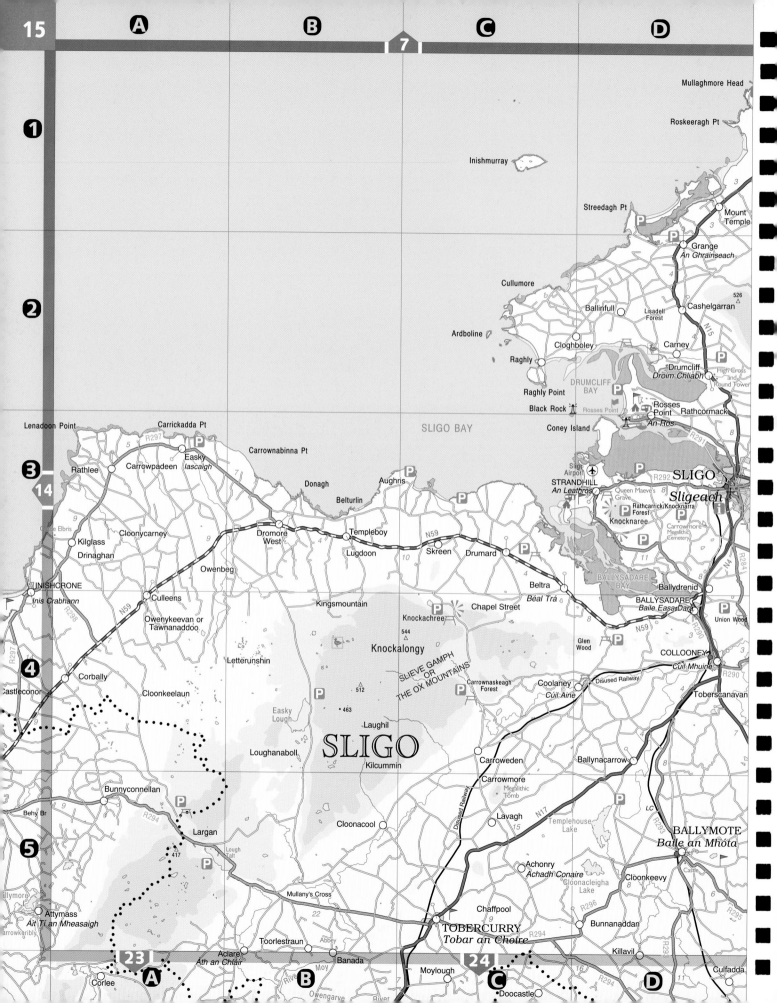

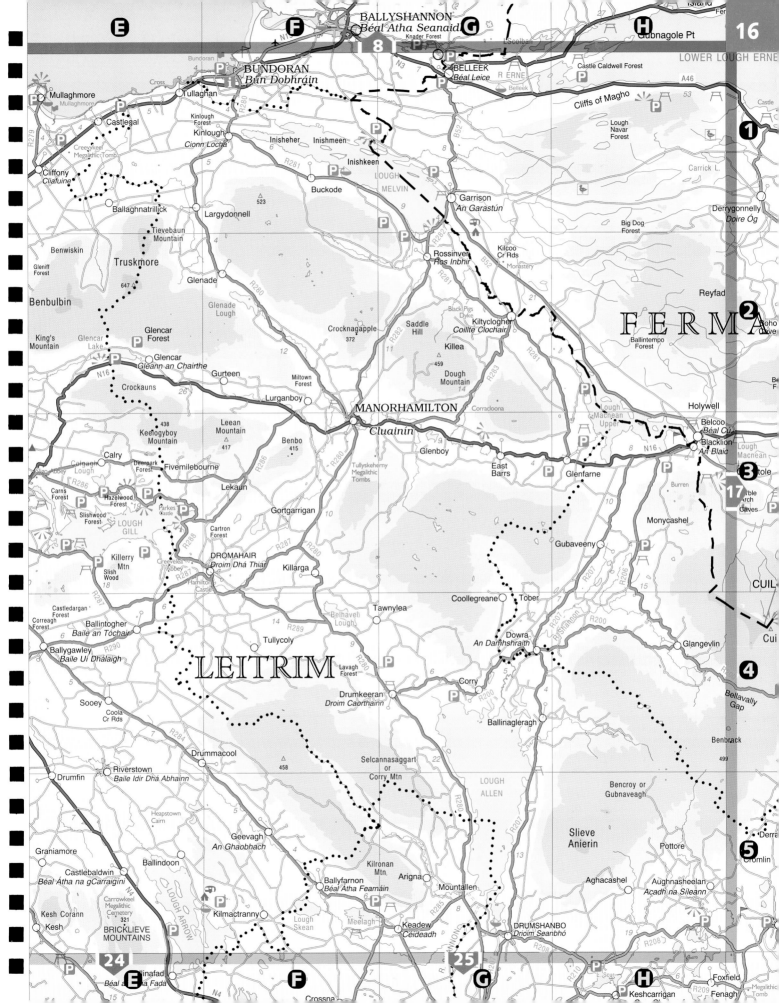

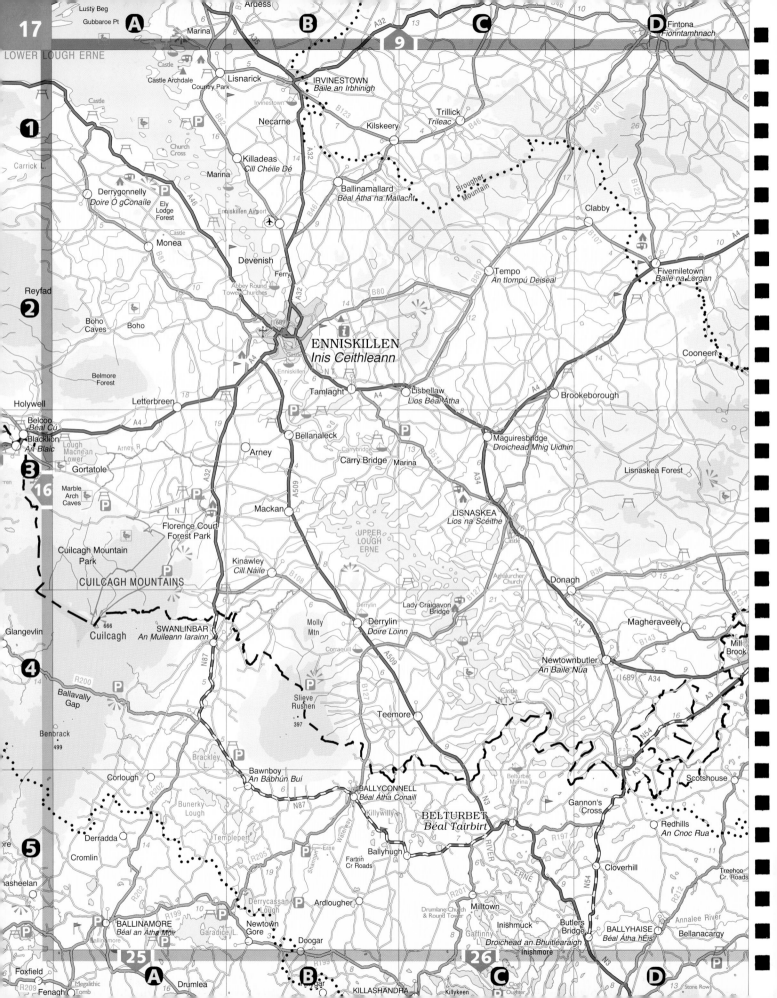

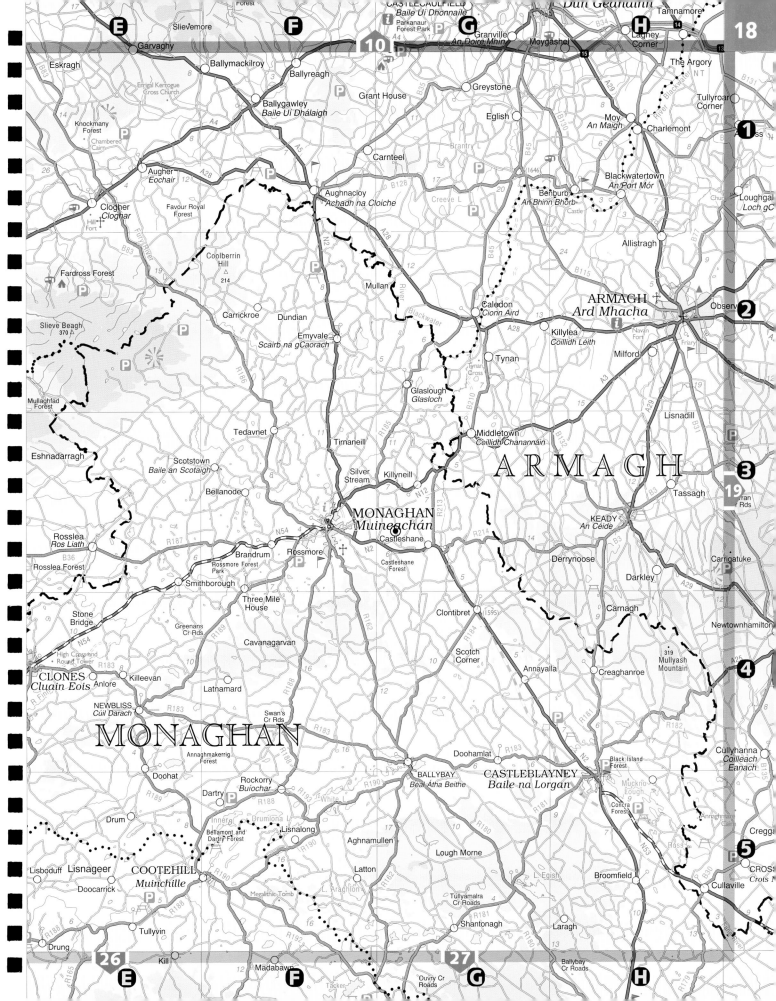

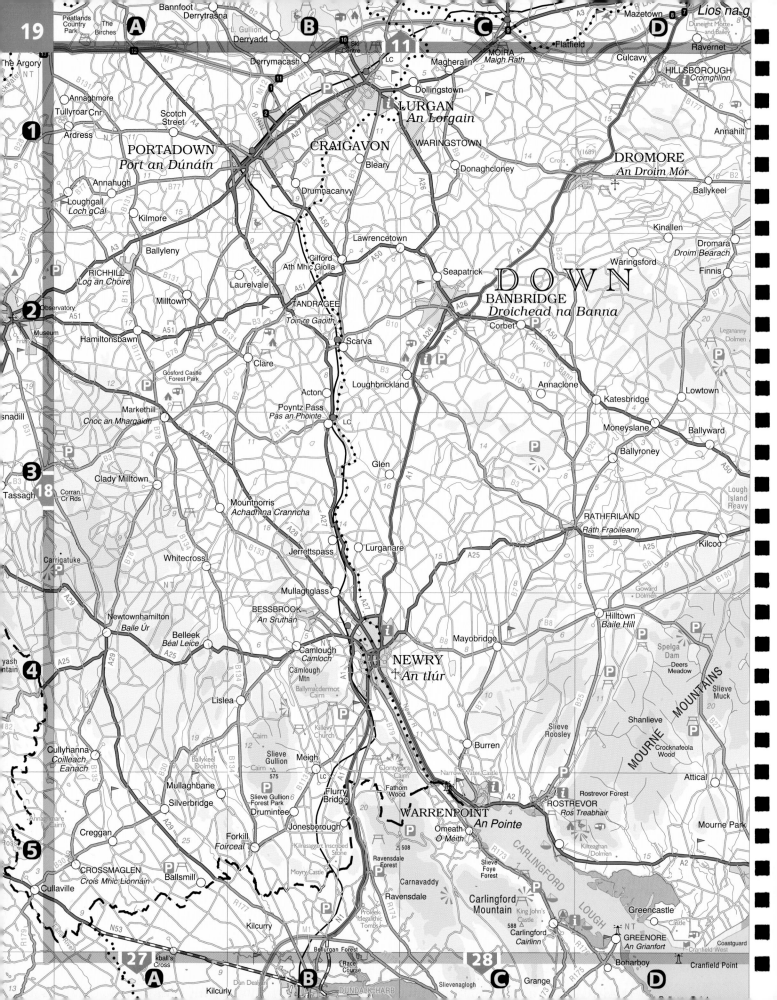

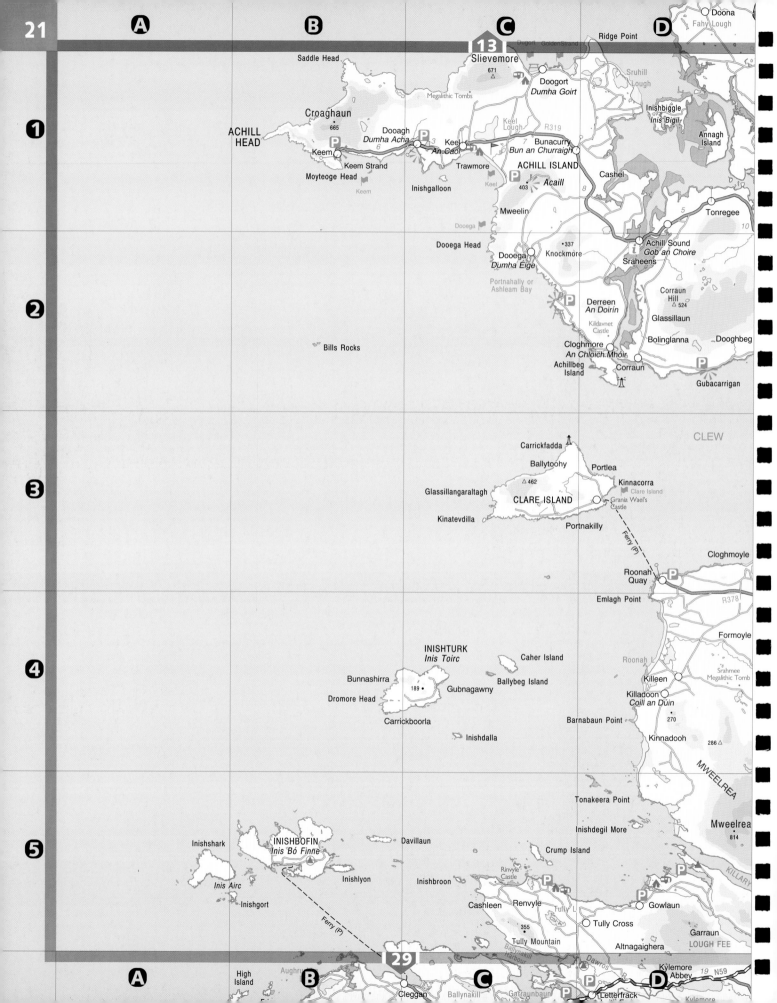

A   B   C   D

1

Doona
Fahy Lough
Ridge Point
Saddle Head
13
Slievemore
671 △
Dugort GoldenStrand
Doogort
Dumha Goirt
Sruhill
Lough
Megalithic Tombs
Inishbiggle
Inis Bigil
Croaghaun
665 •
Dooagh
Dumha Acha
Keel
An Caol
R319
Keel
Lough
7
Bunacurry
Bun an Churraigh
Annagh
Island
**ACHILL
HEAD**
P
6
P
13
Trawmore
ACHILL ISLAND
Cashel
Keem
Keem Strand
Keel
8
Moyteoge Head
Inishgalloon
P
403 •
Acaill
Mweelin
Tonregee
Keem
Q
5
10
Dooega Head
Dooega
Dumha Eige
•337
Knockmore
Achill Sound
Gob an Choire
i
Sraheens
Corraun
Hill
△ 524

2

Portnahally or
Ashleam Bay
P
Derreen
An Doirín
Glassillaun
Bills Rocks
Kildavnet
Castle
Cloghmore
An Chloich Mhóir
Bolinglanna
Dooghbeg
Achillbeg
Island
Corraun
P
Gubacarrigan

CLEW

Carrickfadda

3

Ballytoohy
△ 462
Portlea
Kinnacorra
Glassillangaraltagh
CLARE ISLAND
Clare Island
Grania Wael's
Castle
Kinatevdilla
Portnakilly
Ferry (P)
Cloghmoyle
Roonah
Quay
P
Emlagh Point
R378

4

Formoyle
Roonah L
Srahmee
Megalithic Tomb
INISHTURK
Inis Toirc
Caher Island
Killeen
Bunnashirra
189 •
Ballybeg Island
Killadoon
Coill an Dúin
Dromore Head
Gubnagawny
270 •
Carrickboorla
Barnabaun Point
Inishdalla
Kinnadooh
286 △
MWEELREA

Tonakeera Point

5

Mweelrea
814 •
Inishdegil More
Inishshark
INISHBOFIN
Inis 'Bó Finne
Davillaun
Crump Island
Rinvyle
Castle
P
KILLARY
Inis Airc
Inishlyon
Inishbroon
P
Inishgort
Cashleen
Renvyle
Tully L
Gowlaun
Garraun
Ferry (P)
355 •
Tully Cross
Altnagaighera
LOUGH FEE
Tully Mountain

A   B   C   D

High
Island
Aughrus
Ballynakill
Harbour
Kylemore
Abbey
19 N59
Cleggan
Ballynakill
Garraunbaun
P
Letterfrack
Dawros
Kylemore

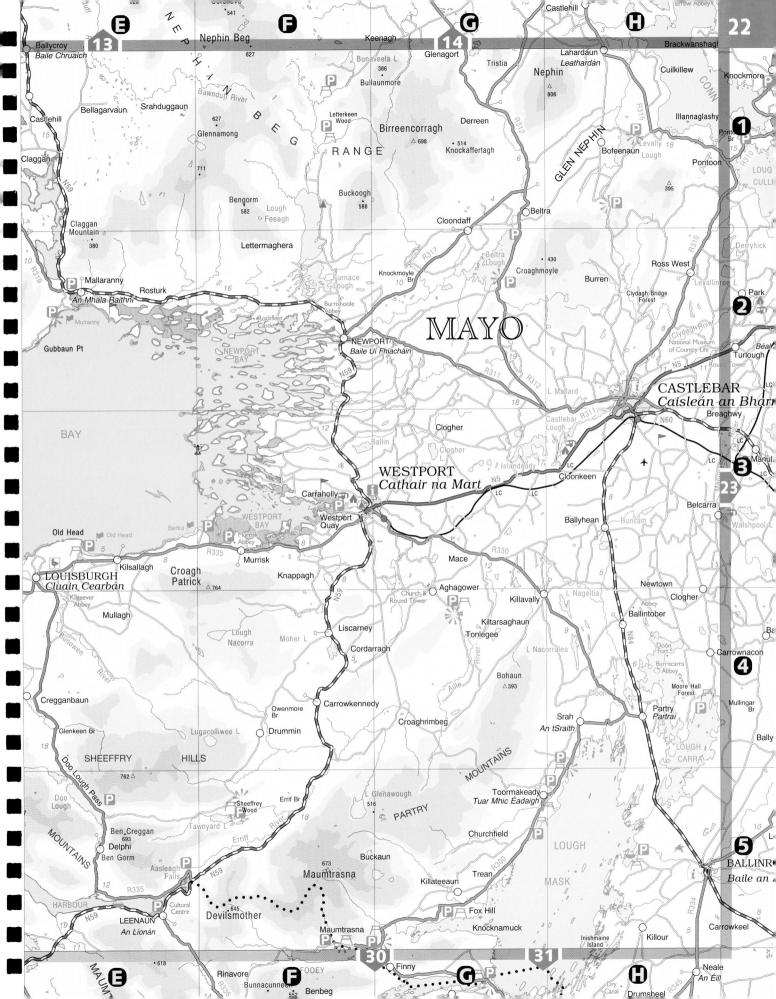

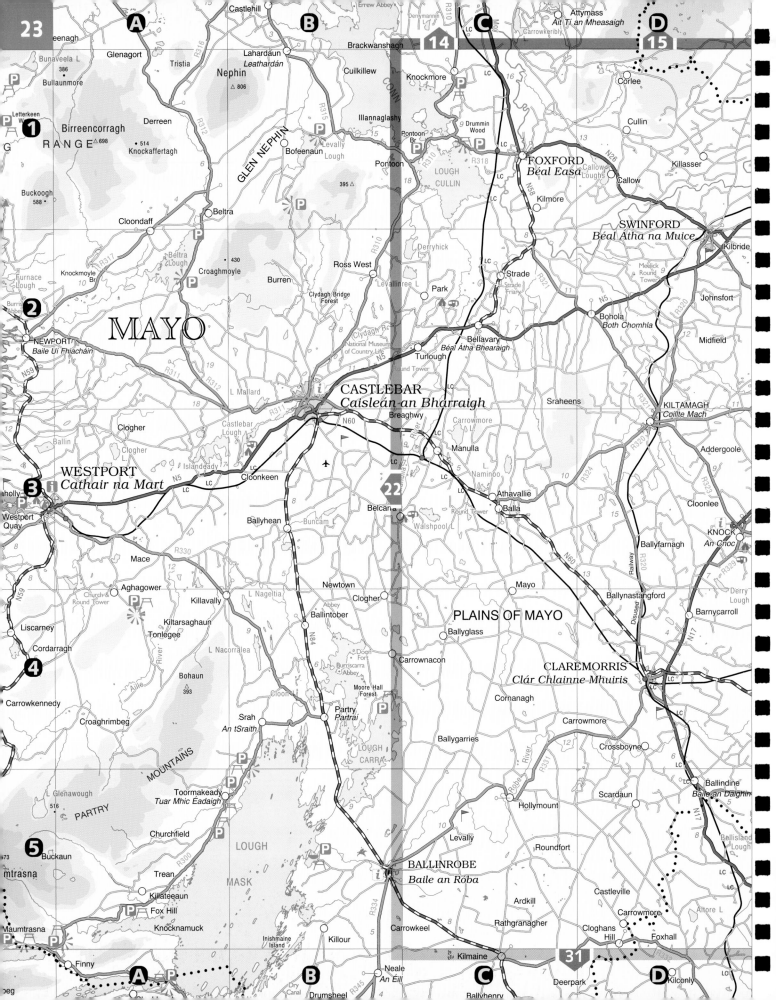

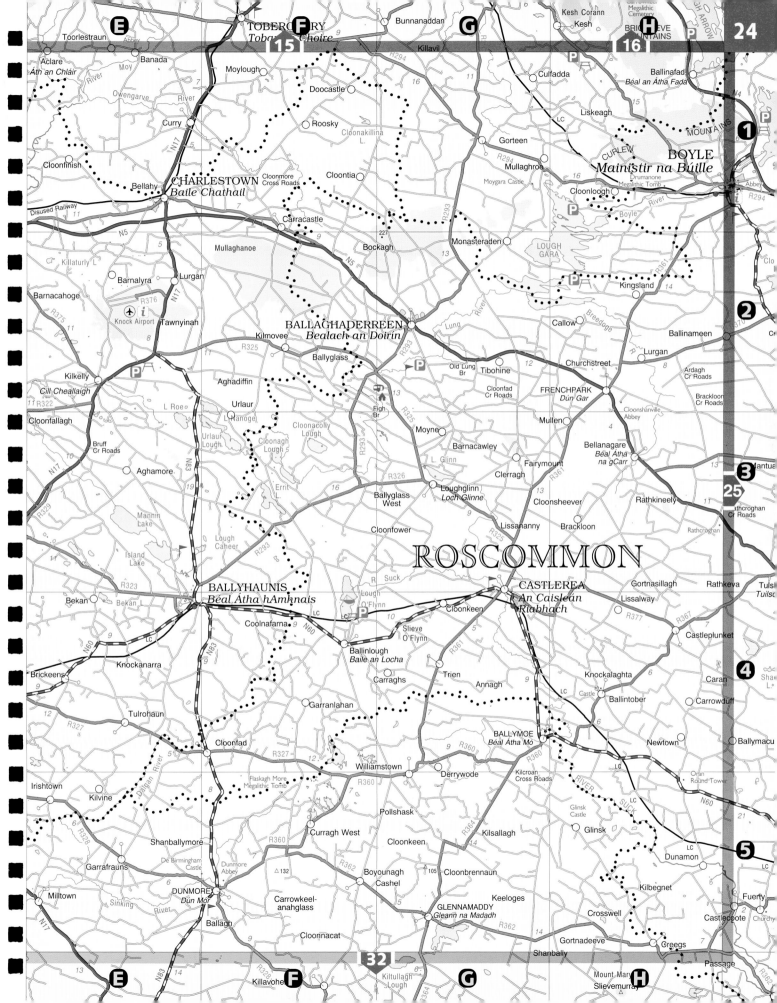

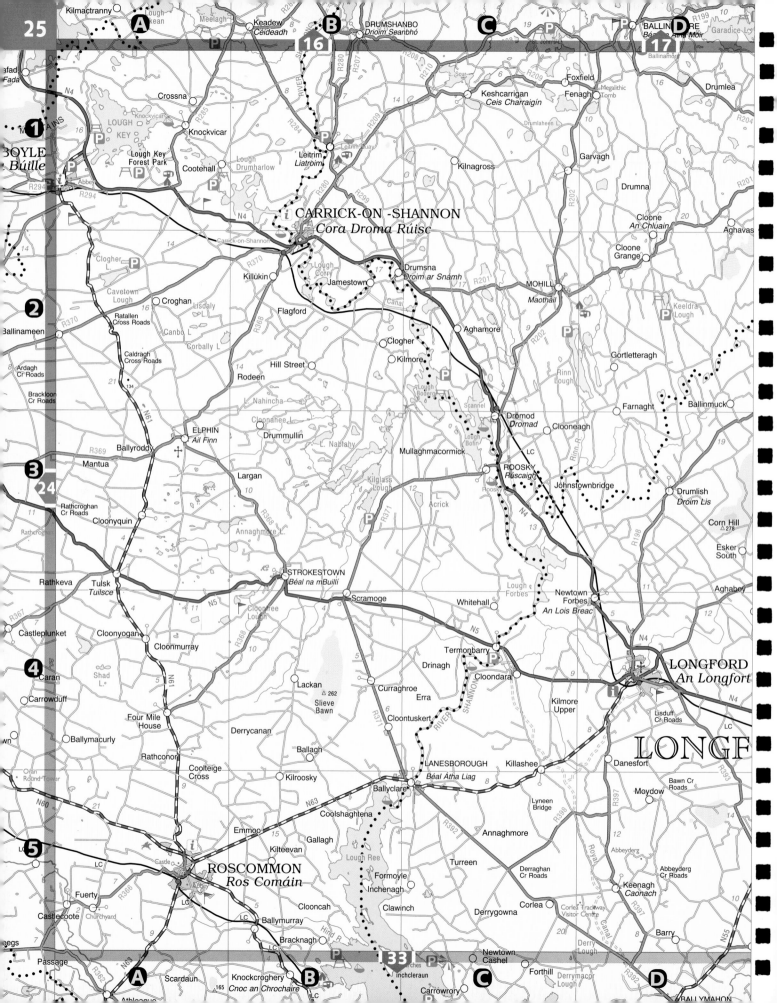

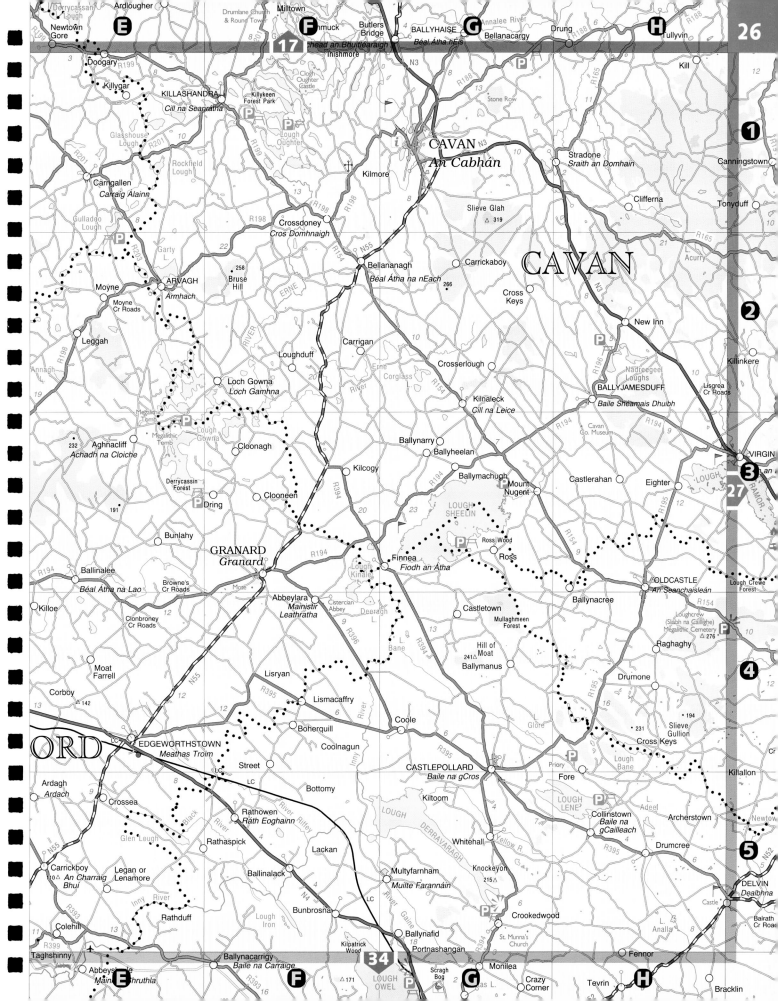

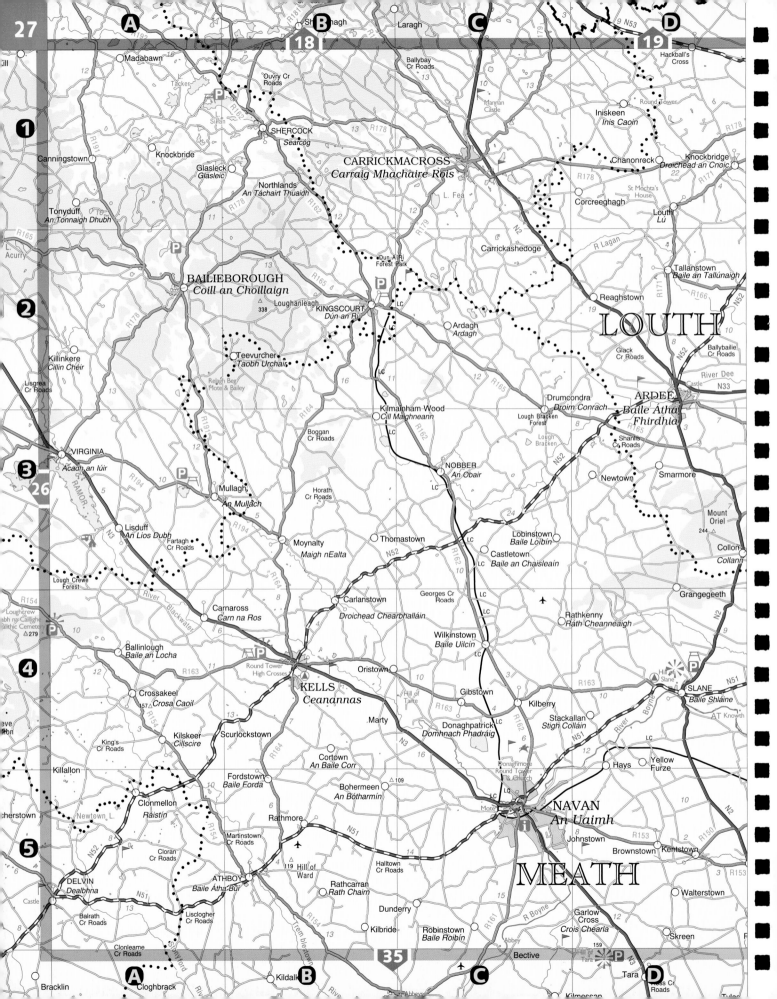

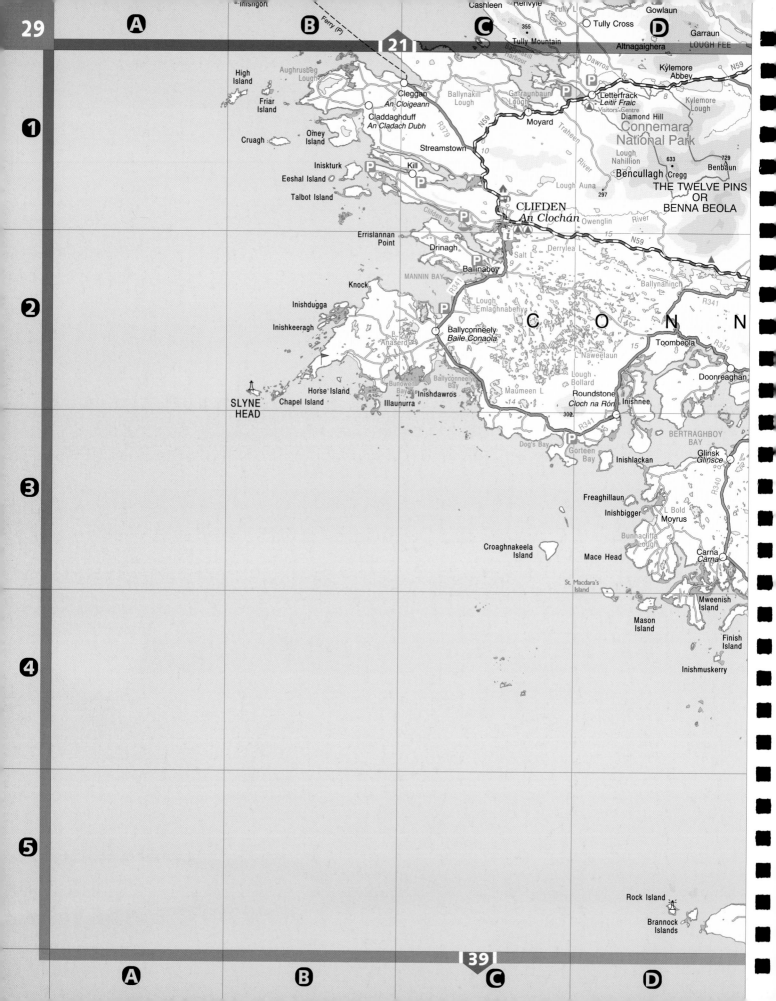

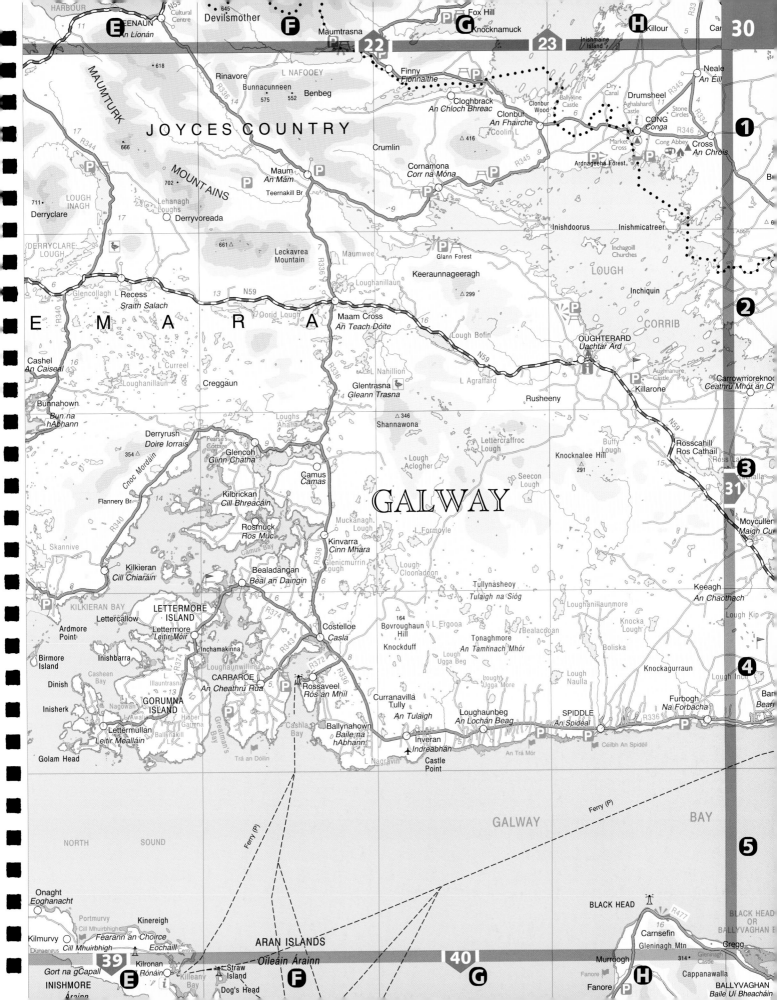

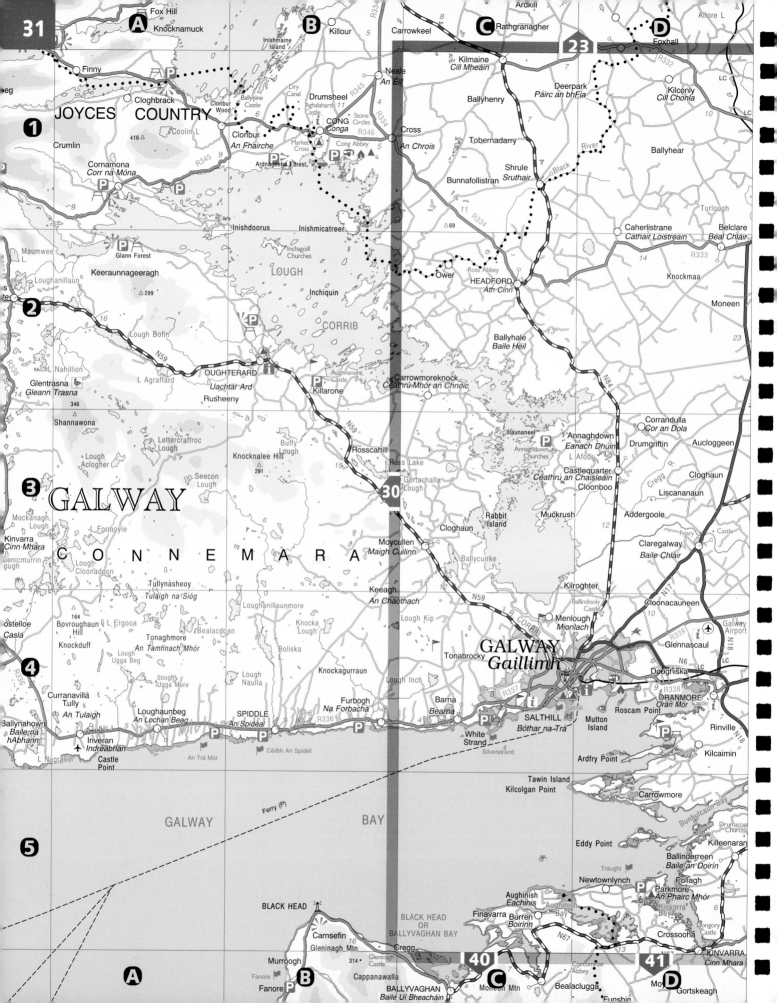

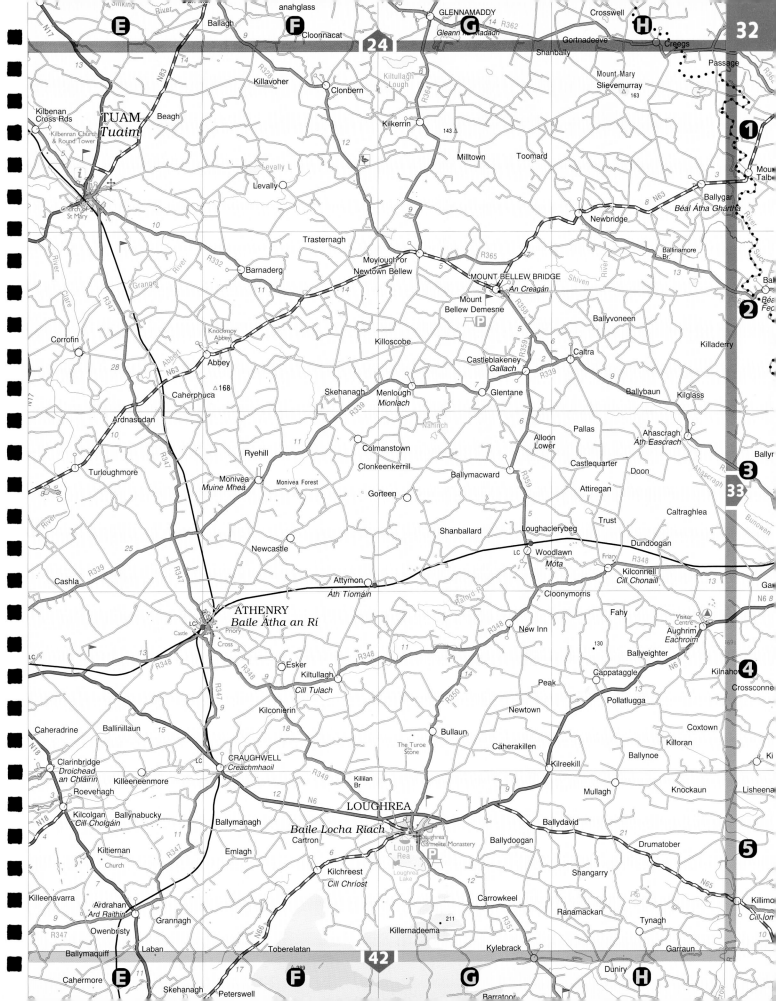

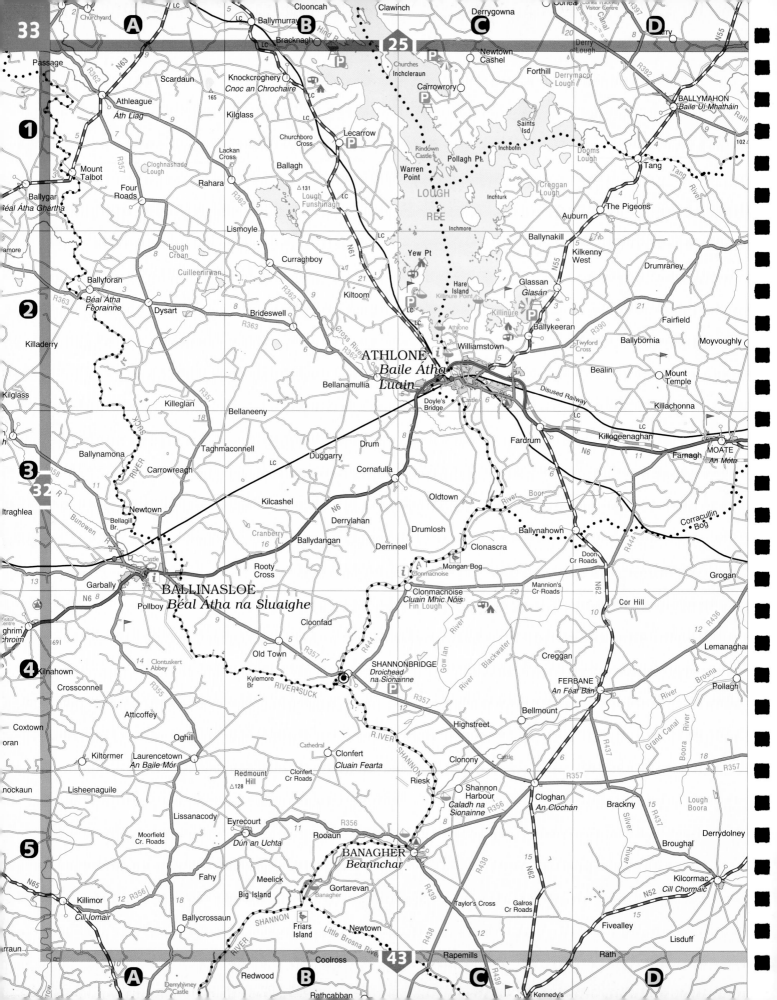

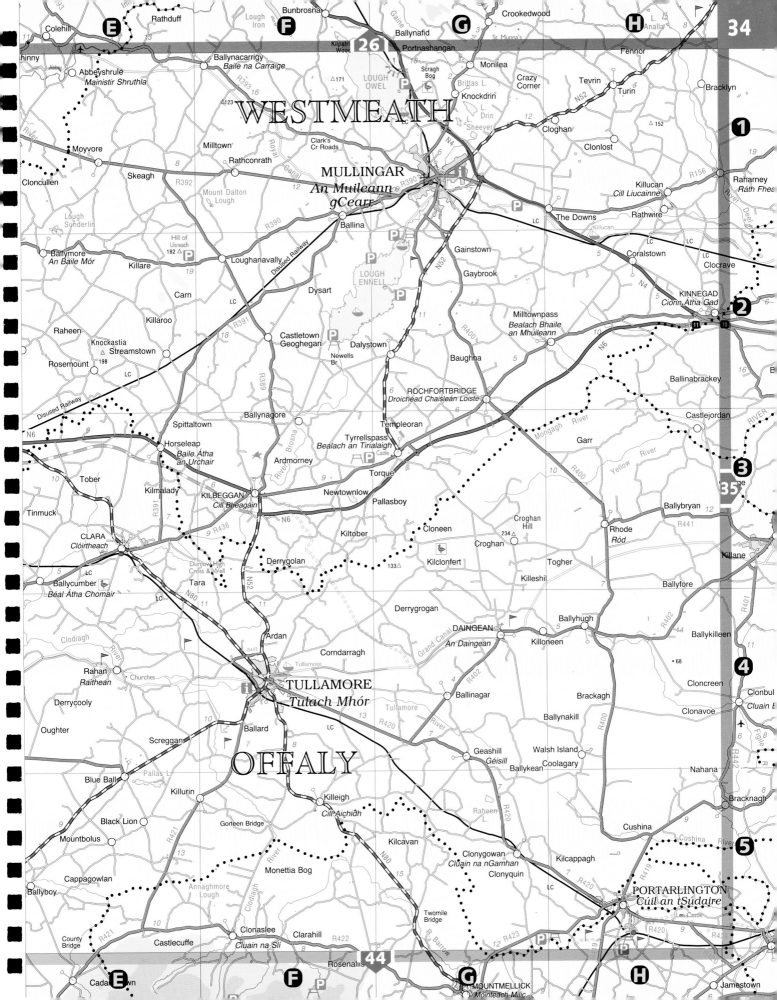

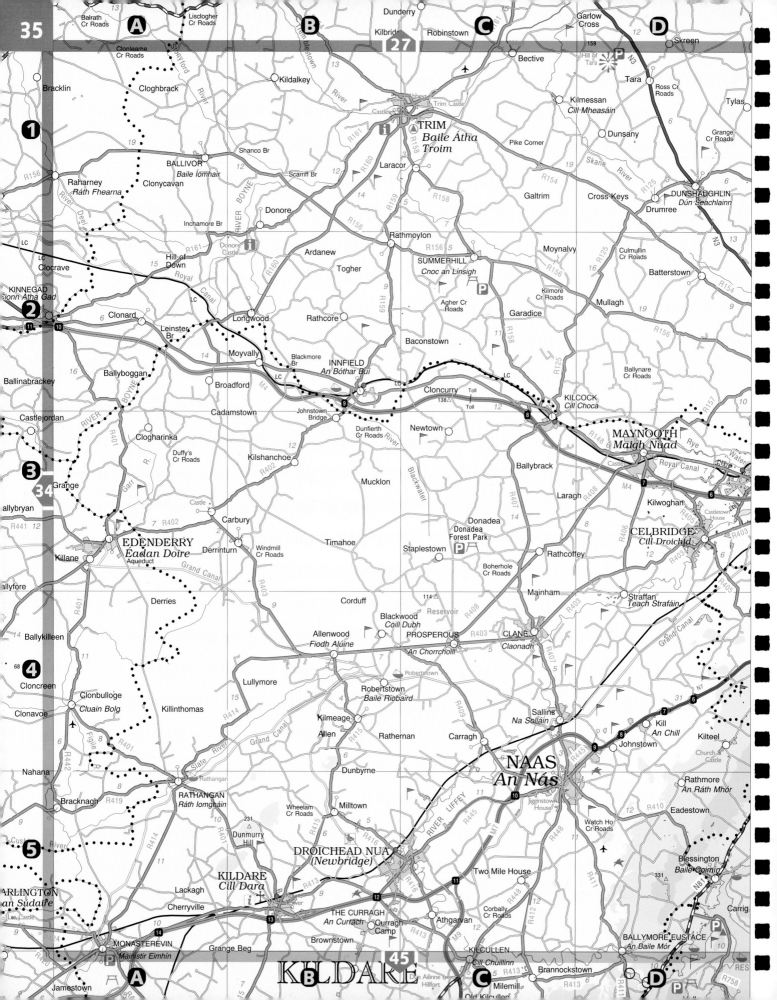

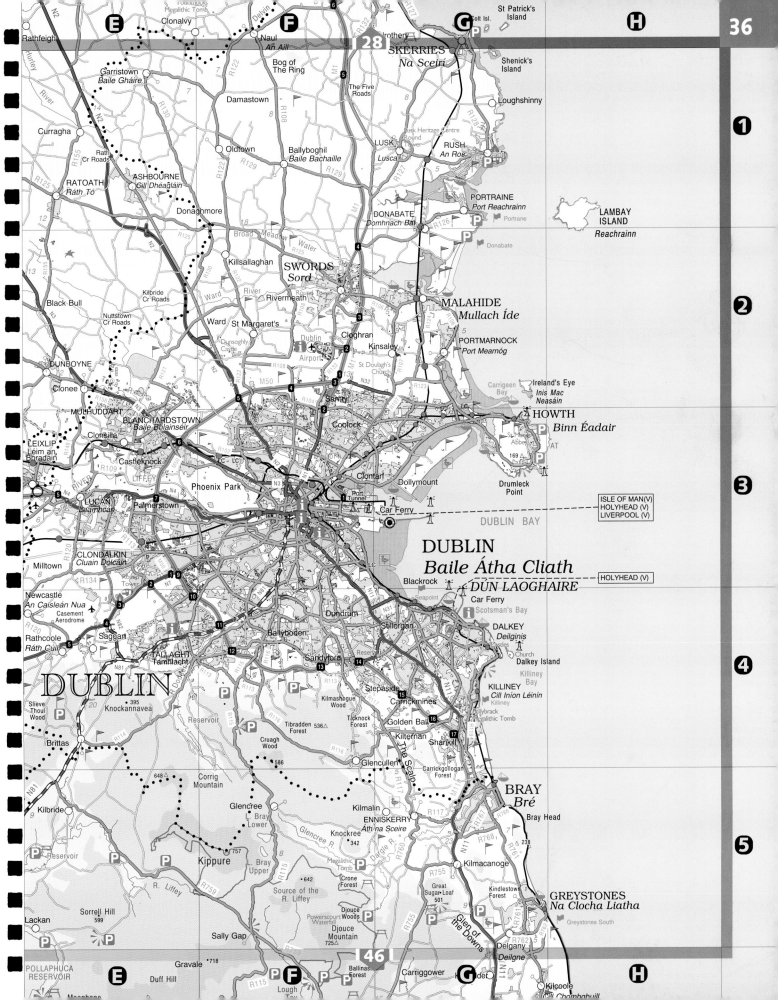

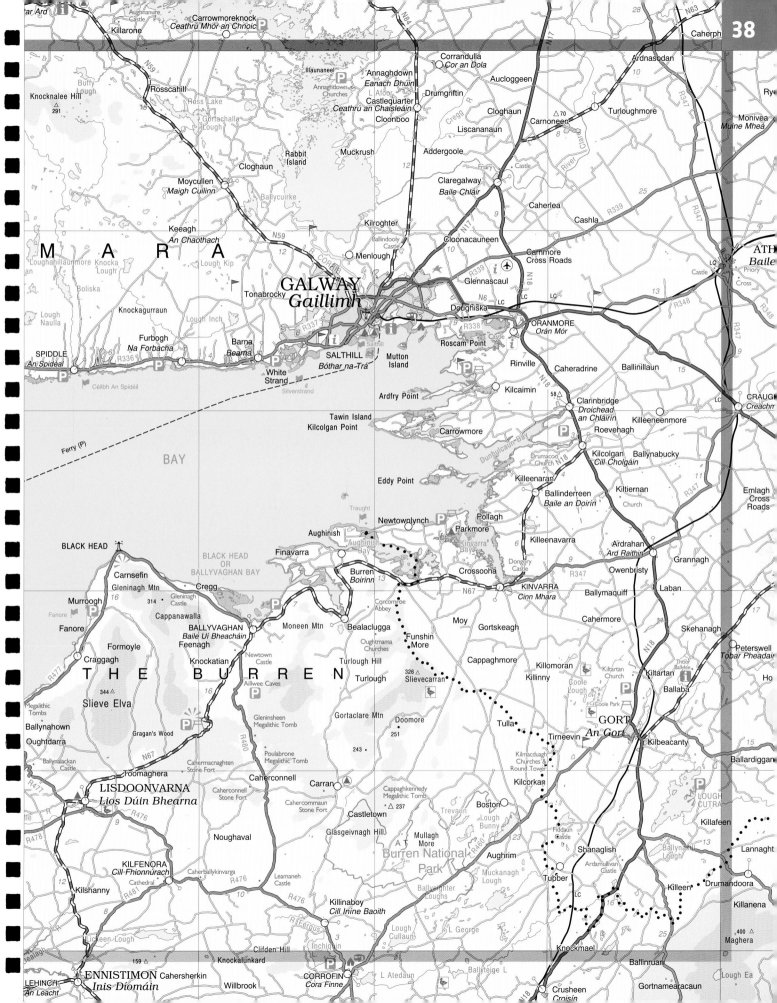

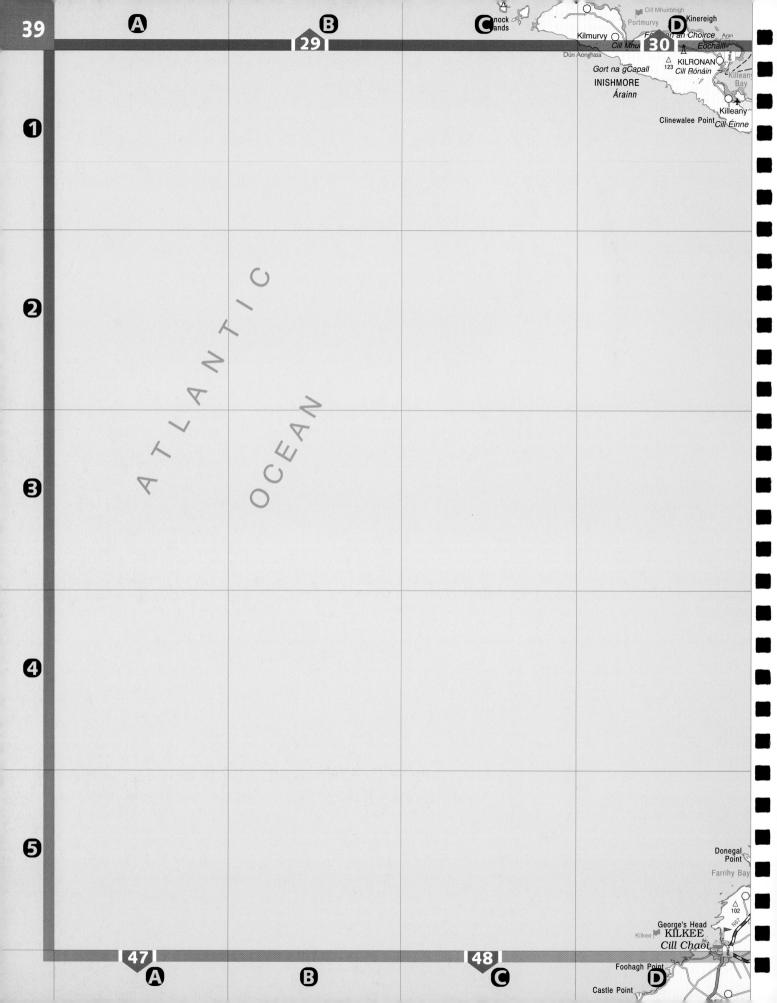

1

2

3

4

5

ATLANTIC

OCEAN

Knock
Islands

Portmurvy
Cill Muirbhigh
Kilmurvy
Cill Mhuir...
Dún Aonghasa
Gort na gCapall
INISHMORE
Árainn

Kinereigh
Fearann an Choirce
Cill Mhuirbhigh
Aran
123
KILRONAN
Cill Rónáin
Eochaill

i
Killeany
Bay
Killeany
Cill Éinne
Clinewalee Point

Donegal
Point
Farrihy Bay

George's Head
Kilkee
KILKEE
Cill Chaoi
Foohagh Point
Castle Point

102
N67

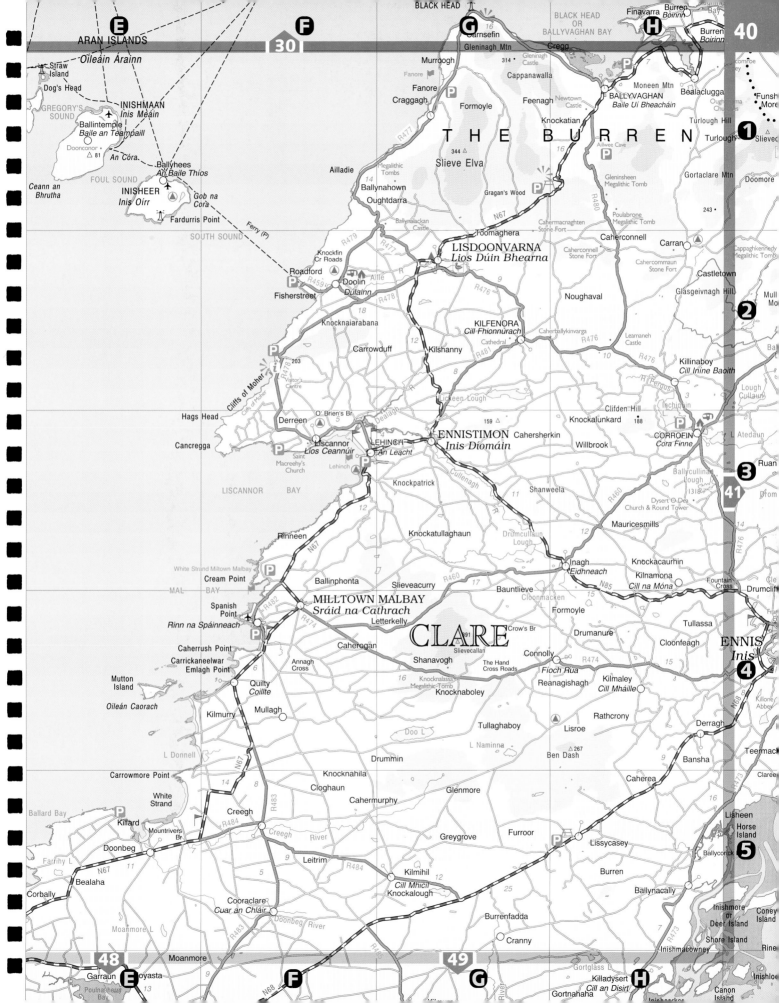

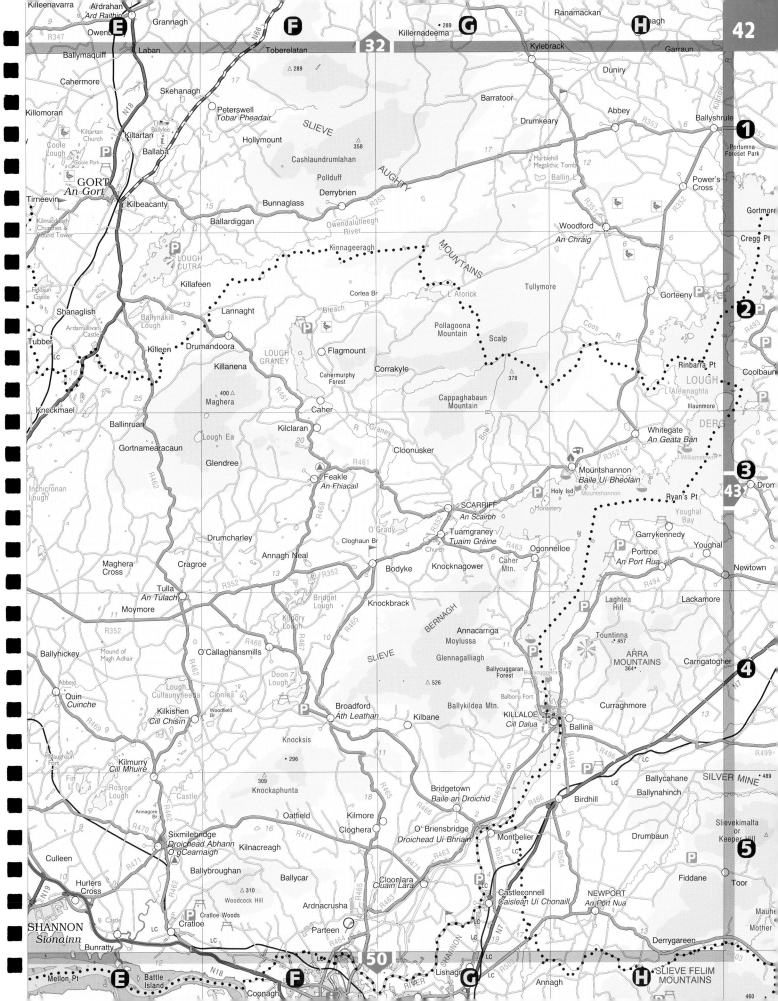

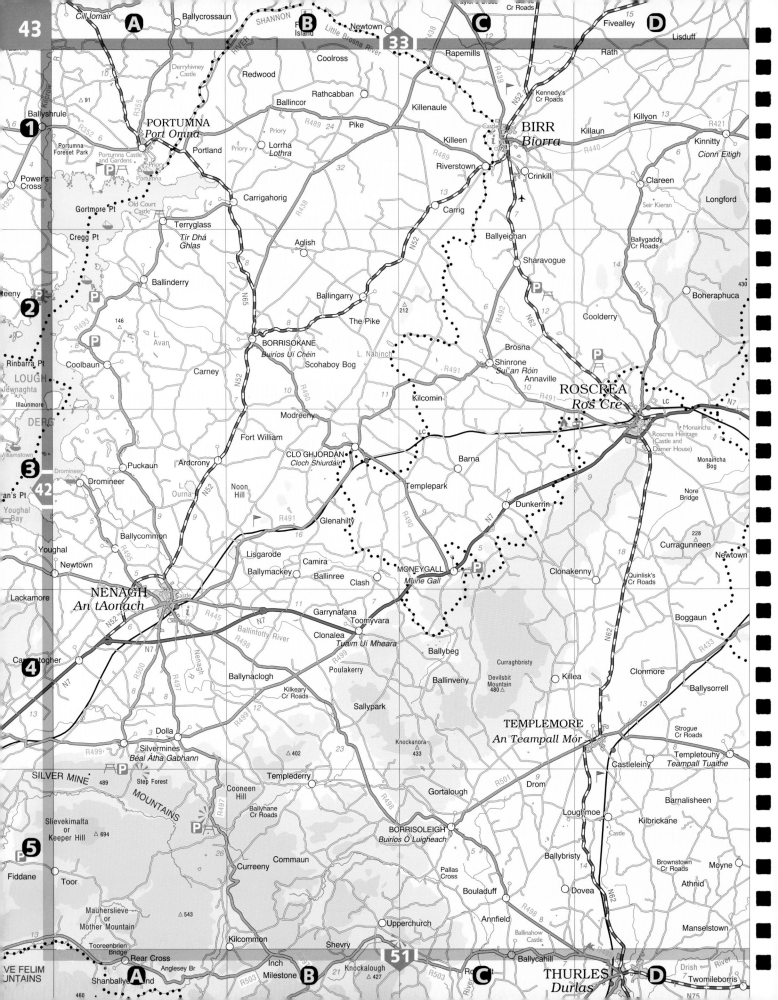

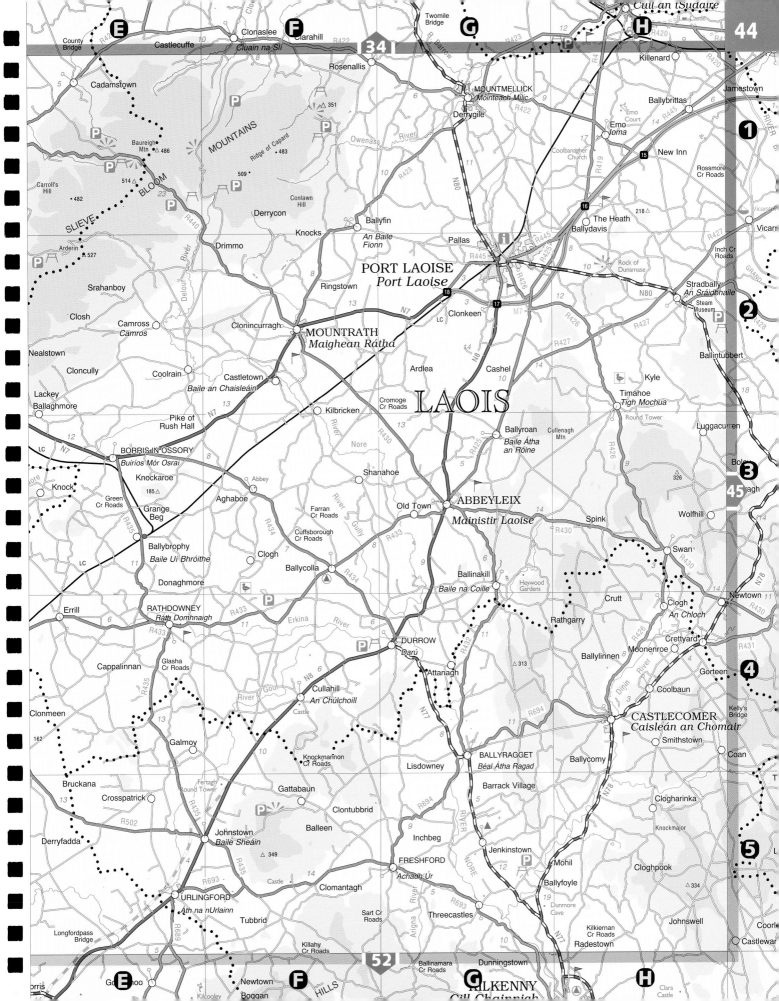

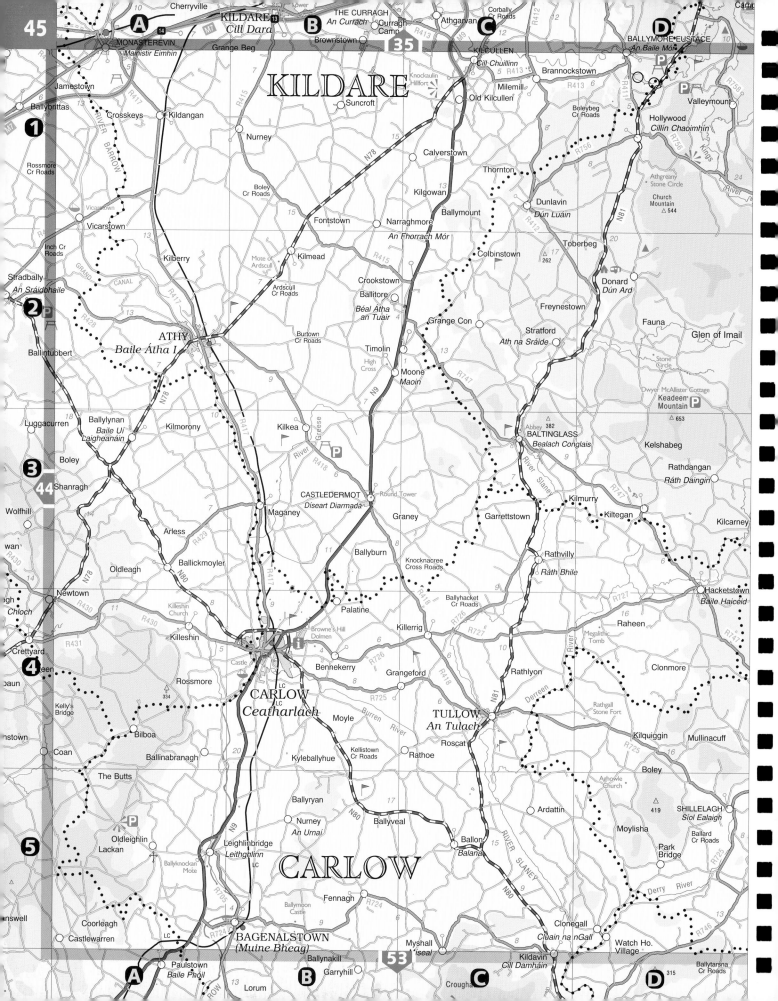

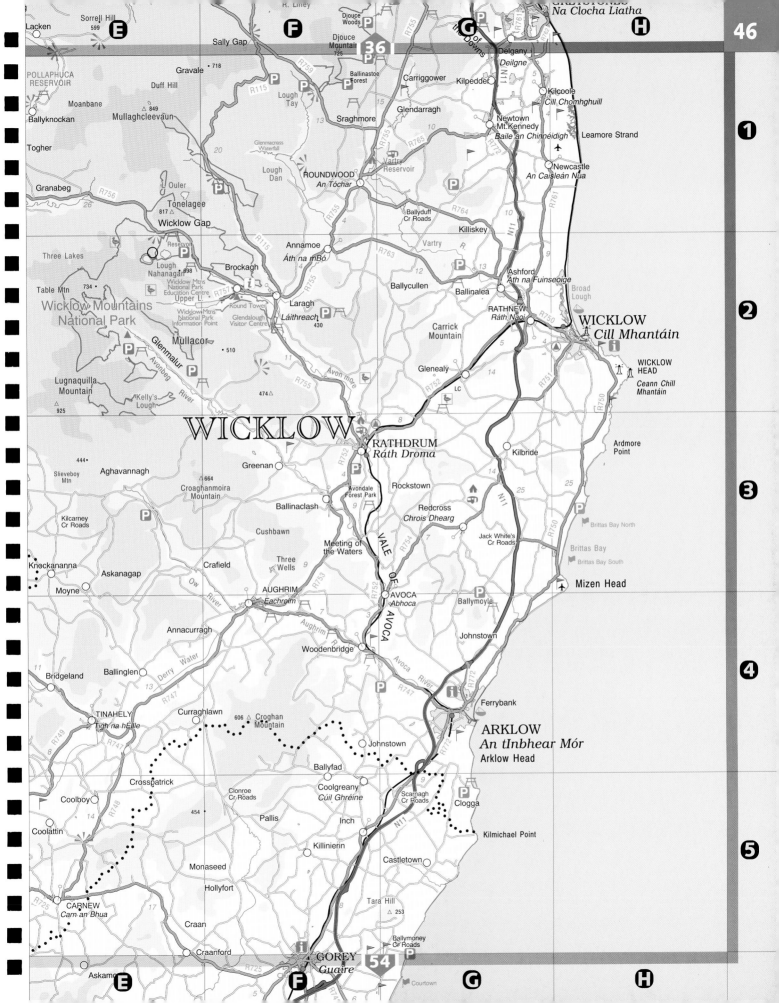

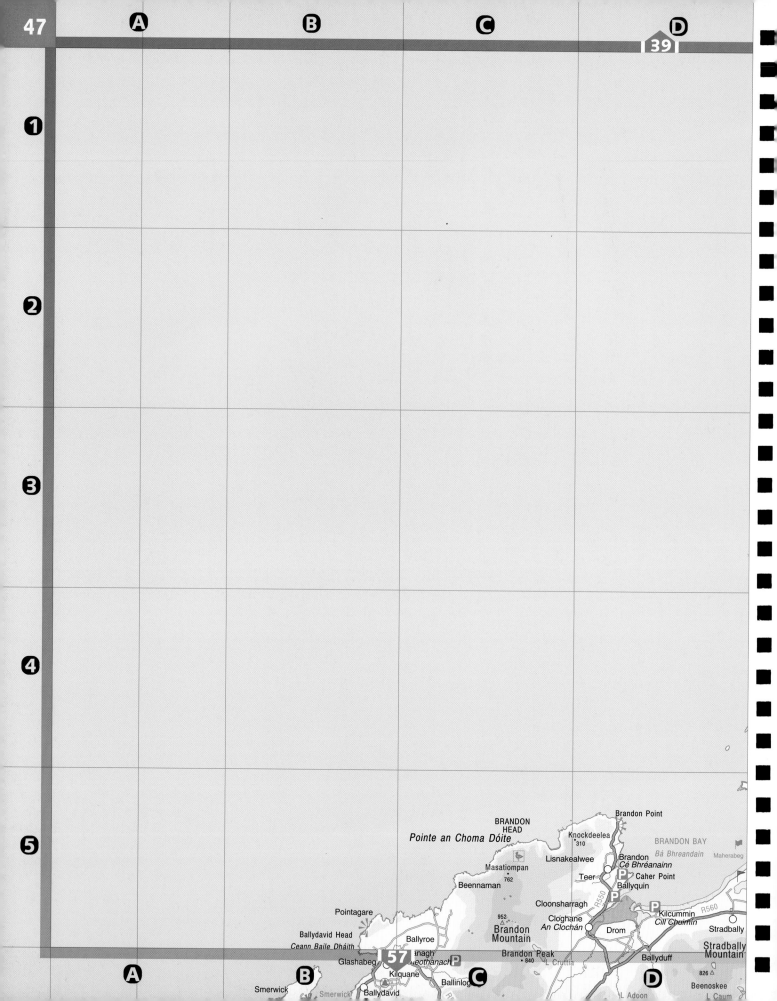

BRANDON
HEAD
Pointe an Choma Dóite

Knockdeelea
·310

BRANDON BAY
Bá Bhreandain   Maherabeg

Lisnakealwee

Brandon
Cé Bhréanainn

Masatiompan

Teer   Caher Point

Beennaman

·762   Ballyquin

Cloonsharragh   Kilcummin
Cill Chuimín

Pointagare   R550   R560

·952   Cloghane
△   An Clochán   Drom

Ballydavid Head   Ballyroe   Stradbally
Ceann Baile Dháith   Brandon   Stradbally
Mountain   Mountain

Glashabeg   57   anagh   Brandon Peak
ueothanach   ·840   L Cruttia   Ballyduff

Smerwick   826 △

Kilquane   Beenoskee
Smerwick?   Ballydavid   Ballinlog

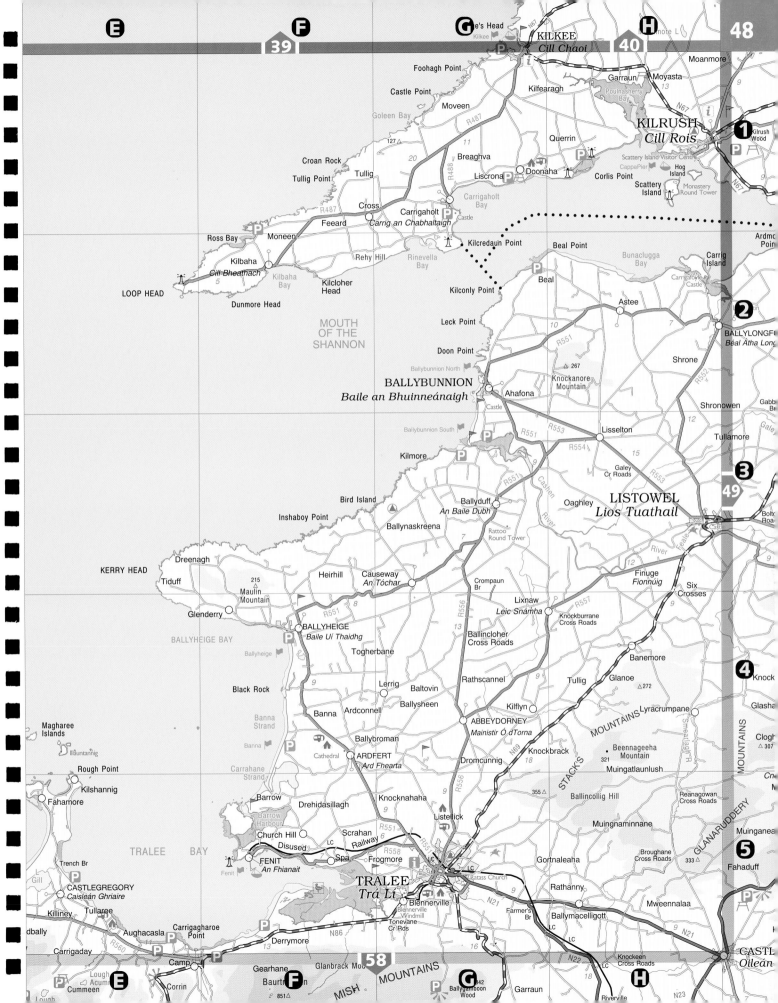

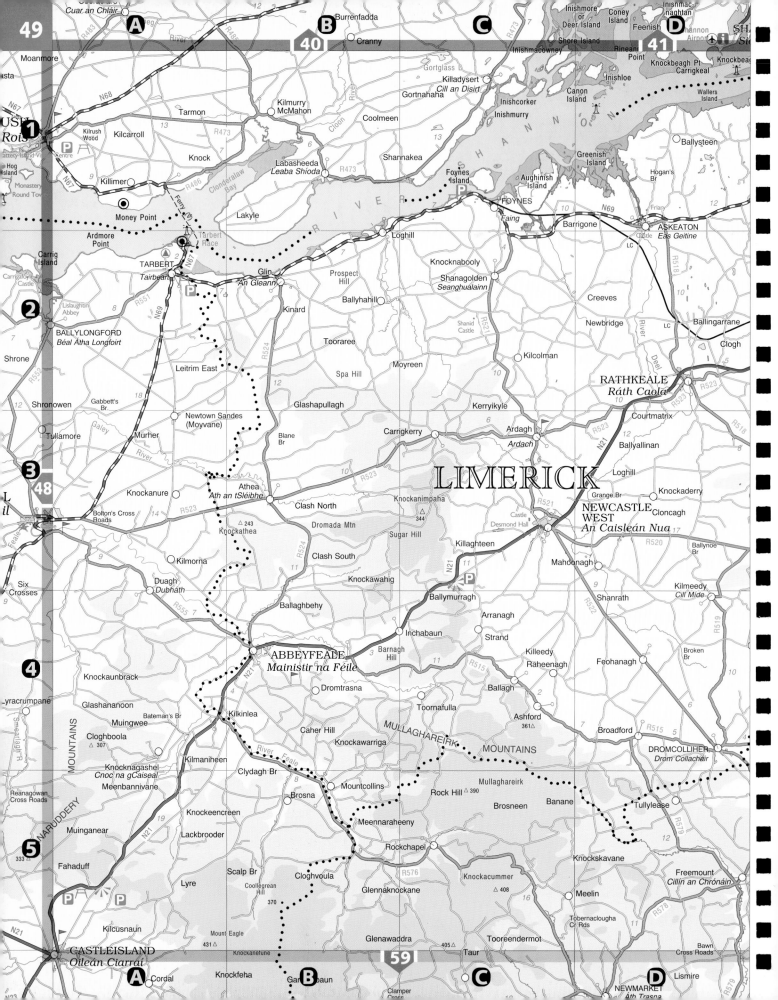

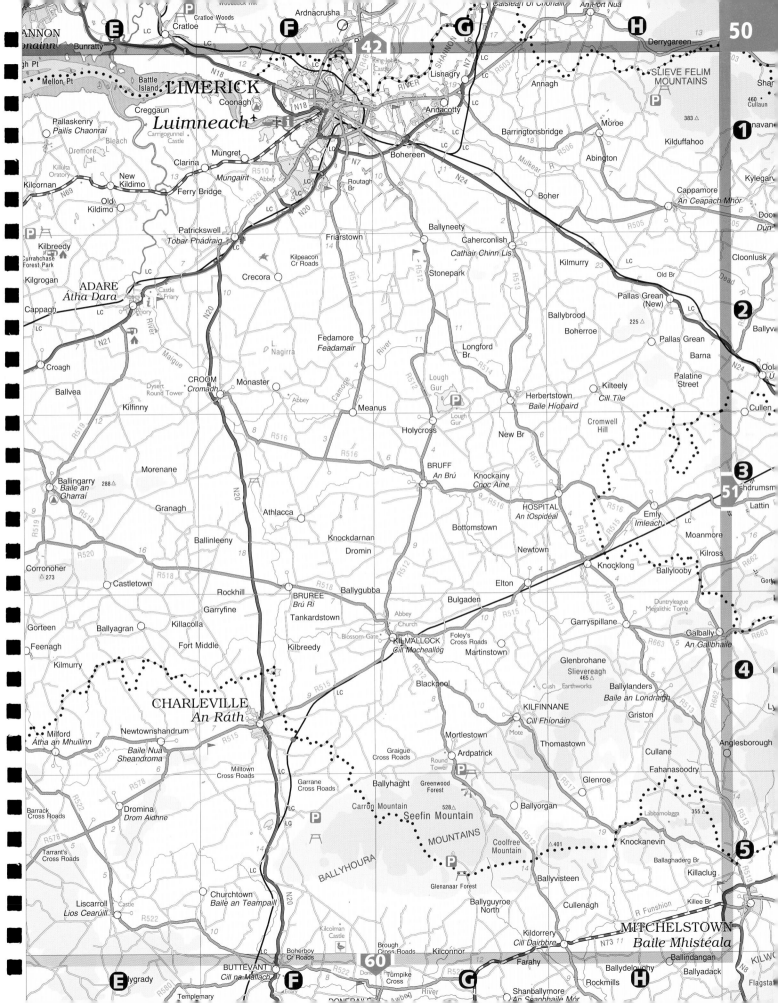

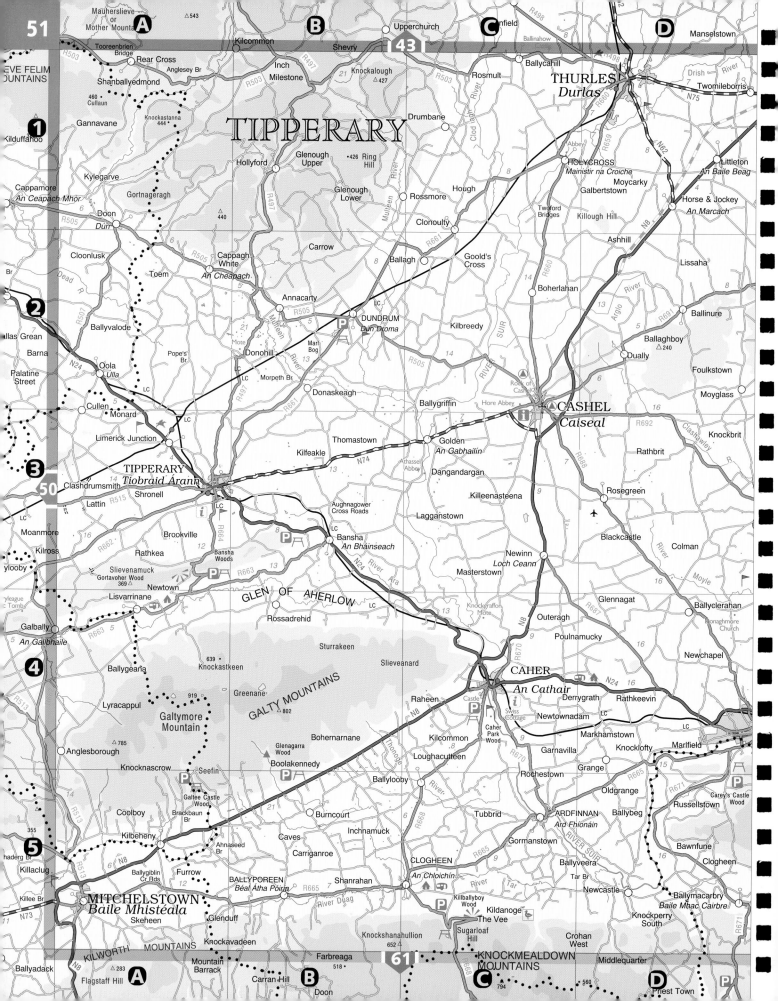

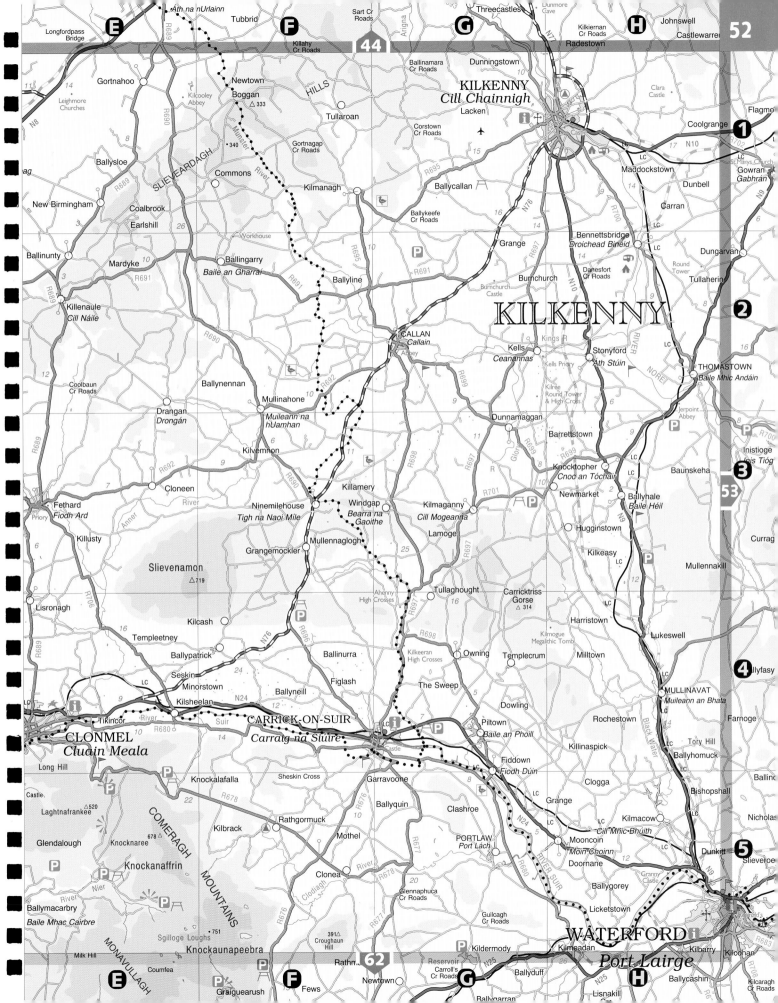

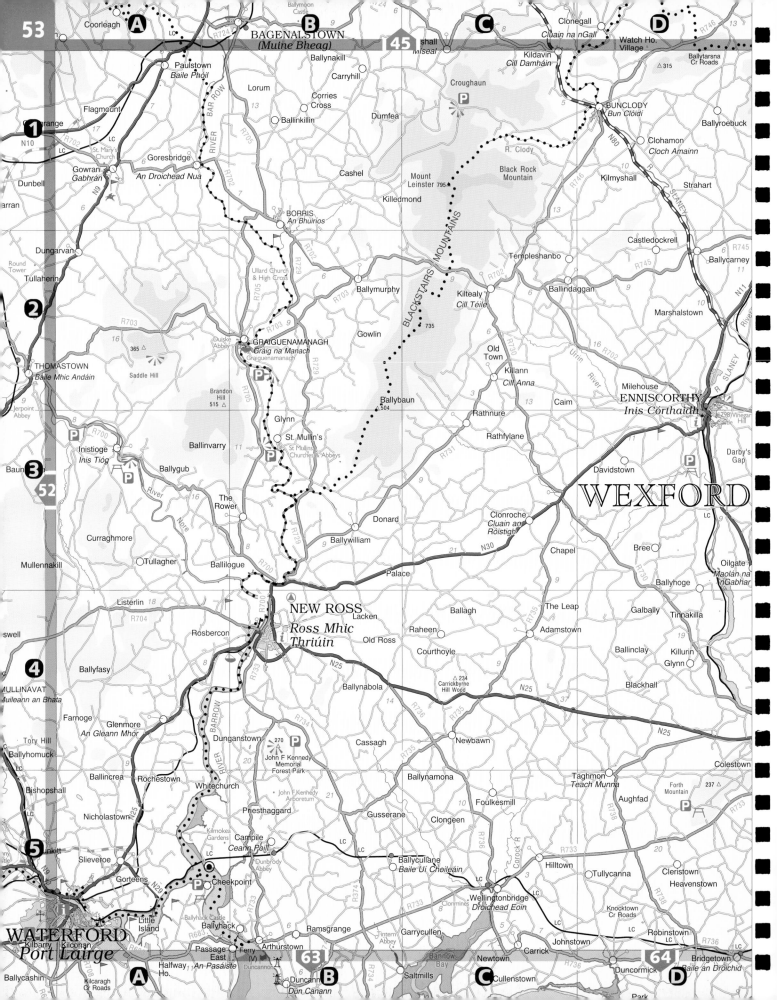

BRANDON
HEAD
Pointe an Choma Dóite

Brandon Point
Knockdeelea
BRANDON BAY
Bá Bhreandain
Maherabeg
Lisnakealwee
Masatiompan
Brandon
Caher Point
Teer
Ballyquin
Beennaman
Cloonsharragh
952 △
Cloghane
Kilcummin
An Clochán
Brandon
Mountain
Drom
Stradbally
Pointagare
Brandon Peak
840 •
L Cruttia
Ballyduff
Stradbally
Mountain
Ballydavid Head
Ceann Baile Dháith
Ballyroe
I   N   G
L   E
△ 826
Feohanagh
An Fheothánach
Beenoskee
Smerwick
Glashabeg
Kilquane
Ballinloghig
L Caum
Araglen
Forest
Sybil Head
Smerwick
Harbour
Ballydavid
Baile na nGall
L Adoon
486
Slievenagower
Dún
an Óir
17
• Kilmalkedar
L Gal
Slievanea
Lough
Anscaul
Murreagh
An Mhuiríoch
Ballysitteragh
623 •
Conair
L Camclaun
Sybil Point
Ballinrannig
Ballynana
Knockmoylemore
Coumanare
Lakes
BALLYFERRITER
Baile an Fheirtéaraigh
Gallans
(Oratory)
Riasc
649
Coumduff
Teeravane
Ballineanig
Ballybowler
Lisdargan
Annagap
Clogher
Head
8
Ballyeightragh
Knockavrogeen
Lispole
Lios Póil
ANASCAUL
Abhainn an Scáil
Croaghmarhin
Milltown
Baile an Mhuilinn
DINGLE
An Daingean
N86   9
9
Dunquin
Dún Chaoin
Ventry
R559   7
Aglish
Inishtooskert
Kildurrihy
The Blasket
Centre
Mount Eagle
△ 516
Ventry
Harbour
Oghan
Stones
Dingle
Harbour
Doonmanagh
Acres Point
GREAT BLASKET
ISLAND
Beginish
BLASKET
SOUND
Ballymacadoyle
Hill
Reenbeg
Point
Bull's
Head
Minard
Head
Gubranna
An Blascaod
Mór
Beenacouma
Fahan
14
Cloghans
Parkmore Pt
Garraun Pt
SLEA HEAD
Ceann Sléibhe
Dunbeg
(Promontory Fort)
Tearaght
Island
Canduff

Inishnabro

DINGLE BAY
Bá an Daingin

Inishvickillane

King's Head
Kells
Gleensk
Wood
Darby's
Br
Kells
Beenmore
Mount Foley
Killurly
Commons
Been Hill
662 •
Mullaghnarakill
Canglass Point
690 △
Knocknadobar
N70
12
Coosfadda
Slievagh
Castlequin
Foilmore Br
Teeromoyle
Leacanabuaile
Stone Fort
DOULUS HEAD
Killelan
Mountain
Coomduff
White Strand-Cahersiveen
V
Beginish
Island
Church
Island
CAHERSIVEEN
Cathair Saidhbhín
Reenadrolaun Pt
VALENCIA
HARBOUR
Reenard
Cross
Ferry V
Knockaneden
Cross
Keelnagore

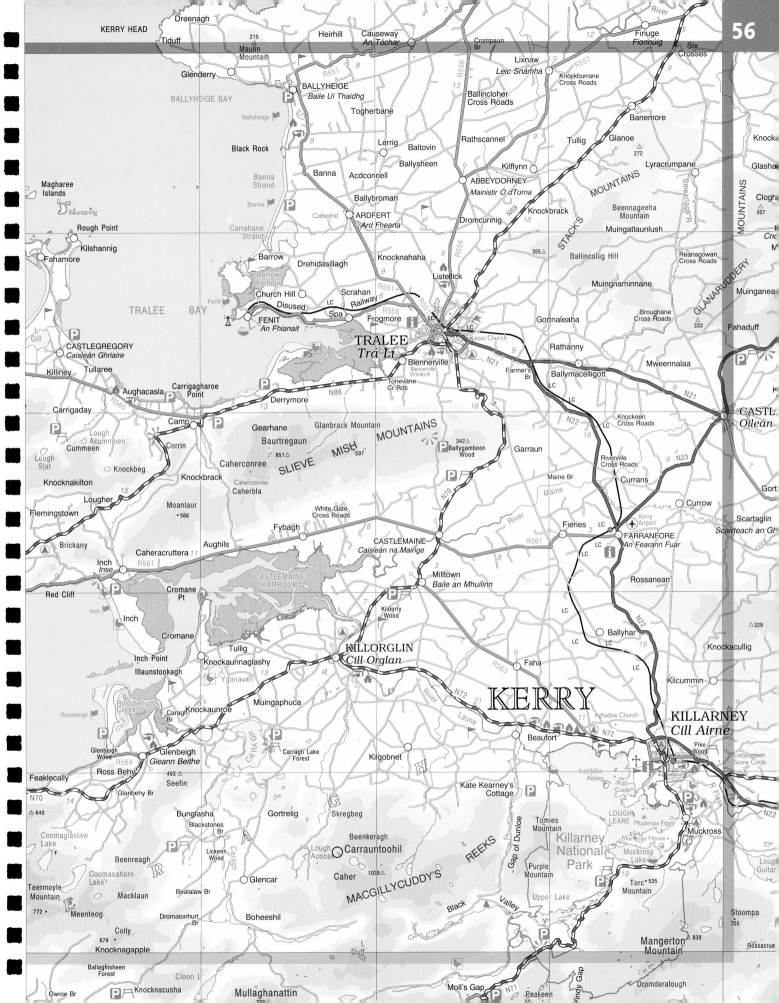

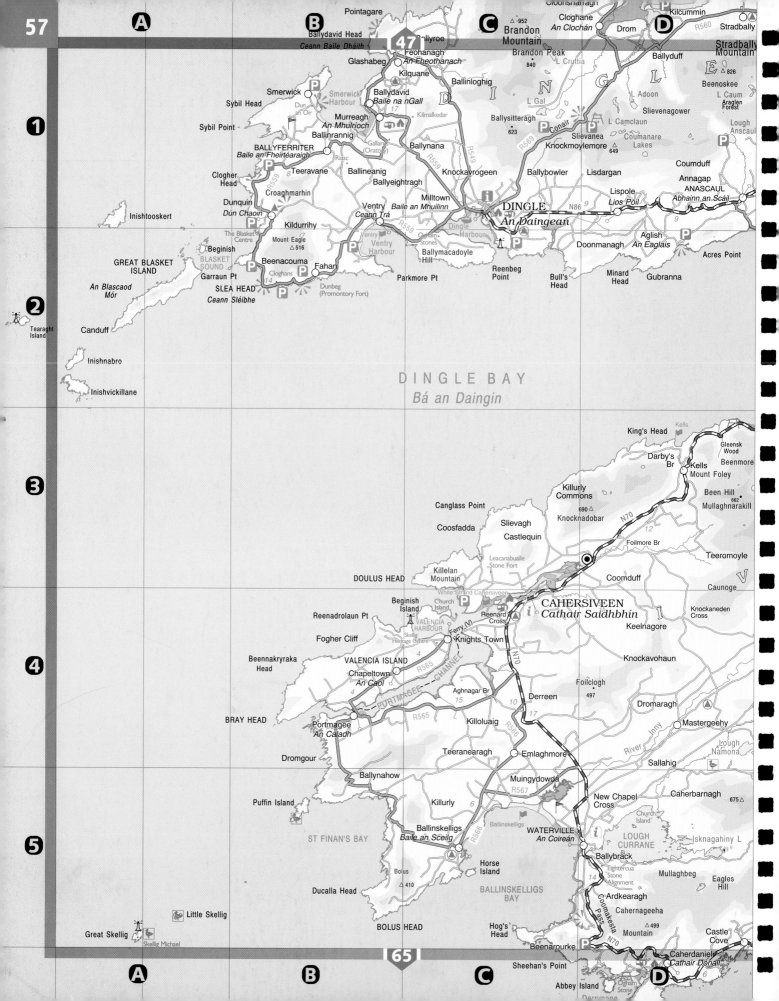

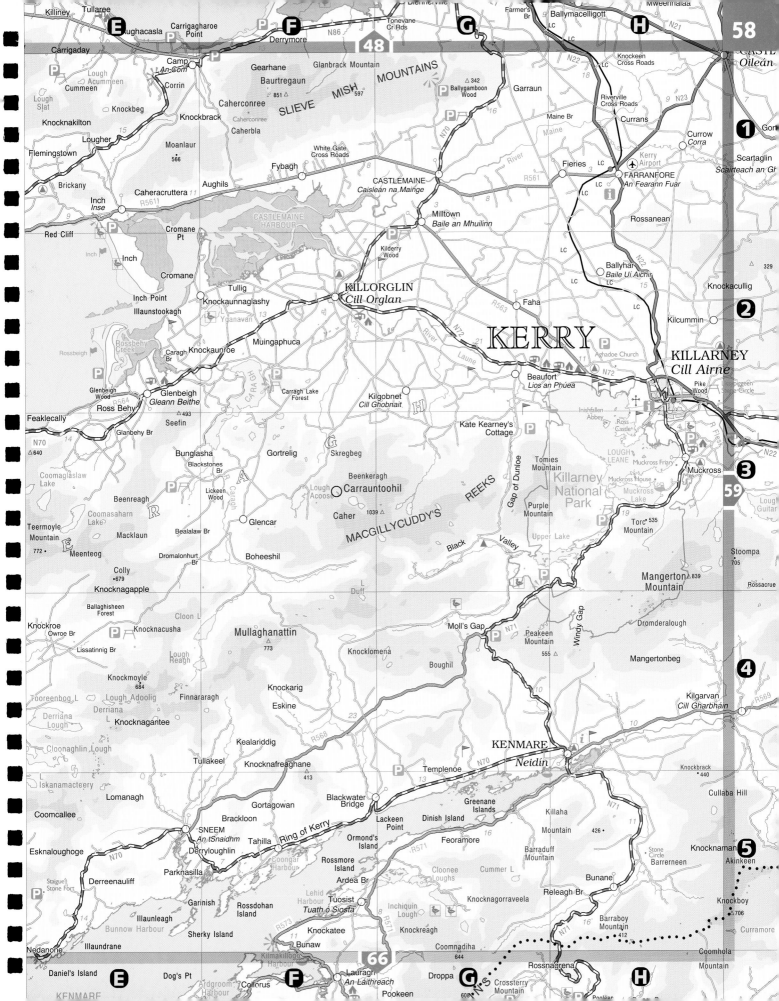

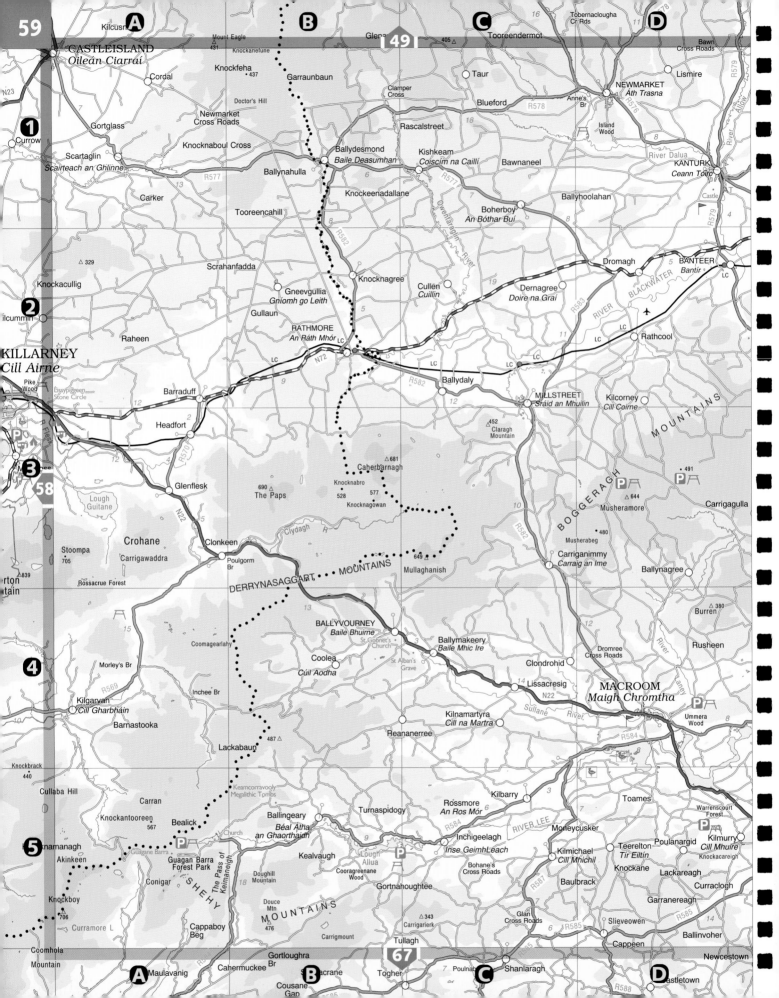

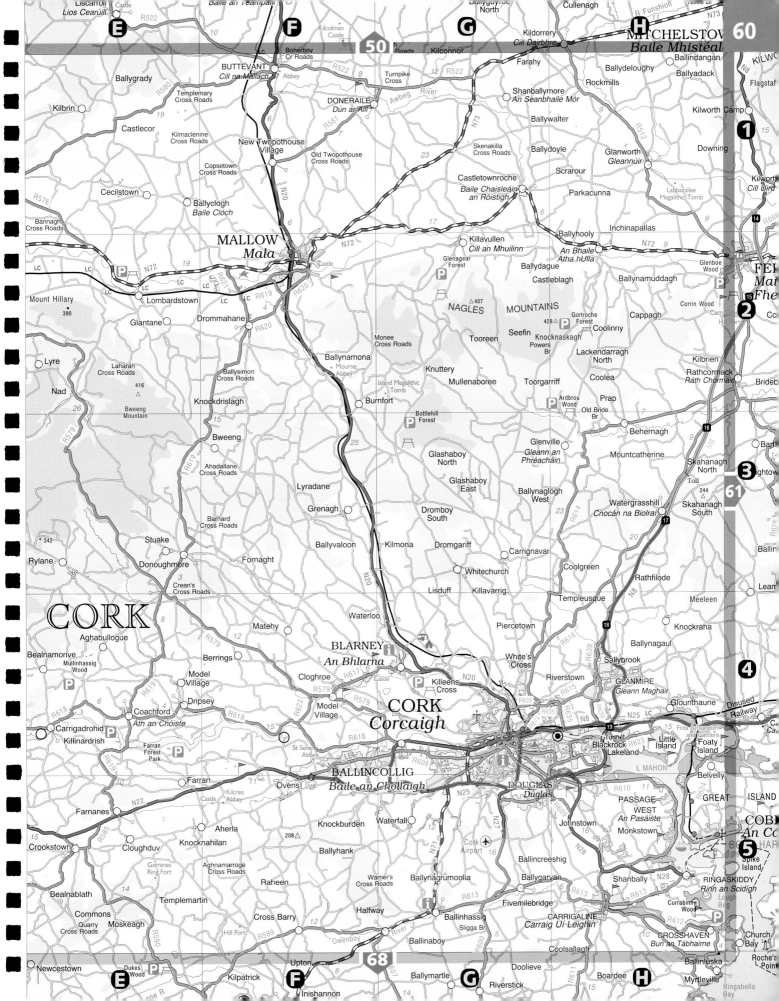

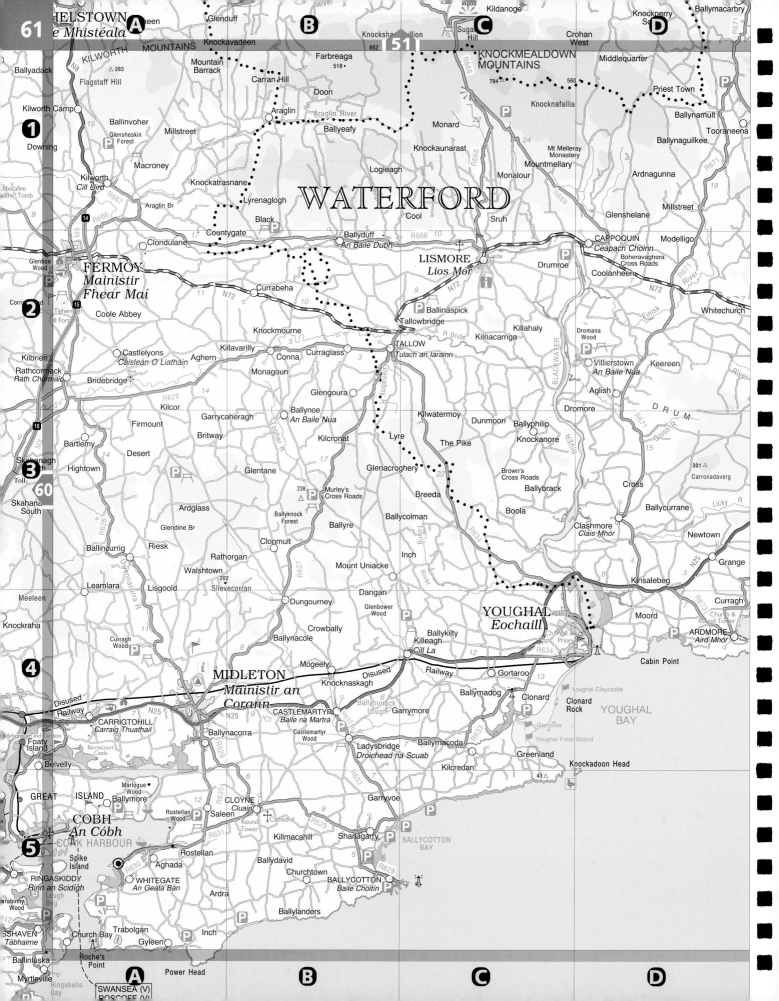

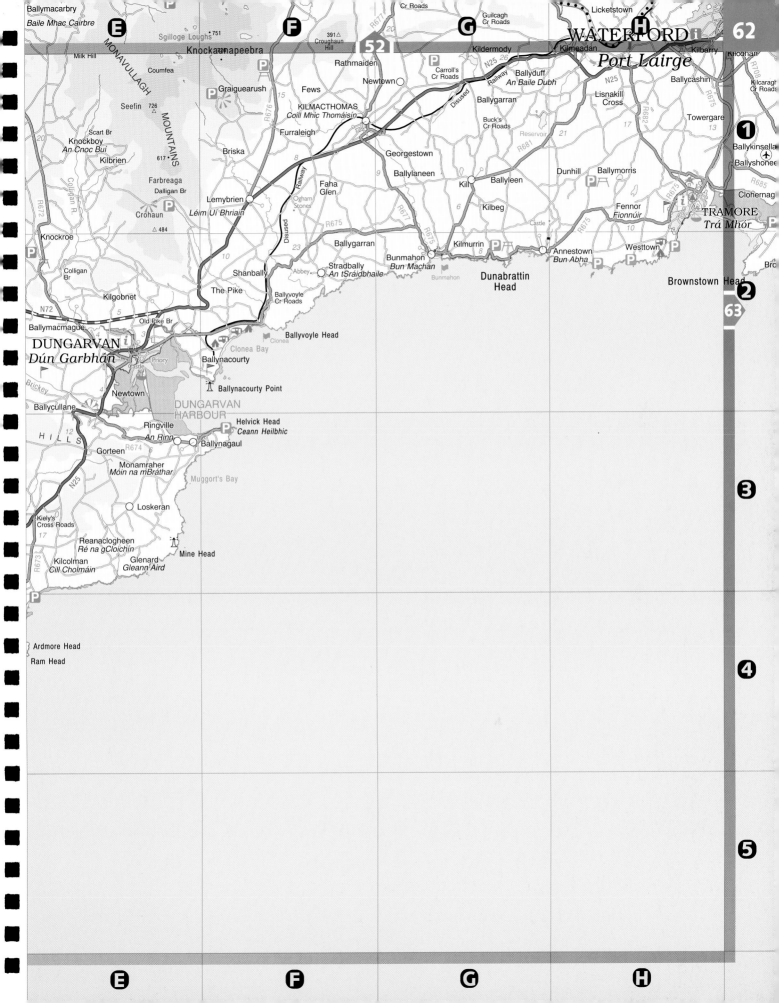

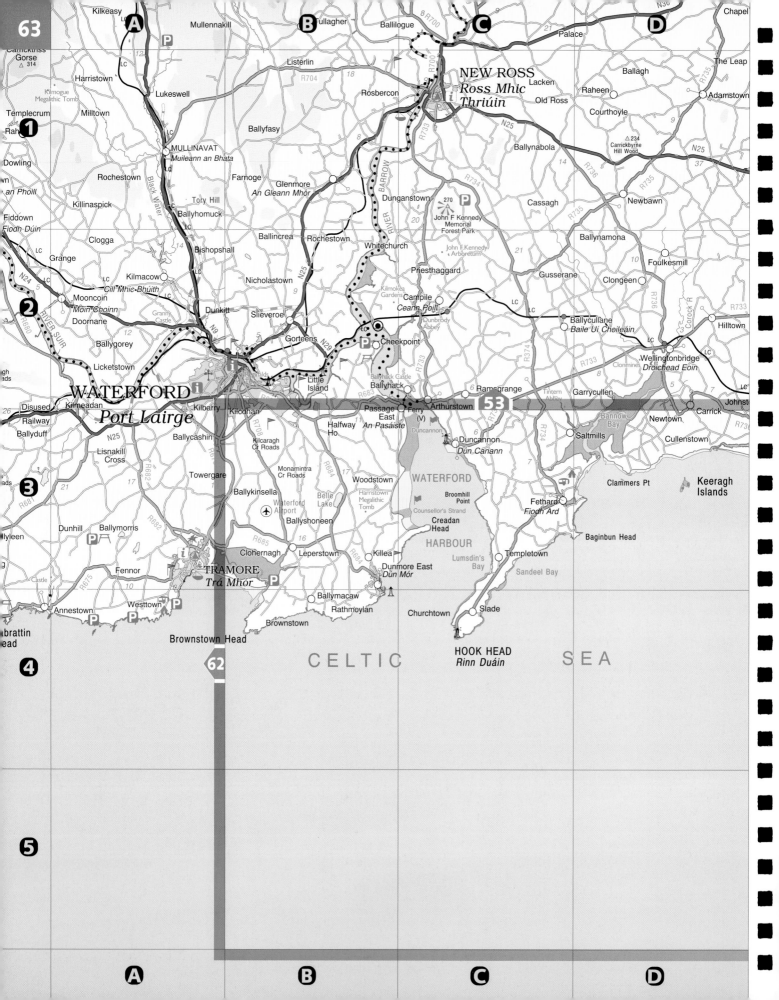

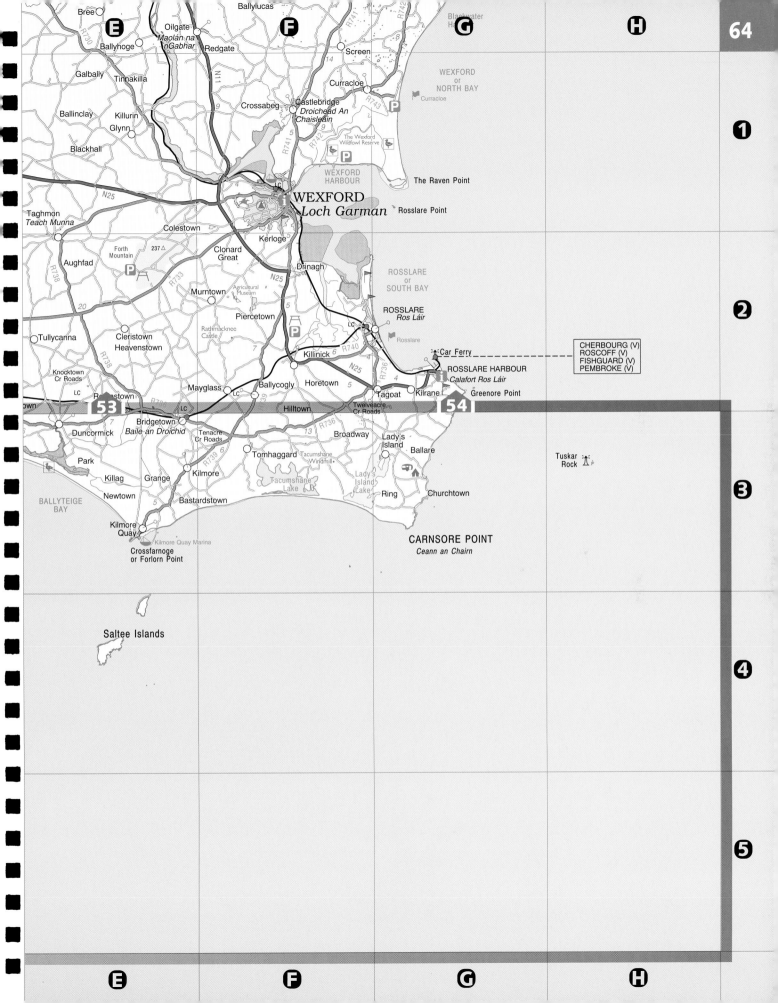

A **B** **C** **D**

Little Skellig
Great Skellig Skellig Michael

BOLUS HEAD

Hog's Head

Castle Cove

Mountain

Caherdaniel
Cathair Donall

Beenarourke

Sheehan's Point

Derrynane
House

Abbey Island
Ogham Stone

Lamb's Head

Deenish
Island

Derrynane
Bay

Scariff Island

1

Cod's Head

R575

Knocknagallaun

Allihies
Na hAilichi

Ballydonegan

2

Garnish Point

Garnish Bay

DURSEY ISLAND

Cable Car

Lackacroghan

260

Cahermore

Ballynacallagh

Firkeel

The Bull

Kilmichael

R572

White Ball Head

The Cow

Black Ball Head

DURSEY HEAD

Crow Head

The Calf

3

A T L A N T I C

4

O C E A N

5

A **B** **C** **D**

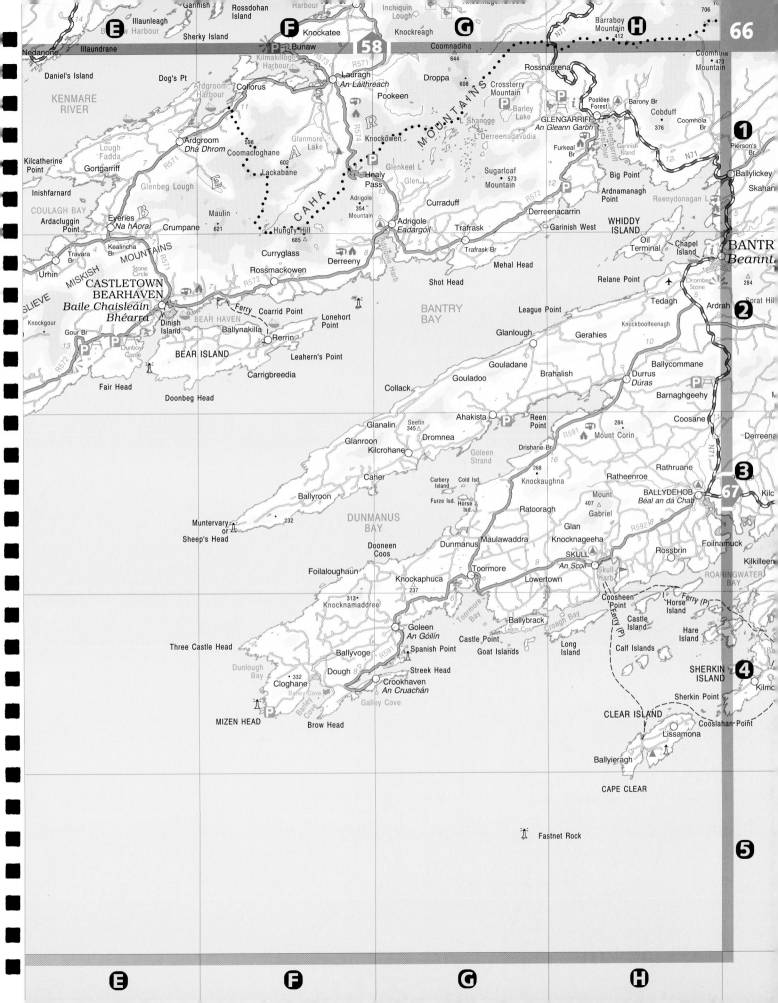

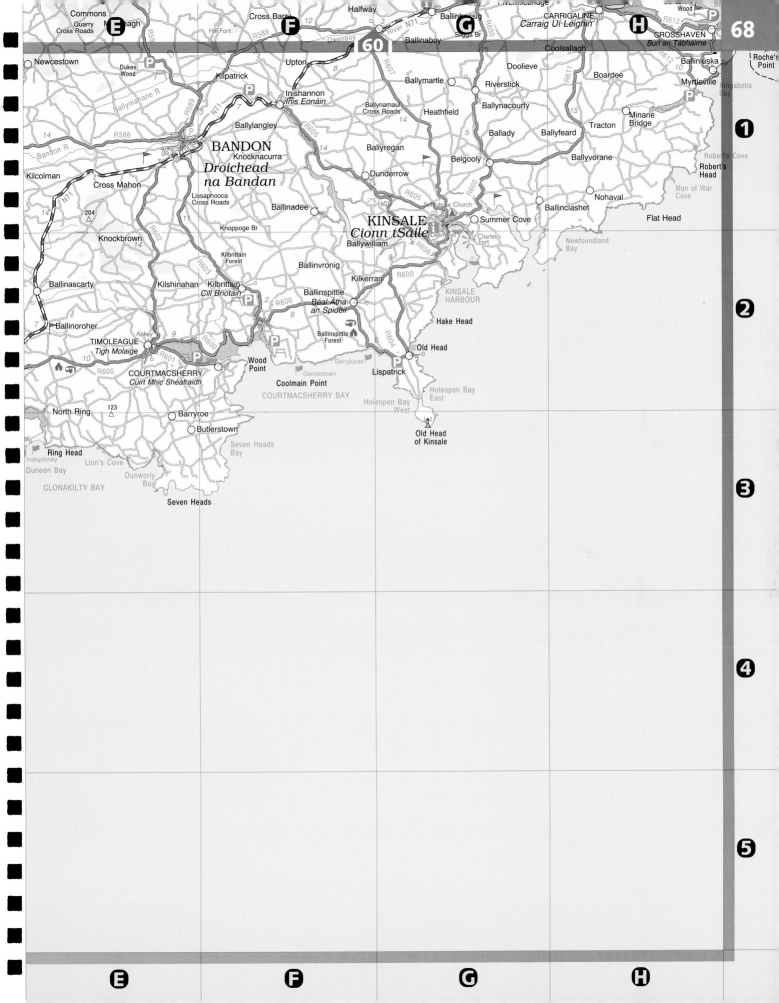

Commons
Quarry
Cross Roads

E

Newcestown

Dukes
Wood

Kilpatrick

Cross Barry

Halfway

Ballinhassig

F 12

Hill Fort

R589

Upton

Inishannon
Inis Eonáin

Owenboy

River N71

Ballinaboy

Sligga Br

G

CARRIGALINE
Carraig Uí Leighin

Coolsallagh

CROSSHAVEN
Bun an Tábhairne

H

R612

Wood

P

10 Ballinluska

Myrtleville

Ringabella
Bay

Roche's
Point

Kilpatrick

Kilpatrick

Ballylangley

R586

BANDON
*Droichead
na Bandan*

Knocknacurra

Lissaphooca
Cross Roads

Ballinadee

R605

Ballymaull
Cross Roads

Ballyregan

Dunderrow

R605

St Multose Church

Ballymartle

Heathfield

Ballynacourty

Riverstick

Dooleive

Ballady

Belgooly

Ballyfeard

Boardee

Minane
Bridge

Tracton

Robert's Cove

Man of War
Cove

Robert's
Head

Kilcolman

Cross Mahon

N71

204
△

Knockbrown

Knoppoge Br

Kilbrittain
Forest

Ballinadee

Ballinvronig

KINSALE
Cionn tSáile

Ballywilliam

Desmond
Castle

Summer Cove

Charles's
Fort

Ballinclashet

Nohaval

Flat Head

Newfoundland
Bay

Ballinascarty

Ballinoroher

Kilshinahan

R602

R603

Kilbrittain
Cill Briotáin

P

R600

Ballinspittle
*Béal Átha
an Spidéil*

Kilkerran

R600

R604

Hake Head

Old Head

KINSALE
HARBOUR

TIMOLEAGUE
Tigh Molaige

Abbey

R601

R600

P

COURTMACSHERRY
Cúirt Mhic Shéafraidh

Wood
Point

Ballinspittle
Forest

Garrylucas

Garretstown

Coolmain Point

Lispatrick

P

Holeopen Bay
East

North Ring

123
△

Barryroe

Butlerstown

Seven Heads
Bay

COURTMACSHERRY BAY

Holeopen Bay
West

Old Head
of Kinsale

Ring Head

Inchydoney

Lion's Cove

Dunworly
Bay

Duneen Bay

CLONAKILTY BAY

Seven Heads

1

2

3

4

5

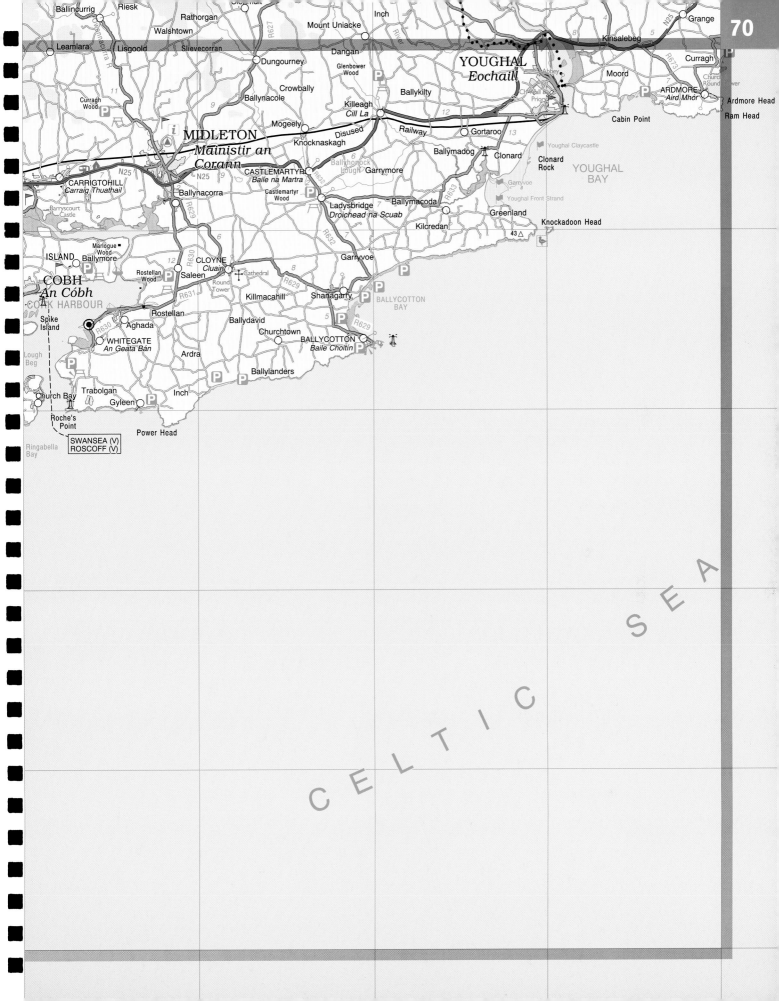

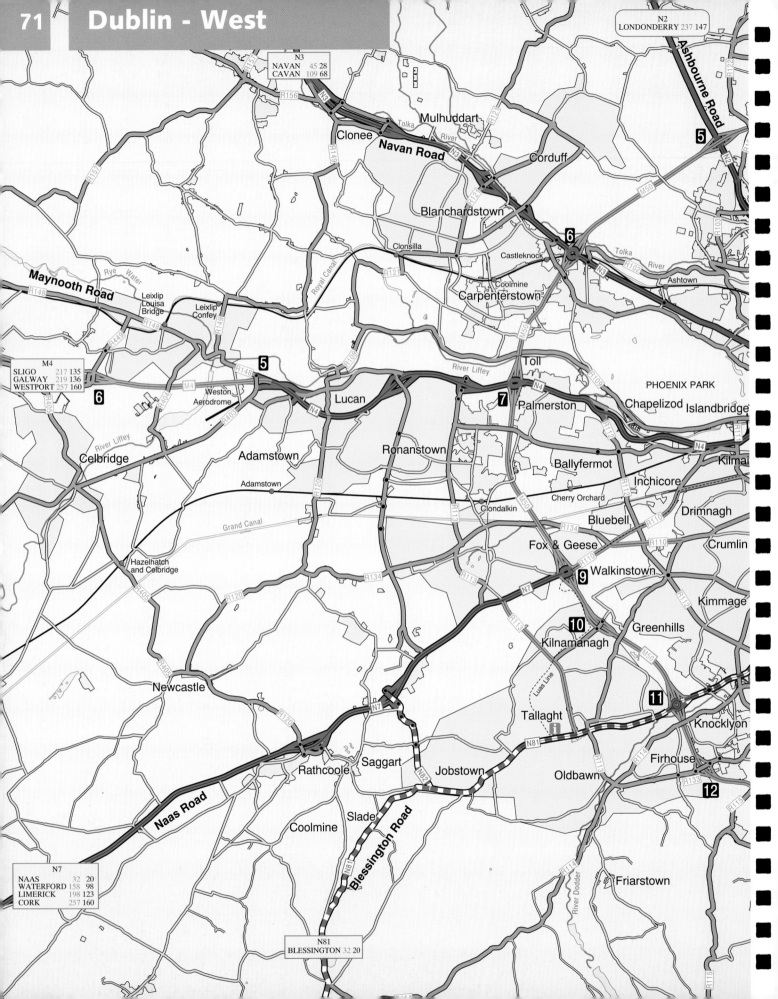

St. Margaret's
Dublin Airport
Swords Road

M1
DROGHEDA 50 31
BELFAST 167 104

Portmarnock
Ireland's Eye
Carrigeen Bay

Poppintree
Santry
Darndale
Donaghmede
Baldoyle

Ballymun
Finglas
Glasnevin North
Kilmore
Beaumont Coolock
Edenmore
Howth Junction
Bayside
Sutton
Howth

Whitehall
Donnycarney
Harmonstown
Raheny
Kilbarrack

Glasnevin
Artane
Killester
Broombridge
Cabra
Drumcondra
Marino
Clontarf
Dollymount

North Bull Island

Heuston
Docklands
Connolly
Tara St.
Pearse
Grand Canal Dock

Ferry Terminal

DUBLIN BAY

FERRIES
Holyhead (V)
Liverpool (V)
Isle of Man (V)
(seasonal)

Irishtown
Lansdowne
Sandymount

Dolphins Barn
Harolds Cross
Ballsbridge
Rathmines
Donnybrook
Clonskeagh
Merrion
Sydney Parade

Booterstown
Blackrock
Seapoint
Salthill & Monkstown

Terenure
Milltown
Windy Arbour
Mount Merrion

Monkstown
Ferry Terminal
Dún Laoghaire
Sandycove/Glasthule

Rathfarnham
Churchtown
Goatstown
Deansgrange
Sallynoggin
Glenageary
Dalkey

Templeogue
Dundrum
Stillorgan

Ballinteer
Sandyford
Foxrock
Leopardstown
Bray Road
Dalkey Island

Edmondstown
14
13
Cabinteely

Killiney Bay
Killiney

Stepaside
Carrickmines
15
16
Loughlinstown

GEORGE'S CHANNEL

0 Km   1   2   3
0 Mls ½   1   1½   2
Scale 1:85 000

M11
BRAY 19 12
WICKLOW 48 30
WEXFORD 142 88

Shankill
Kilternan

--- Inset map (city centre) ---
O'CONNELL STREET
Pro-Cathedral
MARLBOROUGH STREET
TALBOT STREET
EARL ST NORTH
PARNELL STREET
MOORE LANE
Ilac Centre
HENRY STREET
GPO
ABBEY ST
WOLFE TONE STREET
CAPEL STREET
MARY STREET
JERVIS STREET
Jervis Centre
ABBEY STREET
JERVIS
ABBEY ST MIDDLE
EDEN QUAY
LIFFEY
BURGH QUAY
UPPER ORMOND QUAY
LOTTS
BACHELORS WALK
RIVER
POOLBEG ST
Ha'penny Bridge
ASTON QUAY
WESTMORLAND ST
D'OLIER STREET
TARA ST
DART
STRAND STREET GREAT
N4
WELLINGTON QUAY
Temple Bar
FLEET ST
City Hall
ESSEX ST EAST
EUSTACE STREET
Central Bank
DAME STREET
COPE ST
ANGLESEA ST
COLLEGE
GRAFTON STREET
Trinity College
N4
PARLIAMENT STREET
GEORGE'S ST
DAME LANE
SUFFOLK ST
R114
WICKLOW STREET

Ferry Holyhead (V)

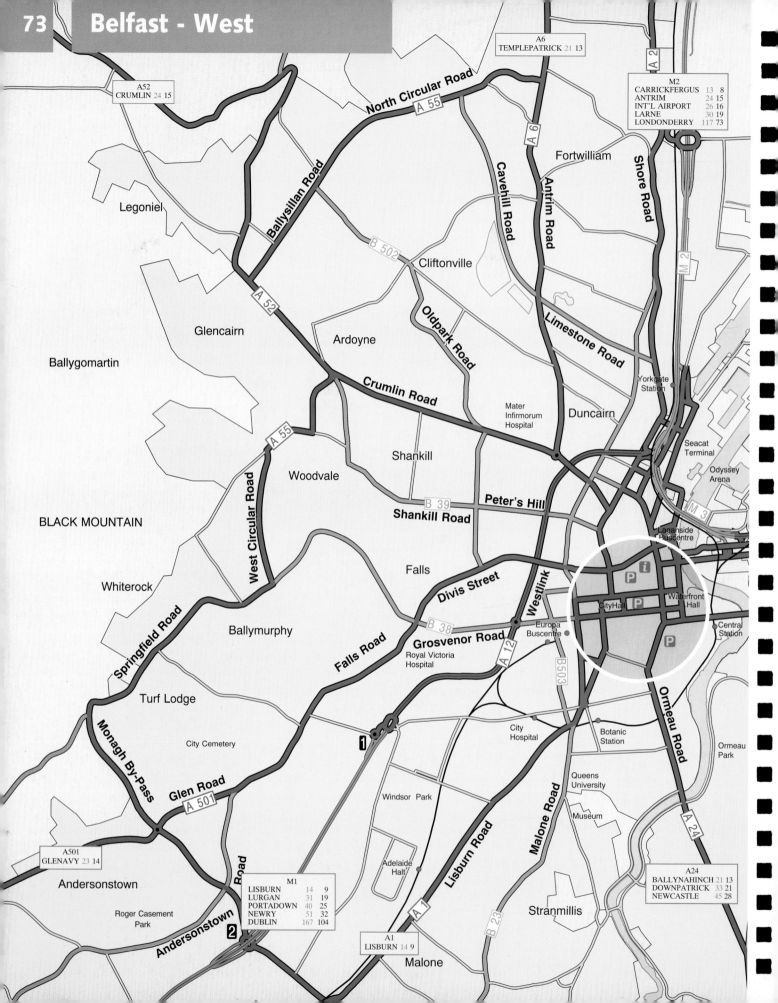

A52
CRUMLIN 24 15

A6
TEMPLEPATRICK 21 13

A 2

M2
CARRICKFERGUS 13 8
ANTRIM 24 15
INT'L AIRPORT 26 16
LARNE 30 19
LONDONDERRY 117 73

Legoniel

North Circular Road

A 55

Fortwilliam

Shore Road

Ballygomartin

Ballysillan Road

A 52

Cavehill Road

Antrim Road

B 502

Cliftonville

Glencairn

Ardoyne

Oldpark Road

Limestone Road

Crumlin Road

Yorkgate Station

Duncairn

Mater Infirmorum Hospital

Seacat Terminal

BLACK MOUNTAIN

A 55

West Circular Road

Shankill

Woodvale

Odyssey Arena

Whiterock

Shankill Road

B 39

Peter's Hill

Laganside Buscentre

Springfield Road

Ballymurphy

Falls

Divis Street

B 38

Westlink

City Hall

Waterfront Hall

Central Station

Falls Road

Grosvenor Road

A 12

Royal Victoria Hospital

Europa Buscentre

B503

Ormeau Road

Turf Lodge

City Cemetery

1

City Hospital

Botanic Station

Ormeau Park

Monagh By-Pass

Glen Road

A 501

Windsor Park

Queens University

Museum

Malone Road

A 24

A501
GLENAVY 23 14

Andersonstown

Roger Casement Park

Andersonstown Road

2

M1
LISBURN 14 9
LURGAN 31 19
PORTADOWN 40 25
NEWRY 51 32
DUBLIN 167 104

Adelaide Halt

Lisburn Road

A 1

B 23

Stranmillis

A24
BALLYNAHINCH 21 13
DOWNPATRICK 33 21
NEWCASTLE 45 28

A1
LISBURN 14 9

Malone

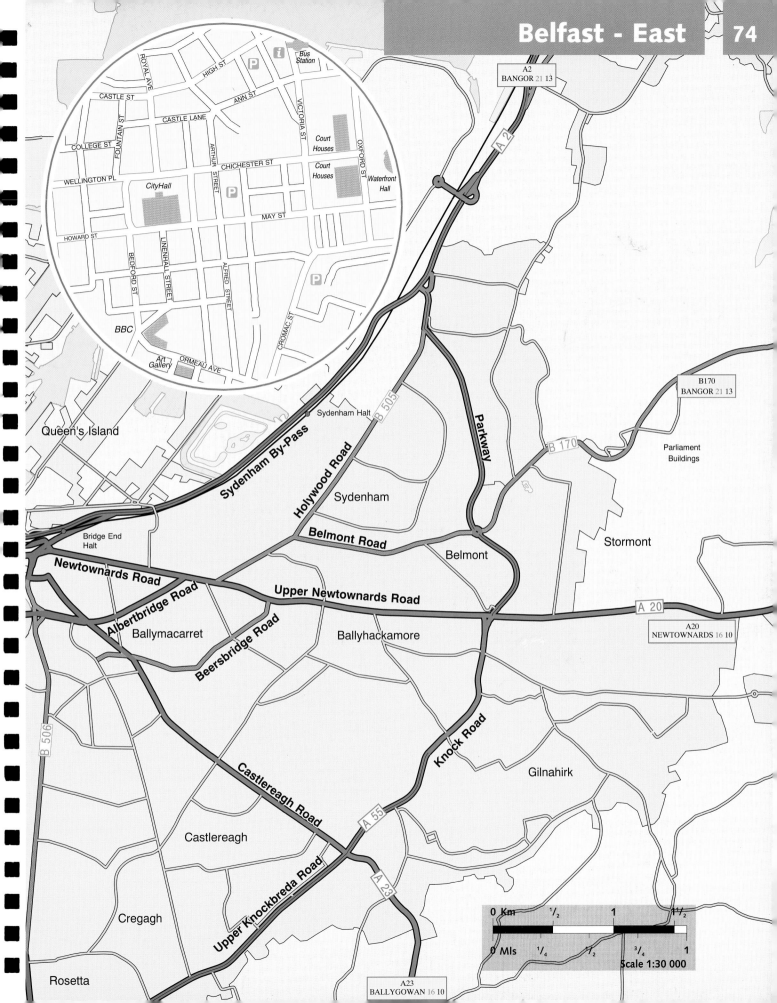

Street map inset:

ROYAL AVE · HIGH ST · i · Bus Station
CASTLE ST · ANN ST · P
CASTLE LANE
FOUNTAIN ST · VICTORIA ST · Court Houses
COLLEGE ST · CHICHESTER ST · Court Houses · OXFORD ST
WELLINGTON PL · ARTHUR STREET · Waterfront Hall
CityHall · P
HOWARD ST
BEDFORD ST · LINENHALL STREET · MAY ST · ALFRED STREET · CHOMAC ST · P
BBC
Art Gallery · ORMEAU AVE

Main map labels:

A2 BANGOR 21 13
A 2
B170 BANGOR 21 13
B 170
Parliament Buildings
Queen's Island
Sydenham Halt
B 505
Sydenham By-Pass
Holywood Road
Sydenham
Parkway
Stormont
Bridge End Halt
Belmont Road
Belmont
Newtownards Road
Albertbridge Road
Upper Newtownards Road
A 20
A20 NEWTOWNARDS 16 10
Ballymacarret
Beersbridge Road
Ballyhackamore
B 506
Knock Road
Gilnahirk
Castlereagh Road
Castlereagh
A 55
Cregagh
Upper Knockbreda Road
A 23
Rosetta
A23 BALLYGOWAN 16 10

0 Km · ½ · 1 · 1½
0 Mls · ¼ · ½ · ¾ · 1
Scale 1:30 000

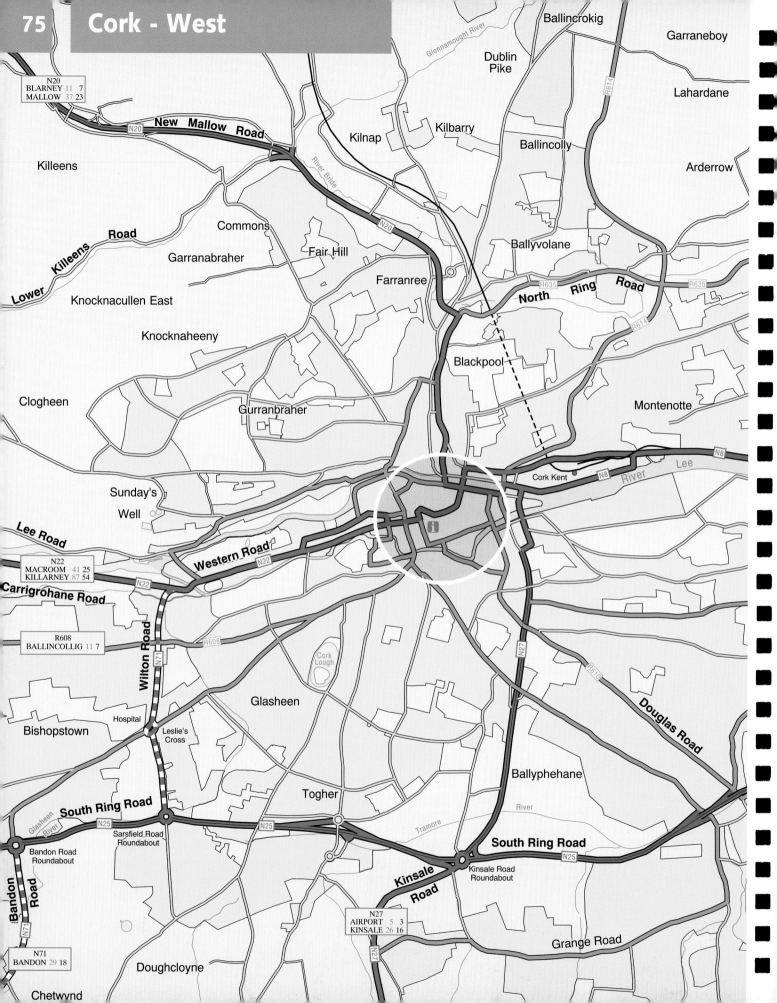

N20
BLARNEY 11 7
MALLOW 37 23

New Mallow Road

N20

Killeens

Commons

Lower Killeens Road

Garranabraher

Fair Hill

Knocknacullen East

Farranree

Knocknaheeny

River Bride

Clogheen

Gurranbraher

Sunday's Well

Lee Road

N22
MACROOM 41 25
KILLARNEY 87 54

Carrigrohane Road

Western Road

N22

Wilton Road

N71

R608
BALLINCOLLIG 11 7

R608

Cork Lough

Glasheen

Bishopstown

Hospital

Leslie's Cross

Togher

N25

South Ring Road

Glasheen River

N25

Sarsfield Road Roundabout

Bandon Road Roundabout

Bandon Road

N71

N71
BANDON 29 18

Doughcloyne

Chetwynd

Kilnap

Kilbarry

Dublin Pike

Ballincrokig

Garraneboy

Ballincolly

Lahardane

Ballyvolane

Arderrow

R614

North Ring Road

R635

R635

R614

Blackpool

Montenotte

Cork Kent

N8

River Lee

N8

N27

R610

Douglas Road

Ballyphehane

River Tramore

South Ring Road

N25

Kinsale Road

Kinsale Road Roundabout

N27
AIRPORT 5 3
KINSALE 26 16

N27

Grange Road

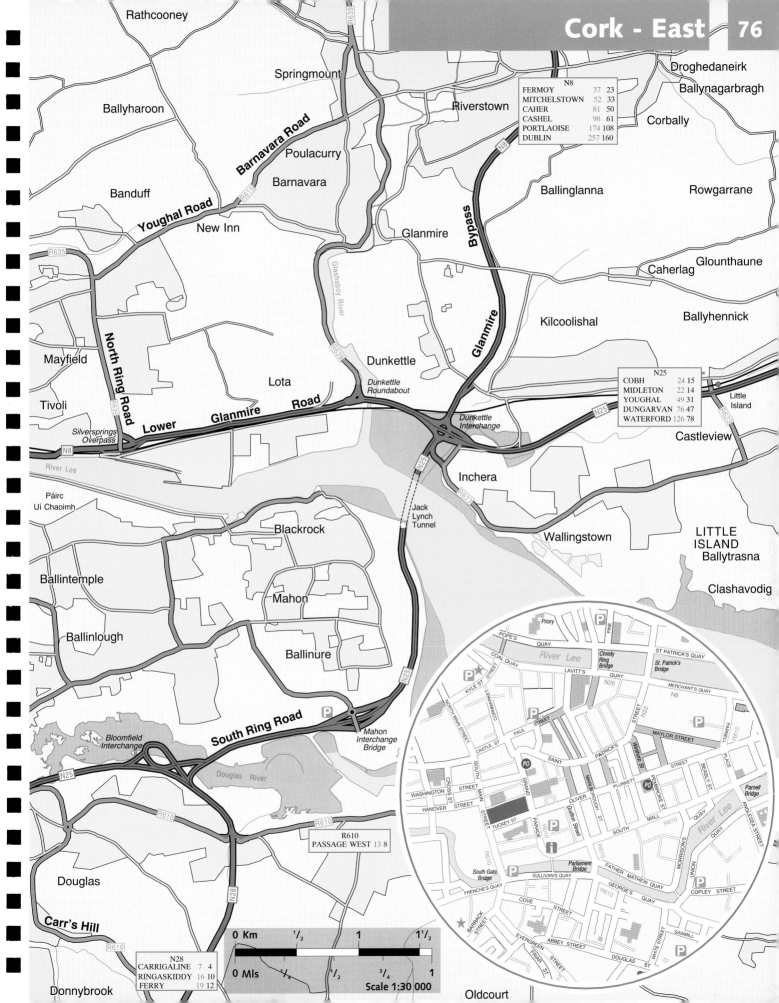

Rathcooney

Springmount

R639

Riverstown

Droghedaneirk

Ballynagarbragh

Ballyharoon

Barnavara Road

Poulacurry

Corbally

N8

N8		
FERMOY	37	23
MITCHELSTOWN	52	33
CAHER	81	50
CASHEL	98	61
PORTLAOISE	174	108
DUBLIN	257	160

Banduff

Barnavara

Ballinglanna

Rowgarrane

R615

Youghal Road

New Inn

Bypass

Glanmire

Caherlag

Glounthaune

R635

Glashaboy River

Glanmire

Kilcoolishal

Ballyhennick

Mayfield

Lota

R639

Dunkettle

Dunkettle Roundabout

N25		
COBH	24	15
MIDLETON	22	14
YOUGHAL	49	31
DUNGARVAN	76	47
WATERFORD	126	78

North Ring Road

R633

Tivoli

Lower   Glanmire   Road

Dunkettle Interchange

N25

R623

Castleview

Little Island

Silversprings Overpass

N8

N25

Inchera

R623

River Lee

Páirc Uí Chaoimh

Jack Lynch Tunnel

Wallingstown

LITTLE ISLAND

Ballytrasna

Blackrock

Clashavodig

Ballintemple

Mahon

Ballinlough

Ballinure

N25

South Ring Road

P

Mahon Interchange Bridge

Bloomfield Interchange

N25

Douglas   River

R610

R610

R610	
PASSAGE WEST	13 8

Douglas

R610

N28

Carr's Hill

N28		
CARRIGALINE	7	4
RINGASKIDDY	16	10
FERRY	19	12

Donnybrook

R610

Oldcourt

0 Km   ½   1   1½

0 Mls   ¼   ½   ¾   1

Scale 1:30 000

Priory

P

P

POPE'S   QUAY

River Lee

Christy Ring Bridge

ST PATRICK'S QUAY

COAL QUAY

LAVITT'S   QUAY

St. Patrick's Bridge

P

KYLE ST   STREET

N20

MERCHANT'S QUAY

N8

P

NORTH MAIN STREET

CORNMARKET STREET

CASTLE ST

PAUL   STREET

PO

SAINT   WINTHROP ST

PATRICK'S

STREET

MAYLOR STREET

PARNELL

PLACE

WASHINGTON   STREET

SOUTH   MAIN

STREET

GRAND   PARADE

OLIVER   PLUNKETT   STREET

MARLBOROUGH ST

PEMBROKE ST

PO

BEASLY ST

Parnell Bridge

CROSS   STREET

HANOVER   STREET

TUCKEY ST

Grafton Street

SOUTH   MALL

R610

MORRISON'S   QUAY

Anglesea Street

River Lee

i

R610

R610

P

Parliament Bridge

FATHER   MATHEW QUAY

South Gate Bridge

P

SULLIVAN'S QUAY

GEORGE'S   QUAY

UNION   QUAY

COPLEY   STREET

FRENCHE'S QUAY

COVE   STREET

BARRACK   STREET

EVERGREEN   STREET

ABBEY STREET

FRIAR ST

DOUGLAS

WHITE STREET

SAWMILL

Ballyarnet
Lake

A2
MOVILLE 32 20

A 515
Culmore Road

Ballyarnet
Country Park

Shantallow

Ballynashallog

B 526

Madam's Bank Road

A 515

Foyle
Bridge

Lough Enagh
(Western)

Gransha

Lough
Enagh
(Easter...

A2
LIMAVADY 26 16

City Inset
P
Museum
Guildhall
Tower
Museum
ROSSVILLE STREET
FAHAN ST
B 507
Bus
Station
FOYLE EMBANKMENT
P
The
Diamond
City Walls
P
P
Court House
St Columb's
Cathedral
P
JOHN ST
P
B 507
ABERCORN ROAD
A40
FOYLE ROAD
P
Craigavon
Bridge
Railway
Station
A2
LETTERKENNY 36 23

Buncrana Rd
B 194
Culmore Road
Strand Road

LONDONDERRY

Northland Road
Pennyburn

Creggan Road
B 527

Leisure
Centre

Rosemount

Limavady Road
Clooney Road
Kilfinnan
Playing Fields
CRESCENT LINK
A 514

Leisure
Centre

Bogside
City Wall
Museum
Kilfennan Link Road
Dungiven Road
Waterside
Lisnagelvin

Creggan

Lone Moor Road
B 524
B 507

Railway
Station
Craigavon
Bridge

Chapel Road

Brandywell
Foyle Road
Victoria Road
Irish Street
B 523
Glenshane Road
Hospital
Altnagelvin

Football
Ground

Foyle Search
and Rescue
Playing
Fields

A40
A5

Gobnascale

River Faughan

A5
A40
RAPHOE 25 15

Prehen

A5
STRABANE 22 14

A5
DUNGIVEN 30 18
BELFAST 117 73

0 Km   ½   1   1½
0 Mls   ¼   ½   ¾   1
Scale 1:30 000

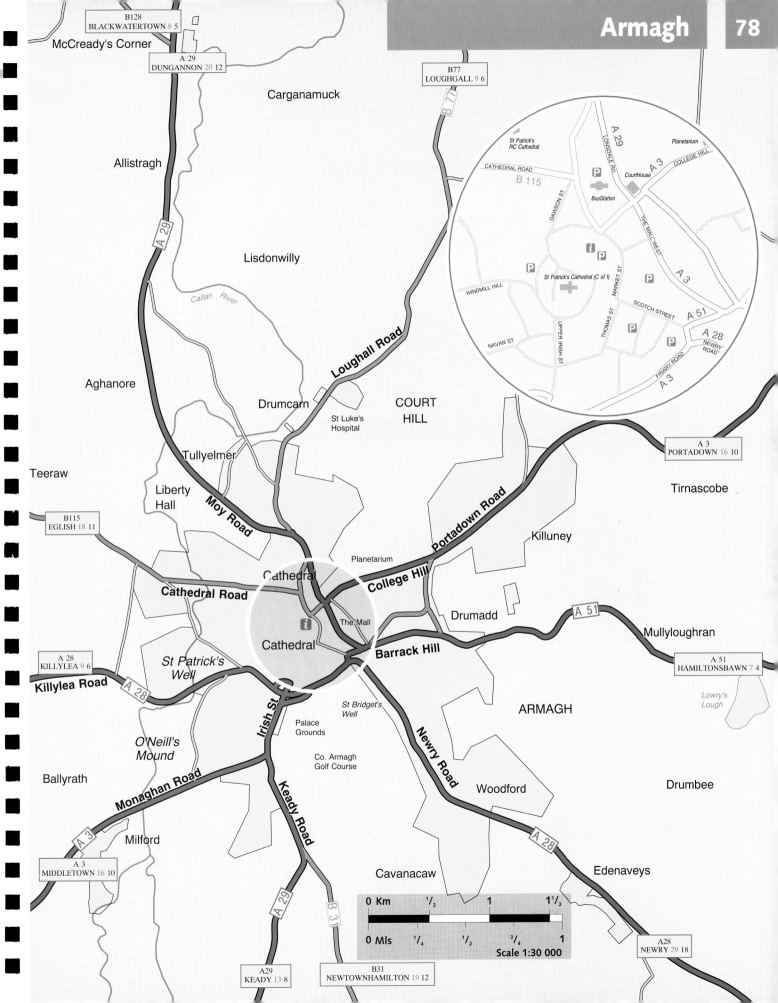

B128
BLACKWATERTOWN 8 5

McCready's Corner

A 29
DUNGANNON 20 12

Carganamuck

B77
LOUGHGALL 9 6

B 77

Allistragh

St Patrick's
RC Cathedral

A 29

Planetarium

CATHEDRAL ROAD

A 3

COLLEGE HILL

B 115

CourtHouse

LONSDALE RD

DAWSON ST

BusStation

Lisdonwilly

THE MALL WEST

Callan River

A 3

St Patrick's Cathedral (C of I)

A 3

Aghanore

WINDMILL HILL

MARKET ST

SCOTCH STREET

A 51

THOMAS ST

Loughall Road

Drumcarn

NAVAN ST

UPPER IRISH ST

A 28

NEWRY
ROAD

St Luke's
Hospital

COURT
HILL

FRIARY ROAD

A 3

Tullyelmer

A 3
PORTADOWN 16 10

Teeraw

Liberty
Hall

Moy Road

Tirnascobe

Portadown Road

Killuney

B115
EGLISH 18 11

Cathedral

Planetarium

College Hill

Drumadd

A 51

Cathedral Road

Mulloughran

i

The Mall

A 28
KILLYLEA 9 6

St Patrick's
Well

Cathedral

Barrack Hill

A 51
HAMILTONSBAWN 7 4

Killylea Road

A 28

Irish St

ARMAGH

Lowry's
Lough

O'Neill's
Mound

St Bridget's
Well

Ballyrath

Monaghan Road

Palace
Grounds

Newry Road

Drumbee

Keady Road

Co. Armagh
Golf Course

Woodford

A 3

Milford

A 3
MIDDLETOWN 16 10

A 29

B 31

Cavanacaw

A 28

Edenaveys

A29
KEADY 13 8

B31
NEWTOWNHAMILTON 19 12

A28
NEWRY 29 18

0 Km		½		1		1½

0 Mls		¼		½		¾		1

Scale 1:30 000

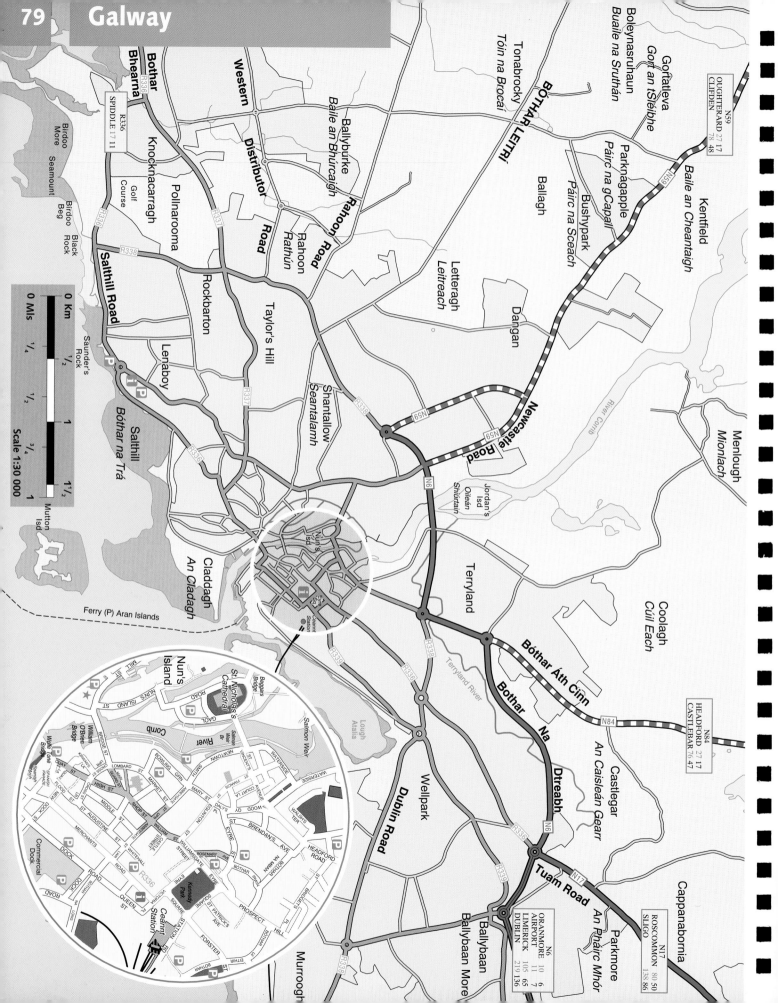

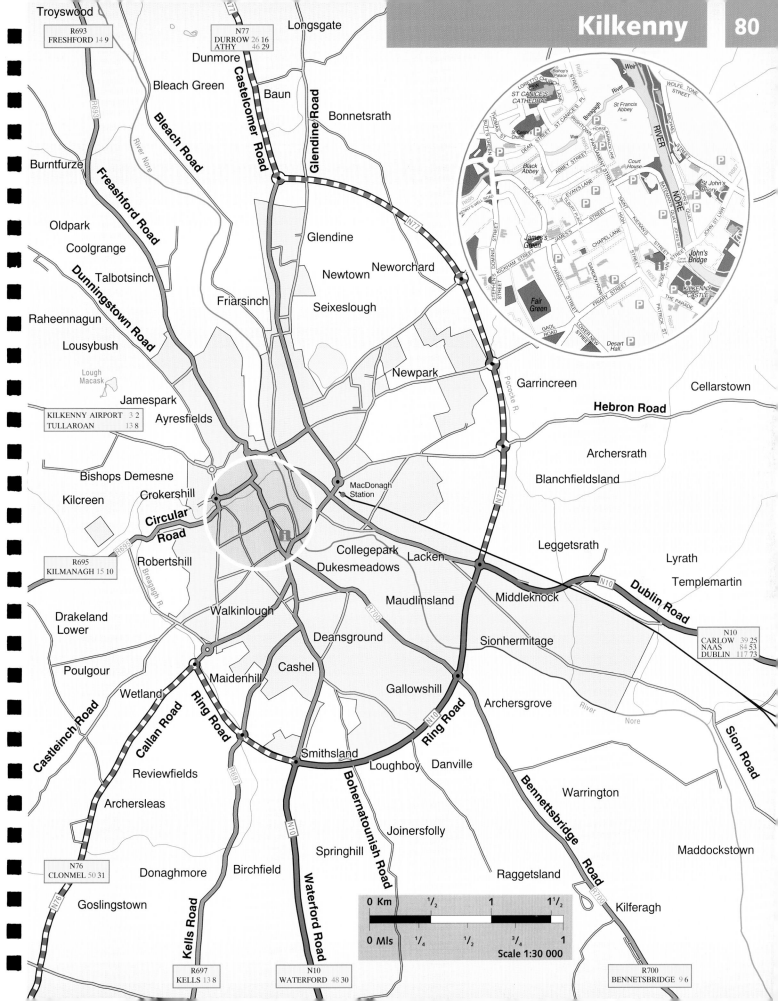

Troyswood
Longsgate
Dunmore
Bleach Green
Baun
Bonnetsrath

R693
FRESHFORD 14 9

N77
DURROW 26 16
ATHY 46 29

Burntfurze
River Nore
Bleach Road
Castlecomer Road
Glendine Road

Oldpark
Freashford Road
Glendine

Coolgrange
Talbotsinch
Newtown
Neworchard

Friarsinch
Seixeslough

Raheennagun
Dunningstown Road

Lousybush

Lough Macask

Jamespark
Newpark
Garrincreen
Cellarstown

KILKENNY AIRPORT 3 2
TULLAROAN 13 8

Ayresfields
Pococke R.
Hebron Road

Archersrath

Bishops Demesne
Blanchfieldsland

Kilcreen
Crokershill
MacDonagh Station

Circular Road

R695
KILMANAGH 15 10

Robertshill
Breagagh R.
Collegepark
Lacken
Leggetsrath
Lyrath

Dukesmeadows
Templemartin

Drakeland Lower
Walkinlough
Maudlinsland
Middleknock
Dublin Road

N10
CARLOW 39 25
NAAS 84 53
DUBLIN 117 73

Deansground
Sionhermitage

Poulgour
Cashel
Gallowshill

Castleinch Road
Maidenhill
Archersgrove

Wetland
Callan Road
Ring Road
Ring Road

Reviewfields
River Nore

Archersleas
Smithsland
Loughboy
Danville
Bennettsbridge Road

N76
CLONMEL 50 31

Warrington

Donaghmore
Birchfield
Bohernatounish Road
Joinersfolly
Maddockstown

Goslingstown
Kells Road
Springhill
Raggetsland
Kilferagh

Waterford Road

R693 FRESHFORD
Sion Road

0 Km   ½   1   1½
0 Mls   ¼   ½   ¾   1
Scale 1:30 000

R697
KELLS 13 8

N10
WATERFORD 48 30

R700
BENNETSBRIDGE 9 6

Inset (Kilkenny city centre):
LORETTO CHURCH LANE
Bishop's Palace
NEW
ST CANICE'S CATHEDRAL
Weir
WOLFE TONE STREET
St Canice's
THOMAS STREET
ST CANICE'S PL
Breagagh
St Francis Abbey
MICHAEL STREET
RIVER NORE
DEAN STREET
IRISHTOWN
BARRACK LANE
PARLIAMENT STREET
Court House
BATEMAN'S QUAY
St John's Priory
Black Abbey
ABBEY STREET
JOHN ST LWR
KENNY'S WELL ROAD
EVAN'S LANE
BLACK MILL STREET
TILBURY PLACE
SAINT KIERAN'S STREET
JOHN ST UPR
STEPHEN'S STREET
DOMINIC STREET
James's Green
JAMES'S STREET
CHAPEL LANE
HIGH STREET
John's Bridge
KICKHAM STREET
GARDEN ROW
Canal Square
KILKENNY CASTLE
PARNELL STREET
FRIARY STREET
THE PARADE
Fair Green
PATRICK ST.
GAOL ROAD
LOWER NEW STREET
Desart Hall.

Goulavoher
St Nessan's Road
Templemungret
Ballykeeffe
Ballygrennan
Redgate
Ballyvrennan
Quinspool South
Ballykeeffe

N69 FOYNES 34 21

Dock Road
Shannon
N69
Clonmacken
Cordell Road
Cratloe Road
Moyross

N18 SHANNON AIRPORT GALWAY 105 65
N18 SHANNON AIRPORT GALWAY 21 13

R445

Dooradoyle Road
Dooradoyle
Ballynaclough River
R526
Derravoher
Ennis Road

Killeely Road
R464

R464 PARTEEN 2 1

N20 CORK KILLARNEY 111 69 105 65

N20
Hospital
River Shannon

N20

Rossbrien
R511
R511 FEDAMORE 9 6
N7
Roxborough Road
R511

Colbert Station

Abbey River

Corbally Road
R463

R463 SCARRIFF 30 18

Rathbane South

Banemore

Kilmallock Road

Crossagalla
Crabb's-Land

Ballysimon Road
R509

Singland

Groody River

Reboge Meadows

Towlerton

R445

R527

Inchmore

R512 KILMALLOCK 32 20

Knockananty

N24 WATERFORD 129 80

N7 DUBLIN 198 123

N24

Ballysir

Dublin Road

Garraun

Scale 1:30,000
0 Km   ½   1   1½
0 Mls   ½   ¾   1   1½

The Shannon Bridge
THE BISHOP'S QUAY
HOWLEYS QUAY
MILL LANE
HENRY ST
GPO
HARVEY'S QUAY
SHANNON
HENRY
BEDFORD
SARSFIELD
Sarsfield Bridge
LUI
N20
MALLOW
HIGH ROAD
O'CONNELL STREET
GLENTWORTH
CECIL ST
ROCHES ST
O'CONNELL STREET
WILLIAM
R527
People's Park
PERY SQ
PERY ST
DAVIS ST
DOMINICK ST
THOMAS STREET
ROW
ARTHUR'S QUAY
PATRICK ST
FRANCIS ST
HYDE RD
PARNELL ST
ANNE ST
DENMARK ST
ELLEN ST
Colbert Station
WICKHAM
R527
MICHAEL STREET
ROXTON ST
HIGH ST
UPR WILLIAM ST
CARR ST
MUNGRET STREET
R527
LWR GERALD GRIFFIN
JAMES ST
SUMMER ST

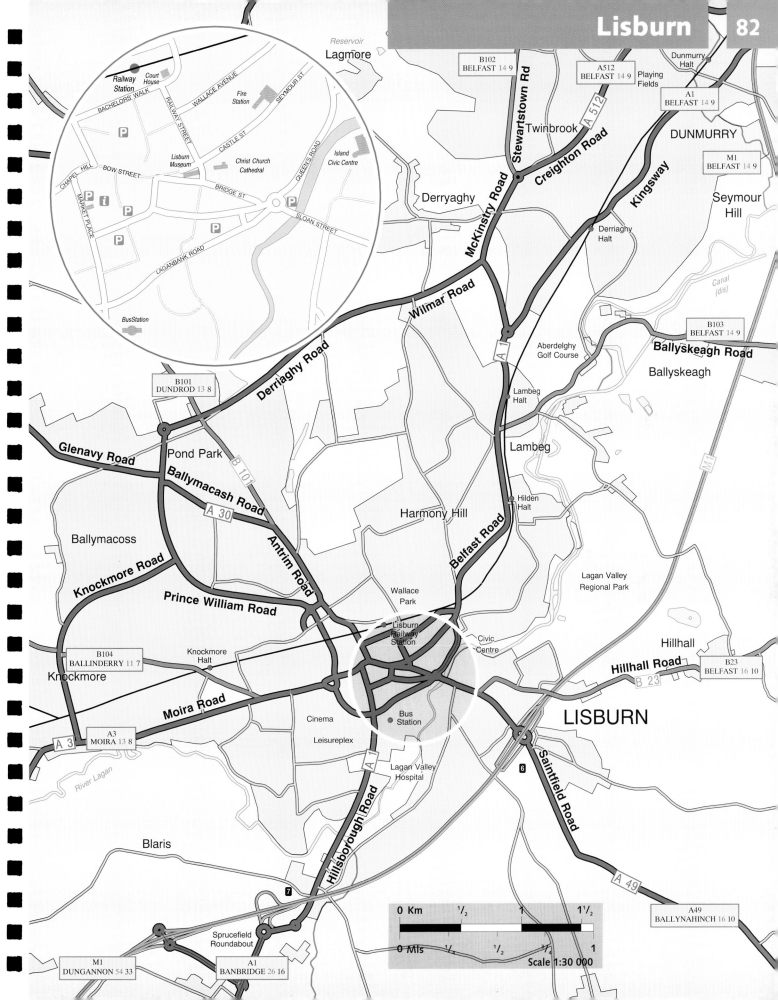

Reservoir
Lagmore

B102
BELFAST 14 9

A512
BELFAST 14 9

Dunmurry
Halt

A1
BELFAST 14 9

Playing
Fields

DUNMURRY

Stewartstown Rd

A 512

Creighton Road

Twinbrook

Kingsway

M1
BELFAST 14 9

Seymour
Hill

Railway
Station

Court
House

Fire
Station

WALLACE AVENUE

SEYMOUR ST.

BACHELORS' WALK

Railway Street

CASTLE ST.

QUEEN'S ROAD

P

Lisburn
Museum

Christ Church
Cathedral

Island
Civic Centre

CHAPEL HILL

BOW STREET

P

i

BRIDGE ST.

P

MARKET PLACE

P

SLOAN STREET

LAGANBANK ROAD

Bus Station

McKinstry Road

Derryaghy

Derriaghy
Halt

Aberdelghy
Golf Course

Lambeg
Halt

Canal
(dis)

B103
BELFAST 14 9

Ballyskeagh Road

Ballyskeagh

Wilmar Road

A 1

Lambeg

M1

Derriaghy Road

B101
DUNDROD 13 8

Glenavy Road

Pond Park

Ballymacash Road

B 101

A 30

Ballymacoss

Knockmore Road

Prince William Road

Antrim Road

Harmony Hill

Belfast Road

Hilden
Halt

Lagan Valley
Regional Park

Hillhall

B104
BALLINDERRY 11 7

Knockmore

Knockmore
Halt

Wallace
Park

Lisburn
Railway
Station

Civic
Centre

Hillhall Road

B23
BELFAST 16 10

B 23

Moira Road

Cinema

Bus
Station

LISBURN

A3
MOIRA 13 8

Leisureplex

A 1

Lagan Valley
Hospital

Saintfield Road

6

A 49

River Lagan

Hillsborough Road

Blaris

7

Sprucefield
Roundabout

A49
BALLYNAHINCH 16 10

0 Km   ½   1   1½

0 Mls   ¼   ½   ¾   1

Scale 1:30 000

M1
DUNGANNON 54 33

A1
BANBRIDGE 26 16

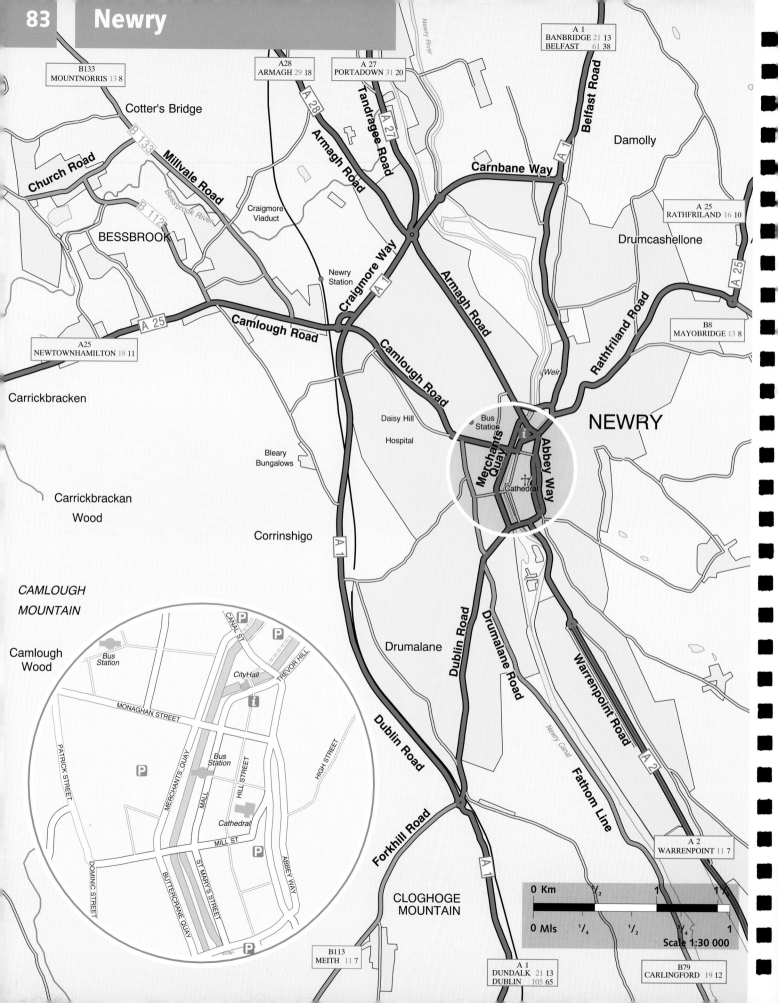

B133
MOUNTNORRIS 13 8

A28
ARMAGH 29 18

A 27
PORTADOWN 31 20

A 1
BANBRIDGE 21 13
BELFAST 61 38

Cotter's Bridge

Damolly

Church Road

Millvale Road

Bessbrook River

Craigmore Viaduct

BESSBROOK

B 133

B 112

Carnbane Way

Newry Station

A 1

Craigmore Way

Tandragee Road

Armagh Road

A 28

A 27

Belfast Road

A 25
RATHFRILAND 16 10

Drumcashellone

A 25

A 25

Camlough Road

A25
NEWTOWNHAMILTON 18 11

Camlough Road

Rathfriland Road

Weir

B8
MAYOBRIDGE 13 8

Carrickbracken

Daisy Hill Hospital

Bleary Bungalows

Bus Station

NEWRY

Abbey Way

Merchants Quay

Cathedral

Carrickbrackan Wood

Corrinshigo

A 1

CAMLOUGH MOUNTAIN

Camlough Wood

Dublin Road

Drumalane

Drumalane Road

Warrenpoint Road

Newry Canal

A 2

CANAL ST

P

P

Bus Station

CityHall

TREVOR HILL

MONAGHAN STREET

i

PATRICK STREET

P

MERCHANTS' QUAY

MALL

Bus Station

HILL STREET

HIGH STREET

DOMINIC STREET

BUTTERCRANE QUAY

ST MARY'S STREET

Cathedral

MILL ST

P

ABBEY WAY

P

Fathom Line

Forkhill Road

Dublin Road

A 1

CLOGHOGE MOUNTAIN

A 2
WARRENPOINT 11 7

0 Km   ½   1   1½

0 Mls   ¼   ½   ¾   1

Scale 1:30 000

B113
MEITH 11 7

A 1
DUNDALK 21 13
DUBLIN 105 65

B79
CARLINGFORD 19 12

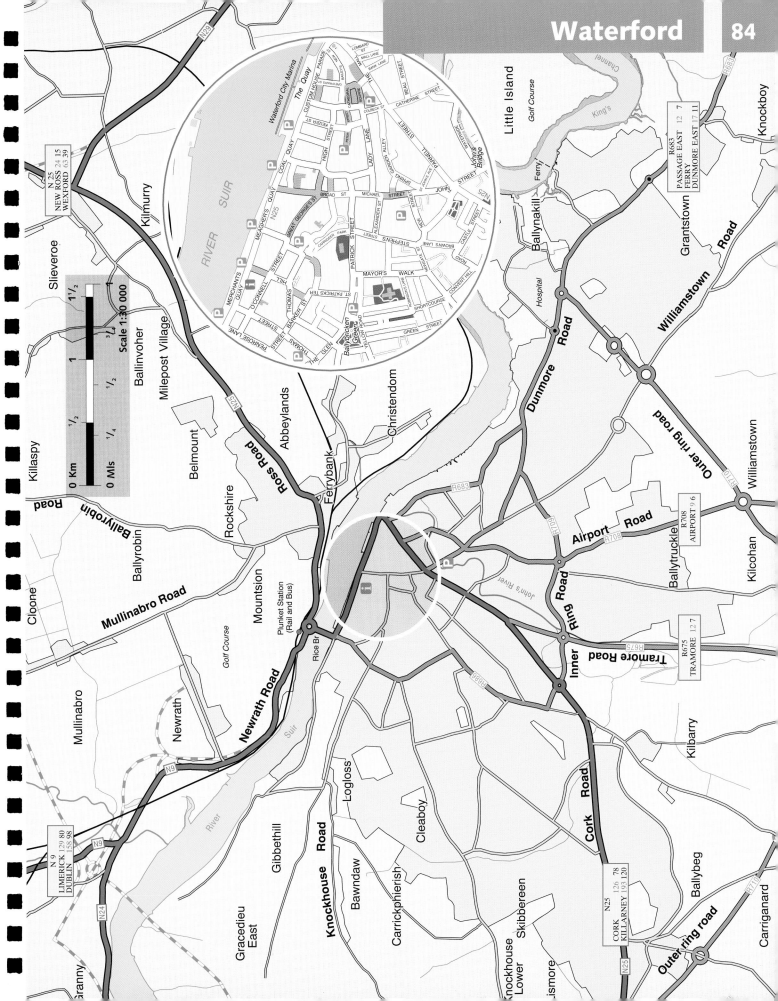

Little Island
Golf Course

King's Channel

R683

R683
PASSAGE EAST 12 7
FERRY DUNMORE EAST 17 11

Knockboy

Grantstown

Williamstown **Road**

Ballynakill

Hospital

Outer ring road

R710

Williamstown

R708
AIRPORT 9 6

Airport R708 **Road**

R709

Kilcohan

Ballytruckle

Ballybeg

Dunmore
Road

R683

John's River

Inner Ring **Road**

Tramore Road
R675
TRAMORE 12 7

Kilbarry

R710

N 25
NEW ROSS 24 15
WEXFORD 63 39

Slieveroe

Kilmurry

RIVER SUIR

Ballinvoher

Milepost Village

Ballyrobin Road

Ballyrobin

Killaspy

Cloone

Mullinabro

Belmount

Rockshire

Abbeylands

Ross Road

Ferrybank

Christendom

Mullinabro Road

Mountsion

Plunket Station
(Rail and Bus)

Rice Br

Golf Course

Newrath

N9

N24

Suir

River

N 9
LIMERICK 129 80
DUBLIN 158 98

Gracedieu East

Granny

Gibbethill

Knockhouse Road

Bawndaw

Logloss

Carrickphierish

Cleaboy

Skibbereen

Knockhouse Lower

Lismore

Cork Road

N25
CORK 126 78
KILLARNEY 193 120

N25

Ballybeg

Outer ring road

Carriganard

R710

Scale 1:30 000

0 Km ¼ ½ 1 1½
0 Mls ½ 1 1½

Newrath Road

City centre inset (magnified circle)

River Suir

The Quay

Waterford City Marina

CUSTOM HOUSE PARADE

LOMBARD ST
MALL LANE
BANK LANE

KEIZER ST

PETER
CATHEDRAL

THE MALL

BEAU STREET

COLBECK ST

CATHERINE STREET

HIGH STREET

COAL QUAY

BROAD ST

GREAT GEORGES ST

MICHAEL ST

LADY LANE

SPRING GARDEN ALLEY

PARNELL STREET

JOHN'S

John's Bridge

JOHN STREET

MEAGHERS QUAY

N25

PATRICK STREET

STEPHEN STREET

ALEXANDER ST

JOHN STREET

BROWNS LANE

CASTLE STREET

MERCHANTS QUAY

O'CONNELL STREET

HILL STREET

THOMAS STREET

BARKER ST

MAYOR'S WALK

CONVENT HILL

GREEN STREET

SHORTCOURSE

ST. PATRICKS TER

THE GLEN

THOMAS STREET

PENROSE LANE

Ballybricken Green

YELLOW ROAD

GREEN STREET

Golfing information

Affiliated to the Golf Union of Ireland. This listing is by Province and County.
The name of the Golf Club is preceded by the number of holes and followed
By a page number and a reference for the grid square in which the golf location symbol appears.

CONNAUGHT

Co. GALWAY
18	Ardacong	32	E1
18	Athenry	32	E4
18	Ballinasloe	33	A4
18	Bearna	31	C4
27	Connemara	29	B2
9	Connemara Isles	30	F3
18	Curra West	32	G5
9	Dunmore Demesne	24	F5
18	Galway	31	C4
18	Galway Bay	31	D4
9	Glenlo Abbey	31	C4
18	Gort	42	E1
18	Loughrea	32	G5
9	Mountbellew	32	G2
18	Oughterard	30	H2
18	Portumna	43	A1
18	Tuam	32	E2

Co. LEITRIM
9	Ballinamore	17	A5

Co. MAYO
9	Achill	21	C1
18	Ballina	14	H5
18	Ballinrobe	22	H5
9	Ballyhaunis	24	E3
18	Belmullet	13	B3
18	Castlebar	22	H3
18	Claremorris	23	D4
9	Mulranny	22	E2
9	Swinford	23	D2
18	Westport	22	F3

Co. ROSCOMMON
18	Athlone	33	C2
9	Ballaghaderreen	24	G2
9	Boyle	25	A1
18	Carrick-on-Shannon	25	A1
9	Castlerea	24	G3
18	Roscommon	25	A5
9	Strokestown	25	B4

Co. SLIGO
9	Ballymote	15	D5
27	Co. Sligo	15	D2
27	Enniscrone	14	H4
18	Strandhill	15	D3
9	Tubbercurry	15	C5

LEINSTER

Co. CARLOW
9	Borris	53	B2
27	Carlow	45	B4
18	Killerig Castle	45	C4
18	Leinster Hills	45	B5

18	Mount Wolseley	45	C4

Co. DUBLIN
18	Balbriggan	28	G5
18	Balcarrick	36	G2
18	Beaverstown	36	G1
18	Beech Park	35	D4
18	Christy O'Connor	36	E4
18	Corballis Links	36	G2
27	Corrstown	36	F2
27	Donabate	36	G2
18	Dublin Mountain	36	E4
18	Dun Laoghaire	36	G4
18	Forrest Little	36	F2
9	Glencullen	36	F2
18	Hermitage	36	E3
27	Hollystown	36	E2
18	Hollywood Lakes	36	F1
18	Island (The)	36	G2
9	Killiney	36	G4
18	Kilternan	36	G4
	Re-relocated during		
	re-development		
18	Lucan	36	E3
18	Luttrellstown	36	E3
27	Malahide	36	G2
27	Portmarnock	36	G2
18	Roganstown	36	F2
9	Rush	36	G1
18	St. Margarets	36	F2
18	Skerries	36	G1
18	Slade Valley	36	E4
18	South County	36	E4
18	Swords	36	F2
18	Turvey	36	G1
18	Westmanstown	36	E3

DUBLIN CITY
9	Ballinascorney	36	F4
9	Carrickmines	36	G4
18	Castle	36	F4
18	Castleknock	36	E3
36	City West	36	E4
18	Clontarf	36	F3
36	Deer Park	36	G3
18	Dublin City	36	E4
18	Edmondstown	36	F4
18	Elmgreen	36	E3
18	Elm Park	36	F4
9	Foxrock	36	G4
18	Grange	36	F4
18	Grange Castle	36	E3
9	Hazel Grove	36	E4
18	Hibernian c/o City West	36	E4
18	Howth	36	G3
9	Kilmashogue	36	F4
18	Leopardstown	36	G4

18	Milltown	36	F4
18	Newlands	36	F4
9	Rathfarnham	36	F4
18	Royal Dublin (The)	36	G3
18	St. Anne's	36	G3
18	Stackstown	36	F4
9	Sutton	36	G3

Co. KILDARE
18	Athy	45	B2
36	Bodenstown	35	C4
36	Carton House	35	D3
18	Castlewarden	35	D4
9	Celbridge	35	D3
9	Cill Dara	35	B5
9	Clane	35	C4
18	Craddockstown	35	D5
18	Curragh	35	B5
18	Dunmurry Springs	35	B5
18	Highfield	35	A3
18	Kilkea Castle	45	B3
18	Killeen	35	D4
18	Knockanally	35	C3
36	K Club (The)	35	D4
18	Millicent	35	C4
18	Naas	35	D4
18	Newbridge	35	D4
18	Palmerstown House	35	D4
18	Woodlands	35	B4

Co. KILKENNY
18	Callan	52	G2
18	Castlecomer	44	H4
18	Gowran Park	53	A1
18	Kilkenny	52	H2
18	Mount Juliet	52	H2
18	Mountain View	52	H3

Co. LAOIS
18	Abbeyleix	44	G3
18	The Heath	44	H1
18	The Heritage	34	H5
18	Mountrath	44	F2
18	Portarlington	34	H5
18	Portlaoise	44	G2
18	Rathdowney	44	E4

Co. LONGFORD
18	Co. Longford	25	D4

Co. LOUTH
18	Ardee	27	D2
18	Co. Louth	28	F4
18	Dundalk	28	E1
18	Greenore	19	D5
18	Killinbeg	28	E1
18	Seapoint	28	F4
9	Townley Hall	28	E4

Co. MEATH
18	Ashbourne	36	E1
27	Black Bush	35	D1
18	County Meath	35	B1
18	Glebe	35	B1
36	Headfort	27	B4
18	Kilock	35	C2
18	Laytown/Bettystown	28	F4
18	Moor Park	27	D5
18	Navan	27	C4
18	Rathcore	35	B2
27	Royal Tara	27	C5
9	South Meath	27	A5
9	Summerhill	35	C2

Co. OFFALY
9	Beechlawn	34	E4
18	Birr	43	C1
18	Castle Barna	34	G4
18	Edenderry	35	A3
18	Esker Hills	34	E4
18	Tullamore	34	F4

Co. WESTMEATH
18	Ballinlough Castle	27	A5
18	Devin Castle	26	H5
18	Glasson	33	C2
18	Moate	33	D3
18	Mount Temple	33	D2
18	Mullingar	34	G2

Co. WEXFORD
18	Courtown	54	F1
18	Enniscorthy	53	D3
18	New Ross	53	A4
30	Rosslare	54	E5
18	Seafield	46	G5
18	St. Helen's Bay	54	F5
9	Tara Glen	54	F1
9	Tuskar Rock	64	G2
18	Wexford	54	E4

Co. WICKLOW
18	Arklow	46	G4
18	Baltinglass	45	C3
18	Blainroe	46	H2
9	Boystown	35	D5
18	Bray	36	H5
18	Charlesland	36	H5
18	Coollattin	46	E5
18	Delgany	36	G5
9	Djouce	46	G1
18	Druid's Glen	46	G1
18	European (The)	46	H3
18	Glen of the Downs	36	G5
18	Glenmalure	46	F3
18	Greystones	36	G5
9	Kilcoole	46	H1

18	Old Conna	36 G4
36	Powerscourt	36 G5
18	Rathsallagh	45 C2
18	Roundwood	46 G1
18	Tulfarris	45 D1
18	Wicklow	46 H2
18	Woodenbridge	46 F4
18	Woodbrook	36 G4

MUNSTER

Co. CLARE

9	Clonlara	42 G5
18	Doonbeg Links	40 E5
18	Dromoland	41 D4
18	East Clare	42 F3
18	Ennis	41 D4
18	Kilkee	36 D5
18	Kilrush	49 A1
36	Lahinch	40 F3
18	Shannon	41 D5
9	Spanish Piont	40 F4
18	Woodstock	41 D4

Co. CORK

18	Bandon	68 E1
18	Bantry Bay	66 H1
9	Berehaven	66 F2
18	Blarney	60 F4
27	Charleville	50 F4
9	Cobh	61 A5
9	Coosheen	66 H3
18	Cork	60 H4
9	Doneraile	60 F1
18	Douglas	60 H5
9	Dunmore	67 D3
18	East Cork	61 A4
18	Fermoy	60 H2
18	Fota Island	60 H4
9	Frankfield	60 G5
9	Glengarriff	66 H1
18	Harbour Point	60 H4
18	Kanturk	59 D1
27	Kinsale	68 G1
18	Lee Valley	60 F4
9	Lisselan	68 E2
18	Macroom	59 D4
18	Mahon	60 H4
18	Mallow	60 F2
18	Mitchelstown	50 H5
18	Monkstown	60 H5
18	Muskerry	60 F4
9	Raffeen Creek	60 H5
18	Skibbereen	67 B3
18	Youghal	61 D4

Co. KERRY

9	Ardfert	48 G4
36	Ballybunion	48 G2
9	Ballyheigue Castle	48 F4
18	Beaufort	58 G2
9	Castlegregory	48 E5
18	Castleisland	49 A5
9	Castlerosse	58 H3
18	Ceann Sibeal	57 B1
18	Dooks	58 E2
9	Dunloe	58 G2
18	Kenmare	58 H4
54	Killarney	58 H2
18	Killorglin	58 G2
9	Listowel	49 A3
18	Parknasilla	58 F5
18	Ring of Kerry	58 G4
9	Ross	58 H3
18	Tralee	48 F5
18	Waterville	57 C5

Co. LIMERICK

9	Abbeyfeale	48 B4
18	Adare	50 E2
18	Adare Manor	50 E2
18	Castletroy	50 G1
18	Limerick	50 F1
18	Limerick Co.	50 G2
18	Newcastle West	49 C3
18	Rathbane	50 F1

Co. TIPPERARY

18	Ballykisteen	51 A3
18	Cahir Park	51 C4
18	Clonmel	52 E4
18	Co. Tipperary	51 B2
18	Nenagh	43 B3
18	Roscrea	43 D3
18	Slievenamon	51 D3
9	Templemore	43 D5
18	Thurles	51 D1
18	Tipperary	51 A3

Co. WATERFORD

18	Carrick-on-Suir	52 F4
18	Dungarvan	62 E2
18	Dunmore East	63 B3
18	Faithlegg	53 A5
18	Gold Coast	62 F2
9	Lismore	61 C2
18	Tramore	62 H1
18	Waterford	53 A5
18	Waterford Castle	53 A5
18	West Waterford	62 E2
18	Williamstown	63 B3

ULSTER

Co. ANTRIM

18	Antrim	11 C3
18	Ballycastle	5 D2
18	Ballyclare	11 D2
18	Ballymena	11 C1
9	Bunfield House	12 E3
9	Bushfoot	4 G2
18	Cairndhu	12 E1
18	Carrigfergus	12 F3
9	Cushendall	6 E4
18	Down Royal	11 D5
18	Galgorm Castle	11 B1
18	Gracehill	4 H3
18	Greenacres	11 D3
9	Greenisland	12 E3
18	Hilton Templepatrick	11 D3
18	Lambeg	11 D5
9	Larne	12 F1
18	Lisburn	11 D5
18	Massereene	11 C3
18	Rathmore	4 F2
45	Royal Portrush	4 F2
18	Whitehead	12 F2

Co. ARMAGH

18	Ashfield	19 A5
18	Cloverhill	19 A5
18	Co. Armagh	18 H2
18	Loughgall	19 A1
18	Lurgan	19 B1
18	Portadown	19 B1
18	Silverwood	19 B1
18	Tandragee	19 B2

BELFAST CITY

18	Balmoral	12 E4
18	Belvoir Park	12 E5
18	Castlereagh Hill	12 F4
9	City of Belfast	12 E3
9	Cliftonville	12 E4
9	Colin Valley	11 D5
18	Dunmurry	12 E5
18	Fortwilliam	12 E4
18	Knock	12 F4
27	Malone	12 E5
18	Mount Ober	12 E5
9	Ormeau	12 E4
18	Rockmount	12 E5
18	Shandon Park	12 E4

Co. CAVAN

9	Belturbet	17 C5
9	Blacklion	16 H3
9	Cabra Castle	27 B2
18	Co. Cavan	26 G1
9	Crover House	26 G3
18	Slieve Russell	17 B4
9	Virginia	27 A3

Co. DONEGAL

18	Ballybofey & Stranorlar	9 A2
36	Ballyliffin	3 A2
9	Buncrana	3 A3
18	Bundoran	8 F5
9	Cloghaneely	2 E3
9	Cruit Island	1 C5
18	Donegal	8 G4
18	Dunfanaghy	2 F3
9	Gweedore	1 D4
18	Greencastle	3 D2
18	Letterkenny	2 H5
18	Narin & Portnoo	8 E2
18	North West	3 A4
9	Otway	3 A3
18	Portsalon	2 H3
9	Redcastle	3 C3
45	Rosapenna	2 G3

Co. DOWN

18	Ardglass	20 G3
9	Ardminnan	20 H1
18	Banbridge	19 C2
18	Bangor	12 G3
18	Blackwood	12 F4
18	Bright Castle	20 F3
18	Carnlea	12 F3
36	Clandeboyne	12 F4
9	Crossgar	20 F1
18	Donaghadee	12 G3
18	Downpatrick	20 G2
18	Edenmore	19 C1
9	Helen's Bay	12 F3
18	Holywood	12 F4
18	Kilkeel	19 D5
18	Kirkistown Castle	20 H1
9	Mahee Island	12 G5
18	Mayobridge	19 C4
18	Mourne	20 E4
18	Ringdufferin	20 G1
18	Royal Belfast	12 F4
36	Royal Co. Down	20 E3
18	Scrabo	12 F4
18	Spa	20 E1
9	Temple	20 E1
18	Warrenpoint	19 C5

Co. FERMANAGH

18	Castle Hume	17 B2
18	Enniskillen	17 B2
9	Lisnarick	17 A1

Co. LONDONDERRY

9	Brown Trout	4 H4
27	Castlerock	4 E3
27	City of Derry	3 B5
18	Faughan Valley	3 B5
18	Foyle	3 B4
9	Kilrea	4 G5
9	Manor	4 G5
18	Moyola Park	11 A2
54	Portstewart	4 E3
18	Roe Park	3 D4
9	Traad Ponds	11 A3

Co. MONAGHAN

9	Castleblaney	18 H5
18	Clones	17 D4
9	Mannan Castle	27 C1
18	Nuremore	27 C1
18	Rossmore	18 F3

Co. TYRONE

9	Aughnacloy	18 F1
9	Clogher Valley	17 D2
18	Dungannon	10 G5
9	Fintona	9 D5
18	Killymoon	10 H4
18	Newtownstewart	9 C3
18	Omagh	9 D4
18	Strabane	9 C2

Gazetteer

This Gazetteer lists cities, towns, villages and selected townlands in alphabetical order. The figure in bold red type immediately following the name is the number of the page on which the place appears and the alphanumeric reference indicates the appropriate grid square.
Example: Allenwood/*Fiodh Alúine* **35** B4 indicates that Allenwood will be found on page **35**, square B4.

A

Abbey/*An Mhainistir*	**32**	F2
Abbey/*An Mhainistir*	**42**	H1
Abbeydorney/*Mainistir Ó dTorna*	**48**	G4
Abbeyfeale/*Mainistir na Feile*	**49**	B4
Abbeylara/*Mainistir Leatghratha*	**26**	F4
Abbeyleix/*Mainistir Laoise*	**44**	G3
Abbeyshrule/*Mainistir Shruthla*	**34**	E1
Abington	**50**	H1
Achill Sound/*Gob an Choire*	**21**	D2
Achonry/*Achadh Conaire*	**15**	C5
Aclare/*Áth An Chláir*	**24**	E1
Acton	**19**	B2
Adamstown/*Maigh Arnai*	**53**	C4
Adare/*Áth Dara*	**50**	E2
Addergoole Co Mayo	**23**	D3
Addergoole Co Galway	**31**	D3
Adrigole/*Eadargóil*	**66**	G1
Aghaboe/*Achadh Bhó*	**44**	F3
Aghaboy	**25**	D3
Aghabullogue/*Achadh Bolg*	**60**	E4
Aghacashel	**16**	H5
Aghada	**61**	A5
Aghadiffin	**24**	F2
Aghadoon	**13**	B3
Aghadowey/*Achadh Dubhtaigh*	**4**	F4
Aghadown	**67**	A3
Aghagallon/*Achadh Gallan*	**11**	C5
Aghagower/*Achadh Ghobhair*	**22**	G3
Aghalee/*Achadh Lí*	**11**	C5
Aghamore/*Achadh Mór*		
Co Leitrim/*Liatroim*	**25**	C2
Aghamore/*Achadh Mór*		
Co Mayo/*Maigh Eo*	**24**	E3
Aghavas/*Achadh an Mheasa*	**25**	D1
Aghern	**61**	A2
Aghleam	**13**	B4
Aghnacliff/*Achadh na Cloiche*	**26**	E3
Aghnamullen/*Achadh na Muileann*	**18**	F5
Agivey	**4**	F4
Aglish/*An Eaglais* Co Kerry/*Ciarraí*	**57**	D2
Aglish/*An Eaglais*		
Co Tipperary/*Tiobraid Árann*	**43**	B2
Aglish/*An Eaglais*		
Co Waterford/*Port Láirge*	**61**	D2
Ahafona	**48**	G2
Ahakista	**66**	G3
Ahascragh/*Áth Eascrach*	**32**	H3
Aherla/*An Eatharla*	**60**	F5
Ahoghill/*Achadh Eochaille*	**11**	B1
Ailladie	**40**	F1
Aldergrove/*An Garrán Fearnóige*	**11**	C4
Allen	**35**	B4
Allenwood/*Fiodh Alúine*	**35**	B4
Allihies/*Na hAitchi*	**65**	D2
Allistragh/*An tAilastrach*	**18**	H2
Alloon Lower	**32**	G3
Altnapaste	**8**	H2
An Greata Mór	**13**	B3
Anascaul/*Abhainn an Scáil*	**57**	D1
Anglesborough	**51**	A4
Anlore	**18**	E4

Annacarriga	**42**	G4
Annacarty/*Áth na Cairte*	**51**	B2
Annaclone/*Eanach Cluana*	**19**	C2
Annacloy/*Áth na Cloiche*	**20**	F2
Annacotty	**50**	G1
Annacurragh	**46**	E4
Annagap	**57**	D1
Annagary/*Anagaire*	**1**	C5
Annagassan/*Áth na gCasán*	**28**	E2
Annagh Co Limerick	**50**	G1
Annagh Co Roscommon	**24**	G4
Annagh Neal	**42**	F3
Annaghdown/*Eanach Dhúin*	**31**	C3
Annaghmore	**19**	A1
Annaghmore/*Eanach Mór*	**25**	C5
Annahilt	**20**	E1
Annahugh	**19**	A1
Annalong/*Áth na Long*	**20**	E5
Annamoe/*Áth na mBó*	**46**	F2
Annaville	**43**	C2
Annayalla/*Eanaigh Gheala*	**18**	G4
Annestown/*Bun Abha*	**62**	H2
Annfield	**43**	C5
Annsborough/*Baile Anna*	**20**	E3
Antrim/*Aontroim*	**11**	C3
Araglin/*Airglinn*	**61**	B1
Archerstown/*Baile an Airsirigh*	**26**	H5
Ardagh/*Ardach*		
Co Limerick/*Luimneach*	**49**	C3
Ardagh/*Ardach*		
Co Longford/*An Longfort*	**26**	E5
Ardagh/*Ardach* Co Meath/*An Mhí*	**27**	C2
Ardnagunna	**61**	D1
Ardan	**34**	F4
Ardanew	**35**	B2
Ardara/*Ard an Rátha*	**8**	E2
Ardattin/*Ard Aitinn*	**45**	C5
Ardbane	**8**	F3
Ardboe	**11**	A4
Ardcath	**28**	E5
Ardconnell	**48**	F4
Ardcrony/*Ard Cróine*	**43**	A3
Ardee/*Baile Átha Fhirdhia*	**27**	D2
Ardfert/*Ard Fhearta*	**48**	F4
Ardfield/*Ard Ó bhFicheallaigh*	**67**	D3
Ardfinnan/*Ard Fhionáin*	**51**	C5
Ardglass/*Ard Ghlais*		
Co Down/*An Dún*	**20**	G3
Ardgroom/*Dhá Dhrom*	**66**	E1
Ardkearagh	**57**	D5
Ardkeen/*Ard Caoin*	**20**	H1
Ardkill	**23**	C5
Ardlea	**44**	G2
Ardlougher/*Ard Luachra*	**17**	B5
Ardmore/*Aird Mhór*	**61**	D4
Ardmorney	**34**	F3
Ardnacrusha	**42**	F5
Ardnasodan	**32**	E3
Ardpatrick/*Ard Pádraig*	**50**	G4
Ardra	**61**	A5
Ardrah Co Cork	**67**	A1
Ardrahan/*Ard Raithin*	**32**	E5

Ardress	**19**	A1
Ardscull	**45**	B2
Ardstraw/*Ard Sratha*	**9**	C3
Ardtrea/*Ard Tré*	**10**	H4
Arigna/*An Airgnigh*	**16**	G5
Arklow/*An tInbhear Mór*	**46**	G4
Arless	**45**	A3
Armagh/*Ard Mhacha*	**18**	H2
Armoy/*Oirthear Maí*	**4**	H3
Arney	**17**	B3
Arranagh	**49**	C4
Arthurstown/*Colmán*	**53**	B5
Articlave/*Ard an Chléibh*	**4**	E3
Artigarvan/*Ard Tí Garbháin*	**9**	C1
Artikelly	**3**	D4
Arvagh/*Ármhach*	**26**	E2
Ashbourne/*Cill Dhéagláin*	**36**	E1
Ashford/*Áth na Fuinseoige*	**46**	G2
Ashford	**49**	C4
Ashhill	**51**	D2
Askamore/*An Easca Mhór*	**54**	E1
Askanagap	**46**	E3
Askeaton/*Eas Géitine*	**49**	D1
Astee/*Eas Daoi*	**48**	H2
Athavallie	**23**	C3
Athboy/*Baile Átha Buí*	**27**	A5
Athea/*Áth an tSléibhe*	**49**	B3
Athenry/*Baile Átha an Rí*	**32**	F4
Athgarvan/*Áth Garbháin*	**35**	C5
Athlacca/*An tÁth Leacach*	**50**	F3
Athleague/*Áth Liag*	**33**	A1
Athlone/*Baile Átha Luain*	**33**	C2
Athnid	**43**	D5
Athy/*Baile Átha Í*	**45**	A2
Attanagh/*Áth Tanaí*	**44**	G4
Attical/*Áth Tí Chathail*	**19**	D5
Atticoffey	**33**	A4
Attiregan	**32**	H3
Attymass/*Áth Tí an Mheasaigh*	**14**	H5
Attymon/*Áth Tiomáin*	**32**	F3
Auburn	**33**	C1
Aucloggeen	**31**	D3
Aughacasla	**48**	E5
Augher/*Eochair*	**18**	E1
Aughfad	**53**	D5
Aughils	**58**	F1
Aughinish/*Eachinis*	**31**	C5
Aughnacloy/*Achadh na Cloiche*	**18**	F1
Aughnacleagh	**11**	A1
Aughnasheelan	**16**	H5
Aughrim Co Clare	**41**	D2
Aughrim/*Eachroim*		
Co Galway/*Gaillimh*	**32**	H4
Aughrim/*Eachroim*		
Co Wicklow/*Cill Mhantáin*	**46**	F4
Avoca/*Abhóca*	**46**	G3

B

Baconstown	**35**	C2
Bagenalstown/*Muine Bheag*	**45**	B5
Baileysmill/*Muileann Bhaile*	**20**	E1
Bailieborough/*Coill an Chollaigh*	**27**	A2

Balbriggan/*Baile Brigin* 28 G5
Balla 23 C3
Ballaba 42 E1
Ballady 68 G1
Ballagh/*An Bealach*
Co Limerick/*Luimneach* 49 C4
Ballagh Co Roscommon 33 B1
Ballagh Co Roscommon 25 B4
Ballagh Co Tipperary 51 B2
Ballagh Co Wexford 53 C4
Ballaghaderreen/*Bealach An Doirín* 24 F2
Ballaghbehy 49 B4
Ballaghboy 51 D2
Ballaghkeen/*An Bealach* 54 E3
Ballaghmore 44 E2
Ballaghnatrillick 16 E1
Ballard 34 F4
Ballardiggan 42 F1
Ballare 64 G3
Balleen 44 F5
Ballickmoyler/*Baile Mhic Mhaoilir* 45 A3
Ballilogue 53 A3
Ballina/*Béal an Átha* Co Mayo/*Maigh Eo* 14 H5
Ballina Co Tipperary 42 H4
Ballina Co Westmeath 34 F1
Ballinaboy Co Cork 60 G5
Ballinaboy Co Galway 29 C2
Ballinabrackey/*Buaile na Bréachmhaí* 34 H2
Ballinabranagh 45 A4
Ballinaclash/*An Chlais* 46 F3
Ballinadee/*Baile na Daibhche* 68 F1
Ballinafad/*Béal an Átha Fada* 24 H1
Ballinagar/*Béal na Glarr* 34 G4
Ballinagleragh/*Baile na gCléireach* 16 G4
Ballinakill/*Baile na Coille* 44 G3
Ballinalack/*Béal Átha na Leac* 26 F5
Ballinalea 46 G2
Ballinalee/*Béal Átha na Lao* 26 E3
Ballinamallard/*Béal Átha na Mallacht* 17 B1
Ballinameen/*Béal an Átha Mín* 24 H2
Ballinamore/*Béal an Átha Móir* 17 A5
Ballinascarty/*Béal na Scairte* 68 E2
Balinasloe/*Béal Átha na Sluaighe* 33 A3
Ballinaspick 61 C2
Ballinclashet 68 H1
Ballinclay 53 D4
Ballincollig/*Baile an Chollaigh* 60 F4
Ballincor 43 B1
Ballincrea 53 A5
Ballincreeshig 60 G5
Ballincurrig/*Baile an Churraigh* 61 A3
Ballindaggan/*Baile an Daingin* 53 C2
Ballindangan 60 H1
Ballinderreen/*Baile an Doirín* 31 D5
Ballinderry Co Tipperary/*Tiobraid Árann* 43 A2
Ballinderry Upper/*Baile an Doire*
Co Antrim/*Aontroim* 11 C5
Ballinderry Lower/*Baile an Doire*
Co Antrim/*Aontroim* 11 C5
Ballinderry/*Baile an Doire*
Co Tipperary/*Tiobraid Árann* 43 A2
Ballindine/*Baile an Daighin* 23 D5
Ballindoon 16 E5
Ballindrait/*Baile an Droichid* 9 C2
Ballydrenid 15 D3
Ballineanig 57 B1
Ballineen/*Béal Átha Fhínín* 67 D1
Ballinfull 15 D2

Ballingarrane/*Baile an Gharraín* 49 D2
Ballingarry/*Baile an Gharraí*
Co Tipperary/*Tiobraid Árann* 52 F2
Ballingarry/*Baile an Gharraí*
Co Tipperary/*Tiobraid Árann* 43 B2
Ballingarry/*Baile an Gharrai*
Co Limerick/*Luimneach* 50 E3
Ballingeary/*Béal Átha an Ghaorthaidh*
Co Mayo/*Maigh Eo* 59 B5
Ballinglen/*Baile an Gleanna* 14 F3
Ballinglen Co Wicklow 46 E4
Ballingurteen 67 C2
Ballinhassig/*Béal Átha an Cheasaigh* 60 G5
Ballinillaun 32 E4
Ballinkillin 53 B1
Ballinleeny 50 E3
Ballinloghig 57 C1
Ballinlough/*Baile an Locha*
Co Meath/*An Mhí* 27 A4
Ballinlough/*Baile an Locha*
Co Roscommon/*Ros Comáin* 24 F4
Ballinluska 68 H1
Ballinmuck 25 D2
Ballinoroher 68 E2
Ballinphonta 40 F3
Ballinran/*Baile an Raithin* 20 E5
Ballinrannig 57 B1
Ballinree 43 B3
Ballinrobe/*Baile an Róba* 23 C5
Ballinruan/*Baile an Ruáin* 42 E3
Ballinskelligs/*Baile an Sceilg* 57 C5
Ballinspittle/*Béal Átha an Spidéil* 68 F2
Ballintemple/*Baile An Teampaill* 40 E1
Ballintober/*Baile an Tobair*
Co Mayo/*Maigh Eo* 22 H4
Ballintober/*Baile an Tobair*
Co Roscommon/*Ros Comáin* 24 H4
Ballintogher/*Bailean Tóchair* 16 E4
Ballintoy/*Baile an Tuaighe* 4 H2
Ballintra/*Baile an tSratha* 8 G5
Ballintubbert 45 A2
Ballinunty/*Baile an Fhantaigh* 52 E2
Ballinure/*Baile an Iúir* 51 D2
Ballinurra 52 F4
Ballinvarry 53 A3
Ballinveny 43 C4
Ballinvoher Co Cork 61 A1
Ballinvoher Co Cork 59 D5
Ballinvronig 68 F2
Ballitore/*Béal Átha an Tuair* 45 B2
Ballivor/*Baile Íomhair* 35 A1
Ballon/*Balana* 45 C5
Balloo 12 F5
Ballsmill/*Baile an gCléireach* 19 A5
Ballure 8 F5
Ballyagran/*Béal Átha Gran* 50 E4
Ballyallinan 49 D3
Ballybaun 53 B2
Ballybay/*Béal Átha Beithe* 18 G5
Ballybeg Co Tipperary 43 C4
Ballybeg/*An Baile Beag*
Co Tipperary/*Tiobraid Árann* 51 D5
Ballyboden/*Baile Baodáin* 36 F4
Ballybofey/*Bealach Feich* 9 A2
Ballyboggan 35 A2
Ballyboghil/*Baile Bachaille* 36 F1
Ballybogy/*Baile an Bhogaigh* 4 G3
Ballybornia 33 D2

Ballybowler 57 C1
Ballyboy 34 E5
Ballybrack Co Kerry 57 D5
Ballybrack Co Kildare 35 C3
Ballybrack Co Waterford 61 C3
Ballybristy 43 C5
Ballybrittas/*Baile Briotais* 44 H1
Ballybrood 50 H2
Ballybrophy/*Baile Uí Bhróithe* 44 E3
Ballybroughan 42 E5
Ballybryan 34 H3
Ballybunnion/*Baile an Bhuinneánaigh* 48 G2
Ballyburn 45 B3
Ballycahane 42 H5
Ballycahill/*Bealach Achaille* 51 C1
Ballycallan 52 C1
Ballycanew/*Baile Uí Chonnmhaí* 54 F1
Ballycar 42 F5
Ballycarney/*Baile Uí Chearnaigh* 53 D2
Ballycarry/*Baile Cora* 12 F2
Ballycashin 62 H1
Ballycastle/*Baile an Chaistil*
Co Antrim/*An Aontroim* 4 H2
Ballycastle/*Baile an Chaisil*
Co Mayo/*Maigh Eo* 14 G3
Ballyclare/*Bealach Cláir* 11 D2
Ballyclerahen 51 D4
Ballyclogh/*Baile Cloch* 60 E1
Ballycogly 54 E5
Ballycolla/*Baile Cholla* 44 F3
Ballycolman 61 B3
Ballycommon/*Baile Uí Chomáin* 43 A3
Ballycomy 44 H4
Ballyconneely/*Baile Conaola* 29 C2
Ballyconnell/*Béal Átha Conaill* 17 B5
Ballycotton/*Baile Choitín* 61 B5
Ballycrossaun/*Baile Crosáin* 33 A5
Ballycroy/*Baile Chruaich* 13 D5
Ballycullane Co Waterford 62 E2
Ballycullane/*Baile Uí Choiléain*
Co Wexford/*Loch Garman* 53 B5
Ballycullen 46 G2
Ballyculter 20 G2
Ballycumber/*Béal Átha Chomair* 34 E3
Ballydague 60 G2
Ballydaly 59 C2
Ballydangan/*Baile Daighean* 33 B3
Ballydavid Co Cork 61 B5
Ballydavid/*Baile an nGall*
Co Kerry/*Ciarraí* 57 B1
Ballydavis 44 H1
Ballydehob/*Béal an Dá Chab* 66 H3
Ballydeloughy 60 H1
Ballydesmond/*Baile Deasumhan* 59 B1
Ballydonegan 65 D2
Ballydoogan 32 G5
Ballydoyle 60 G1
Ballyduff/*An Baile Dubh*
Co Kerry/*Ciarraí* 48 G3
Ballyduff/*An Baile Dubh*
Co Kerry/*Ciarraí* 57 D1
Ballyduff/*An Baile Dubh*
Co Waterford/*Port Láirge* 62 G1
Ballyduff/*An Baile Dubh*
Co Waterford/*Post Láirge* 61 B2
Ballyduff /*An Baile Dubh*
Co Wexford 54 E1
Ballydugennan 11 B3

Ballyea	50	E2
Ballyeafy	61	B1
Ballyeaston/*Baile Uistín*	11	D2
Ballyeighan	43	C2
Ballyeighter	32	H4
Ballyeightragh	57	B1
Ballyfarnagh/*Bealach Fearna*	23	D3
Ballyfarnan/*Béal Átha Fearáin*	16	F5
Ballyfasy	53	A4
Ballyfeard/*Baile Feá Aird*	68	H1
Ballyferriter/*Baile an Fhairtéaraigh*	57	B1
Ballyfin/*An Baile Fionn* Co Laois/*Laois*	44	F1
Ballyfin/*An Baile Fionn* Co Wexford/*Loch Garman*	54	F1
Ballyforan/*Béal Átha Feorainne*	33	A2
Ballyfore	34	H3
Ballyfoyle	44	H5
Ballygalley/*Baile Geithligh*	12	E1
Ballygar/*Béal Átha Ghártha*	32	H1
Ballygarran Co Waterford	62	F2
Ballygarrett/*Baile Ghearóid*	54	F2
Ballygarries	23	C4
Ballygarvan/*Baile Garbháin*	60	G5
Ballygawley/*Baile Uí Dhálaigh* Co Sligo/*Sligeach*	16	E4
Ballygawley/*Baile Uí Dhálaigh* Co Tyrone/*Tír Eoghain*	18	F1
Ballygeana	51	A4
Ballygelly	11	D1
Ballyglass/*An Baile Glas* Co Mayo/*Maigh Eo*	24	F2
Ballyglass/*An Baile Glas* Co Mayo/*Maigh Eo*	14	G3
Ballyglass/*An Baile Glas* Co Mayo/*Maigh Eo*	23	C4
Ballyglass West	24	G3
Ballygorey	52	H5
Ballygorman/*Baile Uí Ghormáin*	3	B1
Ballygortin	54	F2
Ballygowan/*Baile Mhic Gabhann*	12	F5
Ballygrady	60	E1
Ballygriffin	51	C2
Ballygub	53	A3
Ballygubba	50	F3
Ballyguyroe North	50	G5
Ballyhack	53	B5
Ballyhaght	50	F5
Ballyhahill/*Baile Dhá Thuile*	49	B2
Ballyhaise/*Béal Átha hÉis*	17	D5
Ballyhalbert/*Baile Thalbóid*	12	H5
Ballyhale/*Baile Héil* Co Galway/*Gaillimh*	31	C2
Ballyhale/*Baile Héil* Co Kilkenny/*Cill Chainnigh*	52	H3
Ballyhank	60	F5
Ballyhar/*Baile Uí Aichir*	58	H2
Ballyhaunis/*Béal Átha hAmhnais*	24	F3
Ballyhean/*Béal Átha hÉin*	22	H3
Ballyhear	31	D1
Ballyheelan/*Bealach an Chaoláin*	26	G3
Ballyhees /*An Baile Thíos*	40	E1
Ballyheige/*Baile Uí Thaidhg*	48	F4
Ballyhenry	31	C1
Ballyhickey	42	E4
Ballyhoge/*Baile Uí Cheog*	53	D3
Ballyhomuck	52	H4
Ballyhoolahan	59	D1
Ballyhooly/*Baile Átha hUlla*	60	H2
Ballyhornan/*Baile Uí Chornáin*	20	G2
Ballyhugh Co Cavan	17	B5
Ballyhugh Co Offaly	34	H4
Ballyieragh	66	H4
Ballyjamesduff/*Baile Shéamais Dhuibh*	26	H2
Ballykean	34	G4
Ballykeel/*An Baile Caol*	19	D1
Ballykeeran/*Bealach Caorthainn*	33	C2
Ballykelly/*Baile Uí Cheallaigh*	3	D4
Ballykilleen	34	H4
Ballykilty	61	C4
Ballykinler/*Baile Coinnleora*	20	F3
Ballykinsella	63	B3
Ballyknockan	46	E1
Ballylanders/*Baile an Londraigh* Co Cork/*Corcaigh*	61	B5
Ballylanders/*Baile an Londraigh* Co Limerick/*Luimneach*	50	H4
Ballylaneen	62	G1
Ballylangley	68	F1
Ballyleen	62	G1
Ballyleny	19	A2
Ballylesson/*Baile na Leasán*	12	E5
Ballylickey	67	A1
Ballyliffin/*Baile Lifin*	3	A2
Ballyline	52	F2
Ballylinnen	44	H4
Ballylintagh	4	F4
Ballylongford/*Baile Átha Longfoirt*	49	A2
Ballylooby/*Beala Átha Lúbaigh* Co Tipperary/*Tiobraid Árann*	50	H3
Ballylooby/*Beala Átha Lúbaigh* Co Tipperary/*Tiobraid Árann*	51	C5
Ballylucas	54	E3
Ballylumford	12	F1
Ballylynan/*Baile Uí Laigheanáin*	45	A3
Ballymacarbry/*Baile Mhac Cairbre*	51	D5
Ballymacaw/*Baile Mhac Dháith*	63	B4
Ballymacelligot	48	H5
Ballymachugh	26	G3
Ballymackey/*Baile Uí Mhacaí*	43	B3
Ballymackilroy	18	F1
Ballymacmague	62	E2
Ballymacoda/*Baile Mhac Óda*	61	C4
Ballymacurly/*Baile Mhic Thorlaigh*	25	A4
Ballymacward/*Baile Mhic an Bhaird*	32	G3
Ballymagan/*Baile Mhic Cionaoith*	3	A3
Ballymagaraghy	3	C2
Ballymagorry/*Baile Mhic Gofraidh*	9	C1
Ballymahon/*Baile Uí Mhatháin*	33	D1
Ballymakeery/*Baile Mhic Íre*	59	C4
Ballymakenny	28	E3
Ballymanagh	32	F5
Ballymanus	26	G4
Ballymaquiff	42	E1
Ballymartin/ *Baile Mhic Grolla Mhártain*	20	E5
Ballymartle	68	G1
Ballymena/*An Baile Meánach*	11	C1
Ballymoe/*Béal Átha Mó*	24	G4
Ballymoney/*Baile Muine*	4	G4
Ballymoney	46	G5
Ballymore Co Cork	61	A5
Ballymore/*An Baile Mór* Co Donegal/*Dún na nGall*	2	F3
Ballymore/*An Baile Mór* Co Westmeath/*An Iarmhí*	34	E2
Ballymore Eustace/*An Baile Mór*	35	D5
Ballymorris	62	H1
Ballymote/*Baile an Mhóta*	15	D5
Ballymount	45	C1
Ballymurn	54	E3
Ballymurphy/*Baile Uí Mhurchú*	53	B2
Ballymurragh	49	C4
Ballymurray/*Baile Uí Mhuirigh*	25	B5
Ballynabola	53	B4
Ballynabucky	32	E5
Ballynacally/*Baile na Caillí*	40	H5
Ballynacarriga/*Béal na Carraige*	67	C1
Ballynacarrigy/*Baile na Carraige*	34	F1
Ballynacarrow/*Baile na Cora*	15	D4
Ballynaclogh	43	B4
Ballynacole	61	B4
Ballynacorra	61	A4
Ballynacourty Co Waterford	62	F2
Ballynacourty Co Cork	68	G1
Ballynacree	26	H4
Ballynafid	26	G5
Ballynagaul Co Cork	60	H4
Ballynagaul Co Waterford	62	E3
Ballynagore/*Béal Átha na nGabhar*	34	F3
Ballynagree	59	D3
Ballynagrumoolia	60	G5
Ballynaguilkee	61	D1
Ballynahinch/*Baile na hInse* Co Down/*An Dún*	20	E1
Ballynahinch/*Baile na hInse* Co Tipperary/*Tiobraid Árann*	42	H5
Ballynahowan Co Clare	40	F1
Ballynahown/*Baile na hAbhann* Co Galway/*Gaillimh*	30	F4
Ballynahown/*Buaile na hAbhann* Co Westmeath/*An Iarmhí*	33	C3
Ballynahulla	59	B1
Ballynakill Co Carlow	53	B1
Ballynakill Co Offaly	34	H4
Ballynakill Co Westmeath	33	C2
Ballynakilla	66	F2
Ballynakilly	10	H5
Ballynamallaght	9	D2
Ballynamona/*Baile an Móna* Co Cork/*Corcaigh*	60	F2
Ballynamona Co Galway	33	A3
Ballynamona Co Wexford	53	C5
Ballynamuddagh	60	H2
Ballynamult/*Béal na Molt*	61	D1
Ballynana	57	C1
Ballynarry	26	G3
Ballynaskreena	48	G3
Ballynastangford/*Baile na Stanfard*	23	D4
Ballyneaner/*Baile an Aonfhir*	10	E1
Ballyneety/*Baile an Fhaoitigh*	50	G1
Ballyneill/*Baile Uí Néill*	52	F4
Ballynennan	52	F2
Ballynoe/*An Baile Nua* Co Cork/*Corcaigh*	61	B3
Ballynoe Co Galway	32	H4
Ballynure/*Baile an Iuir*	12	E2
Ballyorgan/*Baile Uí Argáin*	50	G5
Ballyoughter	54	F1
Ballyourane	67	A2
Ballypatrick/*Baile Phádraig*	52	E4
Ballyporeen/*Béal Átha Póirín*	51	B5
Ballyquin Co Kerry	47	D5
Ballyquin Co Waterford	52	G5
Ballyragget/*Béal Átha Ragad*	44	G4

Ballyrashane 4 F3
Ballyre 61 B3
Ballyreagh 18 G1
Ballyregan 68 G1
Ballyroan/*Baile Átha an Róine* 44 G3
Ballyrobert 12 F3
Ballyroddy 25 A3
Ballyroe 47 C5
Ballyroebuck 53 D1
Ballyronan/*Baile Uí Rónáin* 11 A3
Ballyroney/*Baile Uí Ruanaí* 19 D3
Ballyroon 66 F3
Ballyryan 45 B5
Ballysadare/*Baile Easa Dara* 15 D4
Ballyscullion 3 D3
Ballyshannon/*Baile Átha Seanaidh* 8 F5
Ballysheen 48 G4
Ballyshoneen 63 B3
Ballyshrule 42 H1
Ballysloe 52 E1
Ballysorrell 43 D4
Ballysteen 49 D1
Ballystrudder 12 F2
Ballyvaghan/*Baile Uí Bheacháin* 40 H1
Ballyvaldon 54 F3
Ballyvalode 51 A2
Ballyvaloon 60 F3
Ballyveal 45 B5
Ballyveera 51 C5
Ballyvisteen 50 H5
Ballyvoge/*Baile Uí Bhuaigh* 66 F4
Ballyvoneen 32 H2
Ballyvonnavaun 41 D4
Ballyvorane 68 H1
Ballyvourney/*Baile Bhuirne* 59 B4
Ballyvoy/*Baile Bhóidh* 5 D2
Ballywalter/*Baile Bháltair* 12 H5
Ballyward/*Baile Mhic an Bhaird* 19 D3
Ballywildrick 4 E3
Ballywilliam Co Wexford 53 B3
Ballywilliam/*Baile Liam* 68 F2
Balnamore/*Béal an Átha Móir* 4 G4
Balrath/*Baile na Ratha* 28 E5
Balrothery 28 G5
Balscaddan 28 F5
Baltimore/*Dún na Séad* 67 A4
Baltinglass/*Bealach Conglais* 45 C3
Baltovin 48 G4
Baltray/*Baile Trá* 28 F4
Banada 15 B5
Banada 24 E1
Banagher/*Beannchar* 33 B5
Banbridge/*Droichead na Banna* 19 C2
Bandon/*Droichead na Bandan* 68 F1
Banemore 48 H4
Bangor/*Beannchar* Co Down/*An Dún* 12 G3
Bangor/*Baingear* Co Mayo/*Maigh Eo* 13 D4
Banna 48 F4
Bannfoot 11 A5
Bansha Co Clare 40 H4
Bansha/*An Bháinseach*
Co Tipperary/*Tiobraid Árann* 51 B3
Banteer/*Bántir* 59 D2
Bantry/*Beanntraí* 67 A2
Baranailt 3 D5
Barefield/*Gort Lomán* 41 D3
Barloge 67 A4
Barna/*Bearna* Co Galway/*Gaillimh* 31 C4

Barna Co Limerick 50 H2
Barna Co Offaly 43 C3
Barnacahoge 24 E2
Barnacawley 24 G3
Barnaderg/*Beara Dhearg* 32 F2
Barnagowlane 67 A1
Barnalisheen 43 D5
Barnalyra 24 E2
Barna Tra 13 C3
Barnesmore 8 H3
Barnycarroll/*Bearna Chearuill* 23 D4
Barrack Village 44 G5
Barraduff 59 A2
Barratoor 42 G1
Barrettstown 52 H3
Barrigone 49 C1
Barringtonsbridge 50 G1
Barrow 48 F5
Barry/*Barraigh* 25 D5
Barryroe 68 E3
Bartlemy 61 A3
Bastardstown 64 E3
Battersstown/*Baile an Bhóthair* 35 D2
Baughna 34 G2
Baulbrack 59 C5
Baunskeha 52 H3
Bauntlieve 40 G3
Bawnaneel 59 C1
Bawnboy/*An Bábhún Búi* 17 B5
Co Cavan/*An Cabhán*
Bawnboy Co Cork 67 A2
Bawnfune 51 D5
Bawnlahan 67 B4
Beagh 32 E1
Beal 48 G2
Bealaclugga/*Béal an Chloga* 40 H1
Bealadangan/*Béal an Daingin* 30 F3
Bealaha 40 E5
Bealin/*Béal Linne* 33 D2
Bealnablath 60 E5
Bealnamorive 60 E4
Beaufort/*Lios an Phúea* 58 G2
Bective 35 C1
Beenacouma 57 B2
Behernagh 60 H3
Bekan/*Béacán* 24 E4
Belcarra 22 H3
Belclare/*Béal Chláir* 31 D2
Belcoo/*Béal Cú* 16 H3
Belderg/*Béal Deirg* 14 E3
Belfast/*Béal Feiriste* 12 F4
Belgooly/*Béal Guala* 68 G1
Bellacorick/*Béal Átha Chomhraic* 14 E5
Bellagarvaun 22 E1
Bellaghy/*Baile Eachaidh* 11 A2
Bellahy 24 E1
Bellanacargy 17 D5
Bellanagare/*Béal Átha na gCarr* 24 H3
Bellananagh/*Béal Átha na nEach* 26 F2
Bellanaleck/*Bealach na Leice* 17 F3
Bellamore 8 G1
Beallanamullia/*Béal Átha na Muille* 33 B2
Bellaneeny 33 B3
Bellanode/*Béal Átha an Fhóid* 18 F3
Bellavary/*Béal Átha Bhearaigh* 23 C2
Belleek/*Béal Leice* 19 A4
Co Armagh/*Ard Mhacha*
Beleek/*Béal Leice*

Co Fermanagh/*Fear Manach* 16 G1
Bellewstown/*Baile an Bheileogaigh* 28 E5
Bellmount 33 C4
Belmullet/*Béal an Mhuirthead* 13 C3
Beltoy 12 F2
Beltra Co Mayo 22 G1
Beltra/*Béal Trá* Co Sligo/*Sligeach* 15 C3
Belturbet/*Béal Tairbirt* 17 C5
Belvelly 60 H4
Benburb/*An Bhinn Bhorb* 18 H1
Bendooragh/*Bun Déurai* 4 G4
Bennekerry 45 B4
Bennettsbridge/*Droichead Binéid* 52 H2
Beragh/*Bearach* 10 E5
Berrings/*Bioráinn* 60 F4
Bessbrook/*An Sruthán* 19 B4
Bettystown/*Baile an Bhiataigh* 28 F4
Bilboa/*Biolbó* 45 A4
Birdhill/*Cnocán an Éin Fhinn* 42 H5
Birr/*Biorra* 43 C1
Bishops Court 20 G2
Bishoppshall 52 H5
Black 61 B1
Black Bull 36 E2
Black Lion 34 E5
Blackcastle/*An Caisleán Dubh* 51 D3
Blackhall 53 D4
Blacklion/*An Blaic* 16 H3
Blackpool/*An Linn Dubh* 50 G4
Blackrock/*An Dúcharraig*
Co Cork/*Corcaigh* 60 H4
Blackrock/*An Charraig Dhubh*
Co Dublin/*Baile Átha Cliath* 36 G3
Blackrock/*Na Creagacha Dubha*
Co Louth/*Lú* 28 E1
Blacksod/*An Fód Dubh* 13 B5
Blackwater/*An Abhainn Dubh* 54 F3
Blackwater Bridge 58 F5
Blackwatertown/*An Port Mór* 18 H1
Blackwood/*Coill Dubh* 35 B4
Blagh 4 F3
Blanchardstown/*Baile Bhlainséir* 36 E3
Blarney/*An Bhlarna* 60 G4
Bleary 19 B1
Blennerville/*Cathair Uí Mhóráin* 48 G5
Blessington/*Baile Coimín* 35 D5
Blue Ball/*An Phailís* 34 E5
Blueford 59 C1
Boardee 68 H1
Boardmills/*An Muileann Adhmaid* 20 E1
Bodyke/*Lúbán Díge* 42 G3
Bofeenaun 22 H1
Bog of the Ring 36 F1
Boggaun 43 D4
Boharboy 28 G1
Boher 50 G1
Boheraphuca 43 D2
Boherboy/*An Bóthar Buí*
Co Cork/*Corcaigh* 59 C1
Bohereen 50 G1
Boherlahan/*An Bóthar Leathan* 51 C2
Bohermeen/*An Bóthar Mín* 27 B5
Bohernarnane 51 B4
Boherquill 26 F4
Boherroe 50 H2
Boho/*Botha* 17 A2
Bohola/*Both Chomhla* 23 D2
Bolea/*Both Liath* 4 E4

Boleran 4 F4
Boley Co Laois 45 A3
Boley Co Wicklow 45 D4
Boleyvogue 54 E2
Bolinglanna 21 D2
Bonnanaboigh 3 D5
Boolakennedy 51 B4
Borris/*An Bhuiríos* 53 B1
Borris in Ossory/*Buiríos Mór Osraí* 44 E3
Borrisokane/*Buiríos Uí Chéin* 43 B2
Borrisoleigh/*Buiríos Ó Luigheach* 43 C5
Boston 41 D2
Bottomstown 50 G3
Bottomy 26 F5
Bouladuff/*An Bhuaile Dhubh* 43 C5
Bovedy 4 F5
Bovevagh/*Boith Mhéabha* 3 D5
Boyle/*Mainistir na Búille* 24 H1
Boyounagh 24 F5
Brackagh 34 H4
Brackloon 24 H3
Bracklyn 34 H1
Bracknagh/*Breacánach*
Co Offaly/*Uíbh Fhailí* 35 A5
Bracknagh Co Roscommon 25 B5
Brackny 33 D5
Brackwanshagh 14 G5
Brahalish 66 G2
Brandon/*Cé Bhréanainn* 47 D5
Brandrum 18 F3
Brannockstown/*Baile na mBreatnach* 45 C1
Bray/*Bré* 36 G5
Bready/*An Bhreadaigh* 9 C1
Breaghna 67 D1
Breaghva 48 G1
Bree/*Brí* 53 D3
Breeda 61 C3
Brickeens/*Na Broicíní* 24 E4
Brideswell/*Tobar Bríde* 33 B2
Bridge End/*Ceann an Droichid* 3 A4
Bridgeland 46 E4
Bridgetown Co Donegal 8 G4
Bridgetown/*Baile an Droichid* 64 E2
Bridgetown/*Baile an Droichid* 42 G5
Brigh 10 H4
Brinlack/*Bun na Leaca* 1 D3
Briska 62 F1
Brittas/*An Briotás* 36 E4
Broadford/*Áth Leathan*
Co Limerick/*Luimneach* 49 D4
Broadford Co Kildare 35 A2
Broadford/*Áth Leathan* 42 F4
Broadway/*Gráinseach Iúir* 64 F3
Brockagh Co Londonderry 4 E5
Brockagh Co Wicklow 46 F2
Brockaghboy 4 F5
Brookeborough/*Achadh Lon* 17 C2
Brookville 51 A3
Broomfield/*Achadh an Bhrúim* 18 H5
Brosna/*Brosnach* Co Kerry/*Ciarraí* 49 B5
Brosna/*An Bhrosnach*
Co Offaly/*Uíbh Fhailí* 43 C2
Broughal 33 D5
Broughshane/*Bruach Sheáin* 11 C1
Brownstown Co Kildare 35 B5
Brownstown Co Waterford 63 B4
Brownstown Co Meath 27 D5
Bruckana 44 E5

Bruckless 8 E4
Bruff/*An Brú* 50 G3
Bruree/*Brú Rí* 50 F3
Bryansford/*Áth Bhriain* 20 E3
Buckna 11 D1
Buckode 16 F1
Bulgaden/*Builgidin* 50 G4
Bullaun 32 G4
Bunacurry/*Bun an Churraigh* 21 C1
Bunane 58 H5
Bunaw 58 F5
Bunbeg/*An Bun Beag* 1 D4
Bunbrosna/*Bun Brosnaí* 26 F5
Bunclody/*Bun Clóidí* 53 D1
Buncrana/*Bun Cranncha* 3 A3
Bundoran/*Bun Dobhráin* 16 F1
Bunglasha 58 E3
Bunlahy 26 E3
Bunmahon/*Bun Machan* 62 G2
Bunnafollistran 31 C1
Bunnaglass 42 F1
Bunnahowen/*Bun na hAbhna* 13 C4
Bunnanaddan/*Bun an Fheadáin* 15 D5
Bunnyconnellan/*Muine Chonalláin* 15 A5
Bunratty 42 E5
Burnchurch 52 G2
Burncourt/*An Chúirt Dóite* 51 B5
Burnfoot/*Bun na hAbhann* 3 A4
Burnfort/*Ráth an Tóiteáin* 60 F2
Burnside 11 D5
Burren/Boirinn Co Clare/*An Clár* 31 C5
Burren/Boirinn Co Clare/*An Clár* 40 H5
Burren/Boirinn Co Down/*An Dún* 19 C4
Burren Bridge 20 E3
Burrenfadda 40 G5
Burt 3 A4
Burtonport/*Ailt an Chorráin* 1 C5
Bushmills/*Muileann na Buaise* 4 G2
Butler's Bridge 17 C5
Butlerstown/*Baile an Bhuitléaraigh* 68 E3
Buttevant/*Cill na Mallach* 60 F1
Bweeng 60 F3

C

Cabragh/*An Chabrach* 10 G5
Cadamstown/*Baile Mhic Ádaim*
Co Kildare/*Cill Dara* 35 A3
Cadamstown/*Baile Mhic Ádaim*
Co Offaly/*Uíbh Fhailí* 44 E1
Caheny 4 F5
Caher/*An Chathair* Co Clare/*An Clár* 42 F2
Caher Co Cork 66 F3
Caher/*An Chathair*
Co Tipperary/*Tiobraid Árann* 51 C4
Caheracruttera 58 E1
Caheradrine 32 E4
Caheragh 67 A2
Caherakillen 32 G4
Caherbarnagh/*An Chatair* 57 D5
Caherconlish/*Cathair Chinn Lis* 50 G2
Caherconnell 40 H2
Caherdaniel/*Cathair Dónall* 65 D1
Caherea 40 H5
Caherlistrane/*Cathair Loistréain* 31 D2
Cahermore/*Cathair Mhór*
Co Cork/*Corcaigh* 65 D2
Cahermore Co Galway 42 E1
Cahermuckee 67 A1

Cahermurphy 40 F5
Caherogan 40 F4
Caherphuca 32 E2
Cahersiveen/*Cathair Saidhbhín* 57 C4
Caim 53 C2
Cairncastle 12 E1
Caledon/*Cionn Aird* 18 G2
Callan/*Callain* 52 G2
Callow/*An Caladh*
Co Mayo/*Maigh Eo* 23 D1
Callow Co Roscommon 24 H2
Calry 16 E3
Caltra/*An Cheatrach* 32 H2
Caltraghlea 32 H3
Calverstown/*Baile an Chalbhaigh* 45 C1
Camira 43 B3
Camlough/*Camloch* 19 B4
Camolin/*Cam Eolaing* 54 E1
Camp/*An Com* 58 E1
Campile/*Ceann Poill* 53 B5
Camross/*Camros* 44 E2
Camus/*Camas* 30 F3
Canningstown/*Baile Chainín* 26 H1
Cape Castle 4 H3
Cappagh Co Cork 60 H2
Cappagh Co Limerick 50 E2
Cappagh/*An Chapóg*
Co Tyrone/*Tír Eoghain* 10 F5
Cappagh White/*An Cheapach* 51 A2
Cappaghmore 41 D1
Cappagowlan 34 E5
Cappalinnan 44 E4
Cappamore/*An Cheapach Mhór* 50 H1
Cappataggle/*Ceapaigh an tSeagail* 32 H4
Cappeen 59 D5
Cappoquin/*Ceapach Choinn* 61 D2
Caran 24 H4
Carbury/*Cairbre* 35 A3
Cargan 5 D5
Carker 59 A1
Carland/*Domnach Carr* 10 G5
Carlanstown/*Droichead Chearbhalláin* 27 B4
Carlingford/*Cairlinn* 19 C5
Carlow/*Ceatharlach* 45 B4
Carn Co Londonderry 10 G1
Carn Co Westmeath 34 E2
Carna/*Carna* 29 D3
Carnagh/*Carranach* 18 H4
Carnalbanagh 11 D1
Carnalbanagh Sheddings 11 D1
Carnanreagh 10 E1
Carnaross/*Carn na Ros* 27 A4
Carndonagh/*Carn Domhnach* 3 B2
Carnew/*Carn an Bhua* 46 E5
Carney/*Fearann Uí Chearnaigh*
Co Sligo/*Sligeach* 15 D2
Carney/*Carnaigh*
Co Tipperary/*Tiobraid Árann* 43 A2
Carnlough/*Carnlach* 6 E5
Carnmoney/*Carn Monaidh* 12 E3
Carnteel/*Carn tSiail* 18 G1
Carracastle/*Ceathrú an Chaisil* 24 F1
Carragh/*Céarach* 35 C4
Carraghs 24 F4
Carraholly/*Ceathrú Chalaidh* 22 F3
Carran/*An Carn* Co Clare/*An Clár* 40 H2
Carran Co Kilkenny 52 H1
Carraroe/*An Cheathrú Rua* 30 F4

Carrick/*An Charraig*	7	C4
Carrick/*An Charraig*	53	C5
Carrick-on-Shannon/*Cora Droma Rúisc*	25	B1
Carrick-on-Suir/*Carraig na Siúire*	52	F4
Carrickaboy/*Carraigigh Bhuí*	26	G2
Carrickart/*Carraig Airt*	2	G3
Carrickashedoge	27	C2
Carrickboy/*An Charraig Bhuí*	26	E5
Carrickfergus/*Carraig Fhearghais*	12	F3
Carrickmacross/*Carraig Mhachaire*	27	C1
Carrickmines/*Carraig Mhaighin*	36	G4
Carrickmore or Termon Rock/		
An Charraig Mhór	10	F4
Carrickroe	18	F2
Carrig	43	C1
Carrigaday	48	E5
Carrigadrohid	60	E4
Carrigagulla	59	D3
Carrigaholt/*Carraig an Chnabhaltaigh*	48	G1
Carrigahorig/*Carraig an Chomhraic*	43	B1
Carrigaline/*Carraig Uí Leighin*	60	H5
Carrigallen/*Carraig Álainn*	26	E1
Carrigan/*An Carraigín*	26	F2
Carriganimmy/*Carraig an Ime*	59	C3
Carriganroe	51	B5
Carrigans/*An Carraigin*	3	A5
Carrigatogher/*Carraig an Tóchair*	42	H4
Carriggower	46	G1
Carrigkerry	49	C3
Carrignavar/*Carraig na bhFear*	60	G3
Carrigtohill/*Carraig Thuathail*	61	A4
Carrow	51	B2
Carrowclare	3	D4
Carrowdore/*Ceathrú Dobhair*	12	G4
Carrowduff Co Clare	40	F2
Carrowduff Co Roscommon	24	H4
Carroweden	15	C4
Carrowkeel/*An Cheathrú Chaol*		
Co Donegal/*Dún na nGall*	2	H3
Carrowkeel Co Galway	32	G5
Carrowkeel Co Mayo	22	H5
Carrowkeelanahglass	24	F5
Carrowkennedy	22	F4
Carrowmenagh	3	C2
Carrowmore Co Galway	31	D5
Carrowmore/*Ceathrú Mhór Leacan*		
Co Mayo/*Maigh Eo*	14	G3
Carrowmore Co Mayo	23	D5
Carrowmore Co Sligo	15	C5
Carrowmoreknock/*Ceathrú Mhór an Chnoic*	31	C2
Carrownacon	23	C4
Carrowpadeen	15	A3
Carrowreagh	33	A3
Carrowrory	33	C1
Carrowteige/*Ceathrú Thaidhg*	13	D2
Carryduff/*Ceathrú Aodha Dhuibh*	11	D5
Carrowkeel	3	B3
Carrowkennedy	22	F4
Cashel Co Carlow	53	B1
Cashel Co Laois	44	G2
Cashel/*An Caiseal* Co Galway/Gaillimh	30	E2
Cashel Co. Galway	24	F5
Cashel/*Caiseal*		
Co Tipperary/*Tiobraid Árann*	51	C2
Cashelgarran/*Caiseal an Ghearráin*	15	D2
Cashel Glebe	2	G2
Cashla	32	E3
Cassagh	53	B4
Castlebaldwin/Béal Átha an gCarraigíní	16	E5
Castlebar/*Caisleán an Bharraigh*	22	H2
Castlebellingham/		
Baile an Ghearlánaigh	28	E2
Castleblakeney/*Gallach*	32	G2
Castleblayney/*Baile na Lorgan*	18	G5
Castlebridge/*Droichead an Chaisleáin*	54	E4
Castlecat/*Caiseal Cait*	4	G3
Castlecaulfield/*Baile Uí Dhonnaile*	10	G5
Castlecomer/*Caisleán an Chomair*	44	H4
Castleconnell/*Caisleán Uí Chonaill*	42	G5
Castleconor	14	H4
Castlecoote	24	H5
Castlecor/*Caisleán na Cora*	60	E1
Castle Cove	57	D5
Castlecuffe	34	E5
Castledawson/*An Seanmhullach*	11	A2
Castlederg/*Caisleán na Deirge*	9	B3
Castledermot/*Diseart Diarmada*	45	B3
Castledockrell	53	D2
Castleellis	54	E3
Castlefinn/*Caisleán na Finne*	9	B2
Castlefreke	67	D3
Castlegal	16	E1
Castlegregory/*Caisleán Ghriaire*	48	E5
Castlehill/*Caorthannán*		
Co Mayo/*Maigh Eo*	22	E1
Castlehill Co Mayo	14	G5
Castleisland/*Oilean Ciarraí*	59	A1
Castlejordan/*Caisleán Shuirdáin*	34	H3
Castleknock/*Caisleán Cnucha*	36	E3
Castleleiny/*Caisleán Laighnigh*	43	D4
Castlelyons/*Caisleán Ó Liatháin*	61	A2
Castlemaine/*Caisleán na Mainge*	58	G1
Castlemartyr/*Baile na Martra*	61	B4
Castleplunket/*Lois Lachna*	24	H4
Castlepollard/*Baile na gCros*	26	G4
Castlequarter /*Ceathrú an Chaisleáin*	31	D3
Castlequin	57	C3
Castlerahan	26	H3
Castlerea/*An Caisleán Riabhach*	24	G3
Castlereagh	12	E4
Castlerock/*Carraig Ceasail*	4	E3
Castleroe	4	F4
Castleshane/*Caisleán an tSiáin*	18	G3
Castletown Co Clare	40	H2
Castletown/*Baile Chaisleáin Chinn Eich*		
Co Cork/*Corcaigh*	67	D1
Castletown/*Baile an Chaisleáin*		
Co Laois/*Laois*	44	F2
Castletown/*Baile an Chaisleáin*		
Co Limerick/*Luimneach*	50	E3
Castletown/*Baile an Chaisleáin*		
Co Meath/*An Mhí*	27	C3
Castletown/*Baile an Chaisleáin*		
Co Westmeath/*An Iarmhí*	26	G4
Castletown/*Baile an Chaisleáin*		
Co Wexford/*Loch Garman*	46	G5
Castletown Bearhaven/		
Baile Chaisleáin Bhéarra	66	E2
Castletown Geoghegan	34	F2
Castletownroche/		
Baile Chaisleáin an Róistigh	60	G1
Castletownshend/*Baile an Chaisleáin*	67	B3
Castleville	23	D5
Castlewarren/*Caisleán an Bhairinnigh*	45	A5
Castlewellan/*Caisleán Uidhilín*	20	E3
Causeway/*An Tóchar*	48	G3
Cavan/*An Cabhán*	26	G1
Cavangarden	8	F5
Caves	51	B5
Ceancullig	67	B2
Cecilstown/*Baile an Bhriotaigh*	60	E1
Celbridge/*Cill Droichid*	35	D3
Chaffpool	15	C5
Chanonrock	27	D1
Chapel	53	C3
Chapel Street	15	C4
Chapeltown/*Baile an tSéipéil*		
Co Down/*An Dún*	20	G3
Chapeltown/*An Caol*		
Co Kerry/*Ciarraí*	57	B4
Charlemont	18	H1
Charlestown/*Baile Chathail*	24	E1
Charleville/*An Ráth*	50	F4
Cheekpoint/*Pointe na Síge*	53	A5
Cherryville	35	A5
Chesney's Corner	11	B2
Church Bay	61	A5
Church Cross/*Cnoc na Rátha*	67	A3
Church Hill/*Min an Lábáin*		
Co Donegal/*Dún na nGall*	2	F5
Church Hill/*An Droim Meánach*		
Co Tyrone/*Tír Eoghain*	9	A4
Church Hill/*Mín an Lábain*	48	F5
Church Town/*Tulaigh an Iúir*	3	A5
Churchboro Cross	33	B1
Churchfield	22	G5
Churchstreet	24	H2
Churchtown	10	H3
Churchtown/*Baile an Teampaill*		
Co Cork/*Corcaigh*	50	F5
Churchtown/*Baile an Teampaill Theas*		
Co Cork/*Corcaigh*	61	B5
Churchtown Co Wexford	64	G3
Churchtown Co Wexford	63	C4
Clabby/*Clabaigh*	17	D1
Claddaghduff/*An Cladach Dubh*	29	B1
Clady Co Londonderry	11	A1
Clady/*Clódigh* Co Tyrone/*Tír Eoghain*	9	B2
Cladymilltown/*Baile an Mhuillinn*	19	A3
Claggan	22	E1
Clane/*Claonadh*	35	C4
Clara/*Clóirtheach*	34	E3
Clarahill	34	F5
Clare/*An Clár*	19	B2
Clarecastle/*Droichead an Chláir*	41	D4
Clareen/*An Cláirín*	43	D1
Claregalway/*Baile Chláir*	31	D3
Claremorris/*Clár Chlainne Mhuiris*	23	D4
Clarina/*Clár Aidhne*	50	E1
Clarinbridge/*Droichead an Chláirín*	32	E4
Clash	43	B3
Clash North	49	B3
Clash South	49	B3
Clashdrumsmith	51	A3
Clashmore/*Clais Mhór*	61	D3
Clashroe	52	G5
Claudy/*Clóidigh*	10	E1
Clawinch	25	B5
Cleggan/*An Cloigeann*	29	C1
Clenagh	41	D5
Clerragh	24	G3
Cleristown	53	D5
Clifden/*An Clochán*	29	C1
Clifferna/*An Chliaifearna*	26	H1

Cliffony/*Cliafuine* 16 E1
Clogga Co Kilkenny 52 H5
Clogga Co Wicklow 46 G5
Clogh/*An Chloch*
Co Antrim/*Aontriom* 4 H5
Clogh/*An Chloch*
Co Kilkenny/*Cill Chainnigh* 44 H4
Clogh Co Laois 44 F3
Clogh Co Limerick 49 D2
Clogh Co Wexford 54 F1
Cloghan/*An Clochan*
Co Donegal/*Dún na nGall* 8 H2
Cloghan/*An Clochán*
Co Offaly/*Uíbh Fhailí* 33 C5
Cloghan Co Westmeath 34 H1
Cloghane Co Cork 66 F4
Cloghane/*An Clochán*
Co Kerry/*Ciarraí* 47 D5
Cloghans Hill 23 D5
Cloghaun Co Clare 40 F5
Cloghaun Co Galway 31 D3
Cloghboley/*Clochbhuile* 15 D2
Cloghbrack/*An Chloch Bhreac*
Co Galway/*Gaillimh* 30 G1
Cloghbrack Co Meath 35 A1
Cloghcor 9 C1
Clogheen/*An Chloichín*
Co Tipperary/*Tiobraid Árann* 51 D5
Clogheen/*An Chloichín*
Co Waterford/*Port Láirge* 51 C5
Clogher Co Mayo 13 B4
Clogher 22 G3
Clogher Co Mayo 22 H4
Clogher Co Roscommon 25 B2
Clogher/*Clochar*
Co Tyrone/*Tír Eoghain* 18 E1
Cloghera 42 F5
Clogherhead/*Ceann Chlochair* 28 F3
Cloghey/*Clochaigh* 20 H1
Cloghfin 10 F5
Cloghjordan/*Cloch Shiurdáin* 43 B3
Cloghmore/*An Chloich Mhóir* 21 C2
Cloghpook 44 H5
Cloghran/*Clochrán* 36 F2
Cloghvoula 49 B5
Clohamon/*Cloch Amainn* 53 D1
Clogharinka Co Offaly 35 A3
Clogharinka Co Kilkenny 44 H5
Clohernagh 63 B3
Clologe 54 E1
Clomantagh 44 F5
Clonakenny/*Cluain Uí Chionaoith* 43 C3
Clonakilty/*Cloich na Coillte* 67 D2
Clonalea 43 B4
Clonalvy/*Cluain Ailbhe* 28 E5
Clonard Co Cork 61 C4
Clonard/*Cluain Ioraird*
Co Meath/*An Mhí* 35 A2
Clonard Great 54 E5
Clonascra 33 C3
Clonaslee/*Cluain na Slí* 34 F5
Clonavoe 34 H4
Clonbern/*Cluain Bheirn* 32 F1
Clonbulloge/*Cluain Bolg* 35 A4
Clonbur/*An Fhairche* 30 G1
Cloncagh/*Cluain Cath* 49 D3
Cloncrave 34 H2
Cloncreen 34 H4

Cloncullen 34 E1
Cloncully 44 E2
Clondalkin/*Cluain Dolcáin* 36 E3
Clondrohid 59 C4
Clondulane 61 A2
Clonea/*Cluain Fhia* 52 F5
Clonee/*Cluain Aodha* 36 E2
Cloneen Co Offaly 34 G3
Cloneen/*An Cluainín*
Co Tipperary/*Tiobraid Árann* 52 E3
Clonegall/*Cluain na nGall* 45 D5
Clonelly 9 A5
Clones/*Cluain Eois* 18 E4
Clonfert/*Cluain Fearta* 33 B4
Clongeen 53 C5
Clonincurragh 44 F2
Clonkeen 44 G2
Clonkeen Co Kerry 59 A3
Clonkeenkerrill 32 F3
Clonlost/*Cluain Loiste* 34 H1
Clonmacnoise/*Cluain Mhic Nóis* 33 C3
Clonmany/*Cluain Maine* 3 A2
Clonmeen 44 E4
Clonmel/*Cluain Meala* 52 E4
Clonmellon/*Ráistín* 27 A5
Clonmore/*Cluain Mhór*
Co Carlow/*Ceatharlach* 45 D4
Clonmore Co Louth 28 E3
Clonmore Co Tipperary 43 D4
Clonmult 61 B3
Clonoe 10 H5
Clonony 33 C4
Clonoulty 51 C1
Clonroche/*Cluain an Róistigh* 53 C3
Clonsilla/*Cluain Saileach* 36 E3
Clontarf/*Cluain Tarbh* 36 F3
Clontibret/*Cluain Tiobrad* 18 G4
Clontubbrid 44 F5
Clonvaraghan 20 E2
Clonycavan 35 A1
Clonygowan/*Cluain na nGamham* 34 G5
Clonyquin 34 G5
Cloonacauneen 31 D4
Cloonacool/*Cluain na Cúile* 15 B5
Cloonagh 26 F3
Cloonbrennaun 24 G5
Clooncah 25 B5
Cloondaff 22 G1
Cloondara/*Cluain Dá Ráth* 25 C4
Cloone/*An Chluain* 25 D1
Cloone Grange 25 D2
Clooneagh 25 C3
Clooneen 26 F3
Clooney 8 E2
Cloonfad Co Roscommon 24 F4
Cloonfad/*Cluain Fada*
Co Roscommon/*Ros Comáin* 33 B4
Cloonfallagh/*Cluain Falach* 24 E3
Cloonfeagh 40 H4
Cloonfinish 24 E1
Cloonfower 24 F3
Cloonkeelaun 15 A4
Cloonkeen Co Galway 24 G4
Cloonkeen Co Mayo 22 H3
Cloonkeen Co Roscommon 24 G5
Cloonkeevy/*Cluain Ciabhaigh* 15 D5
Cloonlara/*Cluain Lára* 42 G5
Cloonlee 23 D3

Cloonloogh/*Cluain Lua* 24 H1
Cloonlusk 51 A2
Cloonmurray 25 A4
Cloonnacat 24 F5
Cloonsheever 24 G3
Cloontia/*Na Cluainte* 24 F1
Cloontuskert 25 B4
Cloonusker 42 G3
Cloonycarney 15 A3
Cloonymorris 32 H4
Cloonyogan 25 A4
Cloonyquin/*Cluain Uí Choinn* 25 A3
Closh 44 E2
Clough/*An Cloch* 20 F2
Cloughduv 60 E5
Cloughmills/*Muileann na Cloiche* 4 H1
Cloverhill 17 D5
Cloyne/*Cluain* 61 B5
Coachford/*Áth an Chóiste* 60 E4
Coagh/*An Cuach* 10 H4
Coalbrook/*Glaise an Ghuail* 52 E1
Coalisland/*Oileán an Ghuail* 10 H5
Coan/*An Cuan* 44 H4
Cobh/*An Cóbh* 61 A5
Caddy 11 B2
Colbinstown/*Baile Choilbín* 45 C2
Colehill/*Cnoc na Góla* 26 E5
Coleraine/*Cúil Raithin* 4 F3
Colestown 53 D4
Collinstown/*Baile na gCailleach* 26 H5
Collon/*Collann* 27 D3
Collooney/*Cúil Mhuine* 15 D4
Colman 51 D3
Colmanstown/*Baile Uí Chlúmháin* 32 F3
Colp 28 F4
Comber/*An Comar* 12 F5
Commaun 43 B5
Commeen 8 H2
Commons Co Cork 60 E5
Commons/*Na Coimíní*
Co Tipperary/*Tiobraid Árann* 52 F1
Cong/*Conga* 30 H1
Conlig/*An Choinleic* 12 G4
Conna/*Conaithe* 61 B2
Connemara 29 C2
Connolly/*Fioch Rua* 40 G4
Connor/*Coinnire* 11 C2
Connonagh 67 C3
Convoy/*Conmhaigh* 9 B1
Cookstown/*An Chorr Chríochach* 10 H4
Cool 61 C1
Coolagary 34 H4
Coolaney/*Cúil Áine* 15 C4
Coolanheen 61 D2
Coolattin 46 E5
Coolbaun/*An Cúl Bán*
Co Tipperary/*Tiobraid Árann* 43 A2
Coolbaun/*An Cúl Bán* 44 H4
Coolboy Co Donegal 2 G5
Coolboy/*An Cúl Buí*
Co Wicklow/*Cill Mhantáin* 46 E5
Coolboy Co Tipperary 51 A5
Coolderry/*Cúl Doire* 43 D2
Coole/*An Chuil* 26 G4
Coole Abbey 61 A2
Coolea/*Cúil Aodha* 59 B4
Coolea 60 H2
Coollegreane 16 G4

Coolgrange 52 H1
Coolgreany/*Cúil Ghréine* 46 F5
Coolgreen 60 H3
Coolinny 60 H2
Coolmeen/*Cúil Mhín* 49 B1
Coolmore 8 F5
Coolnafarna 24 F4
Coolnagun 26 F4
Coolock 36 F3
Coolrain/*Cúil Ruáin* 44 E2
Coolroe 54 F2
Coolross 43 B1
Coolsallagh 60 H5
Coolshaghtena 25 B5
Coomleagh 67 B1
Coonagh 50 F1
Cooneen/*An Cúinnín* 17 D2
Cooraclare/*Cuar an Chláir* 40 F5
Coorleagh 45 A5
Coosane 66 H3
Cootehall/*Uachtar Thíre* 25 A1
Cootehill/*Muinchille* 18 E5
Coralstown/*Baile Mhic Cearúill* 34 H2
Corbally Co Clare 40 E5
Corbally/*An Corrbhaile*
Co Sligo/*Sligeach* 15 A4
Corbet 19 C2
Corclogh 13 B3
Corcreeghagh 27 D1
Corcullin 14 E5
Cordal/*Cordal* 59 A1
Cordarragh 22 F4
Corduff/*An Chorr Dubh* 35 B4
Cork/*Corcaigh* 60 G4
Corkey/*Corcaigh* 4 H4
Corlea 25 C5
Corlee 23 D1
Corlough 17 A5
Cornafulla/*Corr na Fola* 33 B3
Cornamona/*Corr na Móna* 30 G1
Cornanagh 23 C4
Corndarragh 34 F4
Corrakyle 42 G2
Corrandulla/*Cor an Dola* 31 D3
Corraun 21 D2
Correen 11 C1
Corries Cross 53 B1
Corrofin/*Cora Finne* Co Clare/*An Clár* 40 H3
Corrofin Co Galway 32 E2
Corrondher 50 E3
Corry 16 G4
Cortown/*An Baile Corr* 27 B4
Corvoley 14 F4
Costelloe/*Casla* 30 F4
Coumduff 57 D1
Countygate 61 A2
Courthoyle 53 C4
Courtmacsherry/*Cúirt Mhic Shéafraidh* 68 E2
Courtmatrix 49 D3
Courtown/*Baile na Cúirte* 54 F1
Cousane 67 B1
Coxtown 32 H4
Craan 46 E5
Crannford/*Áth an Chorráin* 46 E5
Crafield 46 F3
Craggagh 40 G1
Cragroe 42 E3
Craig 10 E2

Craigavad/*Creig an Bhada* 12 F3
Craigavole 4 F5
Craigavon 19 B1
Craigdarragh 10 E1
Craiggore 4 E5
Craigs/*Na Creaga* 11 B1
Cranagh/*An Chrannóg* 10 E2
Crane 54 E2
Cranford/*Creamhghort* 2 G3
Crannogeboy 7 D2
Cranny/*An Chrannaigh* 54 F2
Co Clare/*An Clár* 40 G5
Cranny Co Londonderry 10 H3
Cratloe/*An Chreatalach* 42 E5
Craughwell/*Creachmhaoil* 32 F4
Crawfordsburn/*Sruth Chráfard* 12 F3
Crazy Corner 34 G1
Creagh Co Cork 67 A3
Creagh/*Créach* 45 A5
Co Fermanagh/*Fear Manach* 17 C2
Creaghanroe/*Crícheán Rua* 18 H4
Crecora/*Craobh Chomhartha* 50 F2
Creegh/*An Chríoch* 40 F5
Creeslough/*An Craoslach* 2 F3
Crettyard 44 H4
Creevagh 14 G3
Creeves 49 D2
Cregg Co Clare 30 H5
Cregg Co Cork 67 C3
Creggan 11 B3
Creggan/*An Creagan* Co Armagh/*Ard Mhaca* 19 A5
Creggan Co Offaly 33 C4
Creggan/*An Creagán*
Co Tyrone/*Tír Eoghain* 10 F4
Cregganbaun/*An Creagán Bán* 22 E4
Creggs/*Na Creaga* 24 H5
Crindle 3 D4
Crinkill/*Crionchoill* 43 C1
Croagh/*An Chruach* 8 E3
Croagh 50 E2
Croaghrimbeg 22 G4
Crockets Town 14 H4
Croghan/*Cruachán*
Co Offaly/*Uíbh Fhailí* 34 G3
Croghan Co Roscommon 25 A2
Crolly 1 D5
Cromane/*An Cromán* 58 E2
Cromlin 17 A5
Crookedwood/*Tigh Munna* 26 G5
Crookhaven/*An Cruachán* 66 G4
Crookstown/*An Baile Gallda*
Co Cork/*Corcaigh* 60 E5
Crookstown Co Kildare 45 B2
Croom/*Cromadh* 50 F2
Cross/*An Chrois* 30 H1
Cross Barry/*Croisan Bharraigh* 60 F5
Cross Keys/*Carraig an Tobair*
Co Cavan/*An Cabhán* 26 G2
Cross Keys Co Meath 26 H4
Cross Keys Co Meath 35 D1
Cross Mahon 68 E1
Cross Roads/*Na Croisbhealaí* 9 A2
Cross/*An Chrois* Co Clare/*An Clár* 48 F1
Crossabeg/*Na Crosa Beaga* 54 E4
Crossakeel/*Crosa Caoil* 27 A4
Crossboyne 23 D4
Crossconnell 33 A4
Crossdoney/*Cros Domhnaigh* 26 F1

Crossea 26 E5
Crosserlough/*Crois ar Loch* 26 G2
Crossgar/*An Chrois Ghearr* 20 F1
Crossgare 4 F4
Crosshaven/*Bun an Tábhairne* 60 H5
Crosskeys/*Na hEochracha* 45 A1
Crossmaglen/*Crois Mhic Lionnáin* 19 A5
Crossmolina/*Crois Mhaoilíona* 14 G5
Crossna 25 A1
Crossooha 31 D5
Crosspatrick/*Crois Phádraig*
Co Kilkenny/*Cill Chainnigh* 44 E5
Crosspatrick Co Wicklow 46 E5
Crosswell 24 H5
Crowbally 61 B4
Crumlin/*Cromghlinn* 11 C4
Crumpane 66 E1
Crusheen/*Croisín* 41 D3
Crutt 44 H4
Cuilkillew 22 H1
Culcavy 19 D1
Culdaff/*Cuil Dábhcha* 3 C2
Culfadda 24 G1
Culkeeny 3 C1
Cullahill/*An Chúlchoill* 44 F4
Cullane 50 H4
Cullaville/*Baile Mhic Cullach* 18 H5
Culleen 42 E5
Culleens/*Na Coillíní* 15 A4
Cullen/*Cuillin* Co Cork/*Corcaigh* 59 C2
Cullen/*Cuilleann*
Co Tipperary/*Tiobraid Árann* 51 A2
Cullenagh 50 H5
Cullenstown 63 D3
Cullin 23 D1
Cullybackey/*Coill na Baice* 11 B1
Cullyhanna/*Coilleach Eanach* 19 A4
Culmore 3 B4
Culnady/*Cúil Chnáidí* 10 H1
Cultra 12 E3
Currabeha/*An Chorr Bheithe* 61 B2
Curracloe/*Currach Cló* 54 E4
Curraclogh 59 D5
Curragh/*An Currach* 61 D4
Curragh Camp 35 B5
Curragh West/*An Currach Thiar* 24 F5
Curragha 36 E1
Curraghalicky 67 C2
Curraghboy/*An Currach Buí* 33 B2
Curraghlawn 46 E4
Curraghmore 53 A3
Curraghroe/*An Currach Rua* 25 B4
Curraglass/*Cora Chlas* 61 B2
Curragunneen/*Currach Guinín* 43 D3
Curran/*An Corrán* 10 H2
Curranavilla 30 G4
Currans 58 H1
Curreeny/*Na Coirríní* 43 B5
Currow/*Corra* 58 H1
Curry/*An Choraidh* 24 E1
Curryglass 66 F2
Cushendall/*Bun Abhann Dalla* 6 E4
Cushendun/*Bun Abhann Duinne* 6 E3
Cushina 34 H5

D

Daingean/*An Daingean* 34 G4
Dalkey/*Deilginis* 36 G4

Dalystown 34 F2
Damastown 36 F1
Damhead 4 F4
Danesfort/*Dún Feart* 25 D4
Dangandargan 51 C3
Darkley/*Dearclaigh* 18 H3
Darragh Cross 20 F1
Dartry 18 F5
Davidstown/*Baile Dháith* 53 D3
Deerpark/*Páirc an bhFia* 31 C1
Delgany/*Deilgne* 36 G5
Delphi 22 E5
Delvin/*Dealbhna* 27 A5
Dernagree/*Doire na Graí* 59 C2
Derradda/*Doire Fhada* 17 A5
Derragh 40 H4
Derreen Co Clare 40 F3
Derreen Co Kerry 57 C4
Derreen/*Dan Doirín*
Co Mayo/*Maigh Eo* 21 D2
Derreenacarrin 66 G1
Derreenard 67 A3
Derreenauliff 58 E5
Derreeny 66 F2
Derries 34 E4
Derrineel 33 B3
Derrinturn 35 A3
Derryadd/*Doire Fhada* 11 B5
Derrybeg/*Doirí Beaga* 1 D4
Derryboye/*Doire Buí* 20 F1
Derrybrien/*Daraidh Braoin* 42 F1
Derrycanan 25 B4
Derryclogh 67 B2
Derrycon 44 F1
Derrycooly 34 E4
Derrycrin 11 A4
Derrydolney 33 D5
Derryfadda 44 E5
Derrygareen 42 H5
Derrygile 44 G1
Derrygolan 34 F3
Derrygonnelly/*Doire Ó gConaíle* 17 A1
Derrygowna 25 C5
Derrygrath 51 C4
Derrygrogan 34 G4
Derrykeighan 4 G3
Derrylahan 33 B3
Derrylin/*Doire Loinn* 17 B4
Derryloughlin 58 E5
Derrymacash 19 B1
Derrymore 48 F5
Derrynacaheragh 67 B1
Derrynoose/*Doire Núis* 18 H3
Derryrush/*Doire Iorrais* 30 E3
Derrytrasna 11 A5
Derrywode 24 G5
Dervock/*Dearbhóg* 4 G3
Derryvoreada 30 E1
Desert 61 A3
Desertmartin/*Diseart Mhártain* 10 H2
Devenish/*Daimhinis* 17 B2
Dingle/*An Daingean* 57 C1
Doagh/*Dumhach* 11 D3
Doagh Beg 2 H2
Dolla/*An Doladh* 43 A4
Dollingstown 19 C1
Dollymount/*Cnocán Doirinne* 36 G3
Donabate/*Domhnach Bat* 36 G1

Donacarney 28 F4
Donadea 35 C3
Donagh 17 C3
Donaghadee/*Domhnach Daoi* 12 G4
Donaghcloney/*Domhnach Cluana* 19 C1
Donaghmore/*Domhnach Mór*
Co Laois/*Laois* 44 E3
Donaghmore Co Meath 36 E1
Donaghmore Co Tyrone 10 G5
Donaghpatrick/*Domhnach Phadráig* 27 C4
Donard Co Wexford 53 B3
Donard/*Dún Ard*
Co Wicklow/*Cill Mhantáin* 45 D2
Donaskeagh 51 B2
Donegal/*Dún na nGall* 8 G4
Doneraile/*Dún ar Aill* 60 F1
Donohill/*Dún Eochaille* 51 B2
Donore Co Meath 35 B1
Donore/*Dún Uabhair* 28 E4
Donoughmore/*Domhnach Mór* 60 E3
Dooagh/*Dumha Acha* 21 B1
Doocarrick 18 E5
Doocastle/*Caisleán an Dumha* 24 F1
Doocharry/*An Dúchoraidh* 8 F1
Dooega/*Dumha Éige* 21 C2
Doogary 26 E1
Dooghbeg 21 D2
Doogort/*Dumha Goirt* 21 C1
Doohamlat 18 G4
Doohat/*Dúháite* 18 E5
Doohooma/*Dumha Thuama* 13 C5
Dooleeg 14 F5
Doolieve 68 G1
Doolin/*Dúlainn* 40 F2
Doon Co Galway 32 H3
Doon/*Dún* Co Limerick/*Luimneach* 51 A1
Doon Co Tipperary 61 B1
Doona 13 C5
Doonaha/*Dún Átha* 48 G1
Doonbeg/*An Dún Beag* 40 E5
Doonmanagh 57 D2
Doonreaghan 29 D2
Doornane 52 H5
Dooyork 13 C5
Dough 66 F4
Doughiska 31 D4
Douglas/*Dúglas* 60 G5
Douglas Bridge 9 C3
Dovea/*Dubhfhéith* 43 C5
Dowling 52 G4
Downhill/*Dún Bó* 4 E3
Downies/*Na Dúnaibh* 2 F3
Downing 60 H1
Downpatrick/*Dún Pádraig* 20 F2
Dowra/*An Damhshraith* 16 G4
Drangan/*Drongan* 52 E2
Draperstown/*Baile na Croise* 10 G2
Dreen 10 F1
Dreenagh 48 E3
Drehidasillagh 48 F5
Driminidy 67 B2
Drimmo 44 F2
Drimoleague/*Drom Dhá Liag* 67 B2
Drinagh/*Draighneagh*
Co Cork/*Corcaigh* 67 B2
Drinagh Co Galway 29 C2
Drinagh Co Roscommon 25 C4
Drinagh Co Wexford 54 E5

Drinaghan 15 A3
Dring/*Droing* 26 F3
Dripsey/*An Druipseach* 60 E4
Drogheda/*Droichead Átha* 28 E4
Droichead Nua (Newbridge) 35 B5
Drom Co Kerry 47 D5
Drom/*An Drom*
Co Tipperary/*Tiobraid Árann* 43 C5
Dromagh 59 D2
Dromahair/*Droim dhá Thiar* 16 F3
Dromara/*Droim Bearach* 19 D2
Dromaragh 57 D4
Dromboy South 60 G3
Dromcolliher/*Drom Collachair* 49 D4
Dromcunnig 48 G4
Dromgariff 60 G3
Dromin Co Limerick 50 G3
Dromin/*Droim Ing* Co Louth/*Lú* 28 E3
Dromina/*Drom Aidhhne* 50 E5
Dromineer/*Drom Inbhir* 43 A3
Dromiskin/*Droim Ineasclainn* 28 E2
Drommahane/*Droim Átháin* 60 F2
Dromnea 66 G3
Dromod/*Dromad* 25 C3
Dromore 67 A2
Dromore West/*An Droim Mór Thiar* 15 B3
Dromore/*Droim an Mór*
Co Down/*An Dún* 19 D1
Dromore/*An Droim Mór*
Co Tyrone/*Tír Eoghain* 9 C5
Dromtrasna 49 B4
Drum/*An Droim*
Co Monaghan/*Muineachán* 18 E5
Drum Co Roscommon 33 B3
Drumahoe 3 B5
Drumandoora/*Drom An Dúdhoire* 42 E2
Drumaness/*Droim an Easda* 20 F2
Drumanure 40 H4
Drumard 15 C3
Drumaroad 20 E2
Drumatober 32 H5
Drumbane/*An Drom Bán* 51 C1
Drumbaun 42 H5
Drumbeg 12 E5
Drumbo 12 E5
Drumcar/*Droim Chora* 28 E2
Drumcharley 42 F3
Drumcliff Co Clare 41 D3
Drumcliff/*Droim Chliabh*
Co Sligo/*Sligeach* 15 D2
Drumcondra/*Droim Conrach* 27 C2
Drumcree/*Droim Cria* 26 H5
Drumfin/*Droim Fionn* 16 E5
Drumfree/*Droim Fraoigh* 3 A3
Drumgriftin 31 D3
Druminnin 8 G3
Drumintee 19 B5
Drumkeary 42 G1
Drumkeen 9 A1
Drumkeeran/*Droim Caorthainn* 16 F4
Drumlea/*Droim Léith* 25 D1
Drumlish/*Droim Lis* 25 D3
Drumlosh 33 C3
Drummacool 16 E4
Drummin Co Mayo 22 F4
Drummin/*An Dromainn* 40 F4
Drummullin/*Droim Ailí* 25 B3
Drumna 25 D1

Drumnagreagh Port 6 F6
Drumnakilly/Droim na Coille 10 E4
Drumoghill 9 B1
Drumone 26 H4
Drumquin/Droim Caoin 9 C4
Drumraney/Droim Raithne 33 D2
Drumree/Droim Rí 35 D1
Drumroe 61 C2
Drumshanbo/Droim Seanbhó 16 G5
Drumskinny/Droim Scine 9 A5
Drumsna/Droim ar Snámh 25 B2
Drumsurn/Droim Sorn 4 E5
Drung 18 E5
Duagh/Dubháth 49 A3
Dually 51 D2
Dublin/Baile Átha Cliath 36 F3
Duggarry 33 B3
Duleek/Damhliag 28 E5
Dumfea 53 B1
Dunadry/Dún Eadradh 11 D3
Dunaff/Dún Damh 3 A2
Dunaghy 4 G4
Dunamon 24 H5
Dunany/Dún Áine 28 F2
Dunbell 52 H1
Dunboyne/Dún Búinne 36 E2
Dunbyrne 35 B4
Duncannon/Dún Canann 63 C3
Duncormick/Dún Chormaic 64 E3
Dundalk/Dún Dealgan 28 E1
Dunderrow/Dún Darú 68 F1
Dunderry 27 B5
Dundian 18 F2
Dundonald/Dún Dónaill 12 F4
Dundoogan 32 H3
Dundrod/Dún dTrod 11 D4
Dundrum/Dún Droma
Co Down/An Dún 20 F3
Dundrum Co Dublin 36 F4
Dundrum Co Tipperary 51 B2
Dunfanaghy/Dún Fionnachaidh 2 F3
Dungannon/Dún Geanainn 10 G5
Dunganstown 53 A4
Dungarvan/Dún Garbháin
Co Kilkenny/Cill Chainnigh 53 A2
Dungarvan/Dún Garbháin
Co Waterford/Port Láirge 62 E2
Dungivin/Dún Geimhin 10 F1
Dunglow/An Clochán Liath 1 C5
Dungourney/Dún Guairne 61 B4
Dunhill 62 H1
Duniry 42 H1
Dunkerrin/Dún Cairin 43 C3
Dunkineely/Dún Cionnaola 8 E4
Dunkitt 52 H5
Dunlavin/Dún Luáin 45 C1
Dunleer/Dún Léire 28 E3
Dunlewy/Dún Lúiche 2 E5
Dunloy/Dún Lúiche 4 H5
Dunmanus 66 G3
Dunmanway/Dún Mánmhaí 67 C1
Dunmoon 61 C3
Dunmore/Dún Mór 24 E5
Dunmore East/Dún Mór 63 B3
Dunmurry/Dún Muirigh 11 D5
Dunnamaggan/Dún Iomagáin 52 G3
Dunnamanagh/Dún na Manach 9 D1
Dunnamore/Domhnach Mór 10 F3

Dunnaval 20 E5
Dunningstown 52 G1
Dunquin/Dún Chaoin 57 B1
Dunsany 35 D1
Dunseverick/Dún Sobhairce 4 G2
Dunshaughlin/Dún Seachlainn 35 D1
Durrow/Darú 44 G4
Durrus/Dúras 66 H2
Dún Laoghaire 36 G4
Dysart/An Diseart 34 F2

E

Eadestown 35 D5
Earlshill 52 E1
Easky/Iascaigh 15 A3
East Barrs 16 G3
East Town/Baile Thoir 1 D2
Eden/An tEadan 12 F3
Edenderry/Éadan Doire 35 A3
Ederney/Eadarnaidh 9 B5
Edgeworthstown/Meathas Troim 26 E4
Eglinton/An Mhagh 3 C4
Eglish/An Eaglais 18 G1
Eighter/Iochtar 26 H3
Ellistrin/Eileastran 2 G5
Elphin/Ail Finn 25 A3
Elton/Eiltiún 50 G3
Emlagh 32 F5
Emlaghmore 57 C4
Emly/Imleach 50 H3
Emmoo 25 B5
Emo/Ioma 44 H1
Emyvale/Scairbh na gCaorach 18 F2
Ennis/Inis 41 D4
Enniscorthy/Inis Córthaidh 53 D2
Enniskean/Inis Céin 67 D1
Enniskerry/Áth an Sceire 36 G5
Enniskillen/Inis Ceithleann 17 B2
Ennistimon/Inis Díomáin 40 G3
Erganagh 9 B3
Erra 25 C4
Errill/Eiréil 44 E4
Esker/An Eiscir 32 F4
Esker South 25 D3
Esknaloughoge 58 E5
Eskragh/Eiscreach 18 E1
Eyeries/Na hAoraí 66 E1
Eyrecourt/Dún an Uchta 33 B5

F

Faha 58 G2
Fahaduff 49 A5
Fahamore 48 E5
Fahan 57 B2
Fahan/Fathain
Co Donegal/Dún na nGall 3 A4
Fahanasoodry 50 H4
Fahy Co Galway 32 H4
Fahy Co Galway 33 A5
Fairfield 33 D2
Fairymount/Mullach na Sí 24 G3
Falcarragh/An Fál Carrach 2 E3
Fanore 40 G1
Farahy 60 G1
Fardrum/Fardroim 33 C3
Farmer's Bridge 48 G5
Farnagh 33 D3
Farnaght 25 D2

Farnanes 60 E5
Farnanes/Na Fearnáin 67 B1
Farnoge 53 A4
Farran/An Fearann 60 E5
Farranfore/An Fearann Fuar 58 H1
Fauna 45 D2
Feakle/An Fhiacail 42 F3
Feaklecally 58 E3
Fedamore/Feadamair 50 F2
Feeard 48 F1
Feenagh Co Clare 40 G1
Feenagh/Fíonach
Co Limerick/Luimneach 50 E4
Feeny/Na Fineadha 10 F1
Fenagh/Fionnmhach 25 C1
Fenit/An Fhianait 48 F5
Fennagh/Fionnmhach 45 B5
Fennor/Fionnúir
Co Waterford/Port Láirge 62 H1
Fennor Co Westmeath 34 H1
Feohanagh/An Fheothanach
Co Kerry/Ciarraí 57 B1
Feohanagh/An Fheothanach
Co Limerick/Luimneach 49 D4
Feoramore 58 G5
Ferbane/An Féar Bán 33 D4
Fermoy/Mainistir Fhear Maí 61 A2
Ferns/Fearna 54 E1
Ferry Bridge 50 E1
Ferrybank/Portan Chalaidh 46 G4
Fethard/Fiodh Ard
Co Tipperary/Tiobraid Árann 52 E3
Fethard/Fiodh Ard
Co Wexford/Loch Garman 63 C3
Fews 62 F1
Fiddane 42 H5
Fiddown/Fiodh Dúin 52 G4
Fieries 58 H1
Figlash 52 F4
Finavarra 31 C5
Finnea/Fiodh an Átha 26 G3
Finnis 19 D2
Finny/Fionnaithe 30 G1
Fintona/Fionntamhnach 9 D5
Fintown/Baile na Finne 8 G1
Finuge/Fionnúig 48 H3
Finvoy/An Fhionnbhoith 4 G5
Firkeel 65 D2
Firmount 61 A3
Fisherstreet 40 F2
Five Corners 11 D2
Fiveally/An Chúirt 33 D5
Fivemilebourne/Abhainn an Chartúin 16 E3
Fivemilebridge 60 G5
Flagford 25 B2
Fivemiletown/Baile na Lorgan 17 D2
Flagmount/Leacain an Éadain
Co Clare/An Clár 42 F2
Flagmount Co Kilkenny 53 A1
Flatfield 11 C5
Flemingstown 58 E1
Florence Court/Mullach na Seangán 17 A3
Foilnamuck 66 H3
Fontstown 45 B1
Fordstown/Baile Forda 27 B5
Fore/Baile Fhobhair 26 H5
Forkhill/Foirceal 19 B5
Formoyle Co Clare 40 G1

Formoyle Co Mayo 21 D4
Formoyle Co Longford 25 B5
Fornaght 60 F3
Fort Middle 50 E4
Fort William 43 B3
Forthill 33 C1
Foulkesmill/Muileann Fúca 53 C5
Foulkstown 51 D2
Four Mile House/
Teach na gCeithre Mhile 25 A4
Four Roads/Tigh Sratha 33 A1
Fox Hill 22 G5
Foxfield/Cnocán an Mhada Rua 25 C1
Foxford/Béal Easa 23 C1
Foxhall 23 D5
Foynes/Faing 49 C1
Freemount/Cillin an Chrónáin 49 D5
Frenchpark/Dún Gar 24 G2
Freshford/Achadh Úr 44 G5
Freynestown 45 C2
Friarstown 50 F2
Frogmore 48 F5
Frosses/Na Frosa 8 F4
Fuerty 25 A5
Funshin More 41 D1
Furbogh/Na Forbhacha 30 H4
Furraleigh 62 F1
Furroor 40 G5
Furrow 51 A5
Fybagh 58 F1

G

Gainstown 34 G2
Galbally/An Gallbhaile
Co Limerick/Luimneach 50 H4
Galbally Co Wexford 53 D4
Galbertstown 51 D1
Galgorm 11 B1
Gallagh 25 B5
Galmoy/Gabhalmhaigh 44 E4
Galtrim 35 D1
Galway/Gaillimh 31 D4
Gannavane 51 A1
Garadice/Garairis 35 C2
Garbally 33 A3
Garlow Cross/Crois Chearla 27 D5
Garnavilla 51 C4
Garr 34 H3
Garrafrauns 24 E5
Garranard 14 G4
Garranereagh 59 D5
Garranlahan/An Garrán Leathan 24 F4
Garraun Co Clare 48 H1
Garraun Co Galway 32 H5
Garraun Co Kerry 58 G1
Garravoone 52 G5
Garrettstown 45 C3
Garrison/An Garastún 16 G1
Garristown/Baile Gháire 36 E1
Garrycaheragh 61 A3
Garrycloonagh 14 G5
Garrycullen 53 C5
Garryduff 4 G4
Garryfine/Garrai Phaghain 50 F4
Garryhill 53 B1
Garrymore 61 B4
Garrynafana 43 B4
Garryspillane 50 H4

Garryvoe 61 B5
Garvagh/Garbhach
Co Leitrim/Liatroim 25 D1
Garvagh/Garbhachadh
Co Londonderry/Doire 4 F5
Garvaghy/Garbhachadh 10 E5
Garvetagh 9 B3
Gattabaun/An Geata Bán 44 F5
Gawleys Gate/Geata Mhic Amhlaí 11 B5
Gaybrook/Baile Réamainn 34 G2
Geashill/Géisill 34 G4
Geevagh/An Ghaobhach 16 F5
Georgestown 62 G1
Gerahies 66 H2
Gibstown 27 C4
Gilford/Áth Mhic Giolla 19 B2
Glanalin 66 G3
Glandart 67 A2
Glandore/Cuan Dor 67 C3
Glangevlin 16 H4
Glanlough 66 G2
Glanmire/Gleann Maghair 60 H4
Glanoe 48 H4
Glanroon 66 F3
Glantane/An Gleanntán 60 E2
Glanworth/Gleannúir 60 H1
Glarryford/An tÁth Glárach 4 H5
Glashabeg 57 B1
Glashaboy East 60 G3
Glashaboy North 60 G3
Glashananoon 49 A4
Glasleck/Glasleic 27 A1
Glaslough/Glasloch 18 G2
Glassan/Glasán 33 C2
Glassillaun 21 D2
Glastry 12 H5
Glebe 3 D3
Glen 19 B3
Glen Of Imail/Gleann Ó Máil 45 D2
Glen Of The Downs 36 G5
Glen/An Gleann
Co Donegal/Dún na nGall 2 G3
Glen Co Londonderry 10 H1
Glenacroghery 61 B3
Glenade 16 E2
Glenagort 22 G1
Glenahilty 43 B3
Glenamoy 14 E3
Glenard/Gleann Aird 62 E3
Glenariff or Waterfoot/Gleann Aireamh 6 E4
Glenarm/Gleann Arma 6 F5
Glenavy/Lann Abhaidh 11 C4
Glenbeigh/Gleann Beithe 58 E2
Glenboy/Gleann Buí 16 G3
Glenbrien/Gleann Bhriain 54 E3
Glenbrohane 50 H4
Glencar Co Kerry 58 F3
Glencar/Gleann an Chairthe
Co Leitrim 16 E2
Glencoh/Glinn Chatha 30 F3
Glencolumbkille/Gleann Cholm Cille 7 C3
Glencree 36 F5
Glencullen 36 F4
Glendalough Co Waterford 52 E5
Glendarragh 46 G1
Glenderry 48 F4
Glendowan/Glenn Domhain 2 F5
Glendree 42 F3

Gleneely/Gleann Daoile 3 C2
Glenealy 46 G2
Glenfarne/Gleann Fearna 16 H3
Glenflesk 59 A3
Glengariff/An Gleann Garbh 66 H1
Glengoura 61 B2
Glenhead 3 D5
Glenhull 10 F3
Glenlara 13 B3
Glenmaquin 9 B1
Glenmore Co Clare 40 G5
Glenmore/An Ghleann Mhór
Co Kilkenny/Cill Chainnigh 53 A4
Glennagat 51 D4
Glennaknockane 49 B5
Glennamaddy/Gleann na Madadh 24 G5
Glennascaul 31 D4
Glenoe 12 F2
Glenough Lower 51 B1
Glenough Upper 51 B1
Glenroe 50 H5
Glenshelane 61 D1
Glentane Co Cork 61 B3
Glentane Co Galway 32 G2
Glenties/Na Gleannta 8 F2
Glentogher/Gleann Tóchair 3 B2
Glentrasna/Gleann Trasna 30 F2
Glenvale 4 H5
Glenvar/Gleann Bhairr 2 H3
Glenville/Gleann an Phréacháin 60 H3
Glin/An Ghleann 49 B2
Glinsk Co Galway 24 H5
Glinsk/Glinsce (Connemara) 29 D3
Glounthaune 60 H4
Glynn/An Gleann
Co Antrim/Aontroim 12 F2
Glynn Co Wexford 53 B3
Glynn Co Wexford 53 D4
Gneevgullia/Gníomh go Leith 59 B2
Golden/An Gabhailin 51 C3
Golden Ball 36 G4
Goleen/An Góilin 66 G4
Goold's Cross/Crois an Ghúlaigh 51 C2
Goresbridge/An Droichead Nua 53 A1
Gorey/Guaire 54 F1
Gormanstown/Baile Mhic Gormáin 28 F5
Gormanstown 51 C5
Gort/An Gort 42 E1
Gortaclady 10 G4
Gortagowan 58 F5
Gortahork/Gort An Choirce 2 E3
Gortalough 43 C5
Gortarevan 33 B5
Gortaroo 61 C4
Gorteen/Goirtín Co Galway/Gaillimh 32 G3
Gorteen Co Kilkenny 44 H4
Gorteen Co Limerick 50 E4
Gorteen Co Sligo 24 G1
Gorteen Co Waterford 62 E3
Gorteens 53 A5
Gorteeny/Goirtíní 42 H2
Gortgarriff 66 E1
Gortgarrigan/Gort Geargáin 16 F3
Gortglass 59 A1
Gortin/An Goirtín 9 D3
Gortleatilla 14 E3
Gortletteragh 25 D2
Gortmore Co Mayo 14 G3

Gortnadeeve	24	H5
Gortnahaha	49	C1
Gortnahey	3	D5
Gortnahoo/*Gort na hUamha*	52	E1
Gortnahoughtee	59	B5
Gortnahurra	14	F4
Gortnaleaha	48	G5
Gortnamearacaun	42	E3
Gortnasillagh	24	H3
Gortreagh/*An Gort Riabhach*	10	G4
Gortrelig	58	F3
Gortskeagh	41	D1
Gowlaun	21	D5
Gowlin	53	B2
Gowran/*Gabhrán*	53	A1
Gracehill/*Baile Uí Chinnéide*	11	B1
Graiguearush	62	F1
Graiguenamanagh/*Gráig na Manach*	53	B2
Granabeg	46	E1
Granagh	50	E3
Granard/*Granard*	26	F3
Graney	45	B3
Grange/*Gráinseach Chuffe*		
Co Kilkenny/*Cill Chainigh*	52	G2
Grange Co Kilkenny	52	H5
Grange Co Louth	28	F1
Grange Co Offaly	35	A3
Grange Co Tipperary	51	D4
Grange/*An Ghráinseach*		
Co Sligo/*Sligeach*	15	D2
Grange/*An Greainsigh*		
Co Waterford/*Port Láirge*	61	D3
Grange Co Wexford	64	E3
Grange Beg Co Kildare	35	A5
Grange Beg Co Laois	44	E3
Grange Con/*Gráinseach Choinn*	45	C2
Grange Corner	11	B2
Grangebellew/*Greainseach an Oísirt*	28	F3
Grangeford/*An Ghráinseach*	45	C4
Grangegeeth	27	D4
Graniamore	16	E5
Grannagh	32	E5
Grant House	18	F1
Granville/*An Doire Mhin*	10	G5
Greenan/*An Grainán*	46	F3
Greenanstown/*Baile Uí Ghrianáin*	28	F4
Greencastle/*An Caisléan Nua*		
Co Donegal/*Dún na nGall*	3	D2
Greencastle/*Caisleán na hOireanaí*		
Co Down/*An Dún*	19	D5
Greencastle Co Tyrone	10	F3
Greenisland/*Inis Glas*	12	E3
Greenland	61	C4
Greenore/*An Grianfort*	19	D5
Grenagh/*Grenach*	60	F3
Greyabbey/*An Mhainistir Liath*	12	G5
Greygrove	40	G5
Greysteel	3	C4
Greystone/*An Chloch Liath*	18	G1
Greystones/*Na Clocha Liath*	36	G5
Griston	50	H4
Grogan	33	D3
Groomsport/*Port an Ghiolla Ghruama*	12	G3
Gubaveeny	16	H3
Gulladuff	10	H2
Gullaun	59	B2
Gurteen/*Goirtín*	16	F2
Gusserane/*Ráth na gCosarean*	53	B5
Gweedore/*Gaoth Dobhair*	1	D4
Gweesalia/*Gaoth Sáile*	13	C5
Gyleen	61	A5

H

Hackball's Cross	27	D1
Hacketstown/*Baile Haicéid*	45	D3
Halfway	60	F5
Halfway House/*Tigh Leath Slí*	63	B3
Hamiltonsbawn/*Bábhún Hamaltún*	19	A2
Hannahstown/*Baile Haine*	11	D4
Harristown	52	H4
Hays	27	D4
Headford/*Áth Cinn*	31	C2
Headfort	59	A3
Heathfield	68	G1
Heavenstown	53	D5
Heirhill	48	F3
Helen's Bay/*Cuan Héilin*	12	F3
Herbertstown/*Baile Hiobaird*	50	G2
Highstreet	33	C4
Hightown	61	A3
Hill of Down/*Cnoc an Dúin*	35	A2
Hill Street	25	B2
Hillhall	11	D5
Hillsborough/*Cromghlinn*	19	D1
Hilltown/*Baile Hill* Co Down/*An Dún*	19	D4
Hilltown Co Wexford	54	E5
Hilltown Co Wexford	53	C5
Hollyford/*Áth an Chuillinn*	51	B1
Hollyfort/*Ráth an Chuillinn*	46	F5
Hollymount Co Galway	42	F1
Hollymount/*Maolla*		
Co Mayo/*Maigh Eo*	23	C5
Hollywood/*Cillín Chaoimhín*	1	D1
Holycross/*Gaile na gCailleach*		
Co Limerick/*Luimneach*	50	G3
Holycross/*Mainstir na Croiche*		
Co Tipperary/*Tiobraid Árann*	51	C1
Holywell	16	H2
Holywood/*Ard Mhic Nasca*	12	F4
Horetown	54	E5
Horse and Jockey/*An Marcach*	51	D1
Horseleap/*Baile Átha an Urchair*	34	E3
Hospital/*An tOspidéal*	50	H3
Hough	51	C1
Howth/*Binn Éadair*	36	G3
Hugginstown	52	H3
Hurlers Cross	42	E5
Hyde Park	11	D3

I

Illaunstookagh	58	E2
Inagh/*Eidhneach*	40	H3
Inch/*An Inis* Co Donegal/*Dún na nGall*	3	A4
Inch/*Inse* Co Kerry/*Ciarraí*	58	E1
Inch Co Tipperary	51	B1
Inch/*An Inis*		
Co Wexford/*Loch Garman*	46	F5
Inchabaun	49	C4
Inchbeg	44	G5
Inchigeelagh/*Inse Geimleach*	59	C5
Inchinapallas	60	H1
Inchnamuck	51	B5
Inishannon/*Inis Eonáin*	68	F1
Inishcrone/*Inis Crabhann*	14	H3
Inishnee	29	D2
Inishrush	11	A1
Iniskeen/*Inis Caoin*	27	D1
Inistioge/*Inis Tíog*	53	A3
Innfield/*An Bóthar Buí*	35	B2
Inver/Inbhear	8	F4
Inveran/*Indreabhán*	30	G4
Irishtown/*An Baile Gaelach*	24	E5
Irvinestown/*Baile an Irbhinigh*	17	B1

J

Jamestown Co Laois	45	A1
Jamestown Co Leitrim	25	B2
Jenkinstown	28	F1
Jenkinstown Co Kilkenny	44	G5
Jerrettspass/*Bealach Sheirit*	19	B3
Johnsfort	23	D2
Johnstown/*Cill Sheanaigh*		
Co Cork/*Corcaigh*	60	H5
Johnstown Co Kildare	35	D4
Johnstown/*Baile Sheáin*		
Co Kilkenny/*Cill Chainnigh*	44	F5
Johstown Co Meath	27	C5
Johnstown Co Wexford	53	C5
Johnstown Co Wicklow	46	F4
Johnstown Bridge	35	B3
Johnstownbridge	25	C3
Johnswell/*Tobar Eoin*	44	H5
Jonesborough/*Baile an Chláir*	19	B5
Julianstown/*Baile Iuiliáin*	28	F4

K

Kanturk/*Ceann Toirc*	59	D1
Katesbridge/*Droichead Cháit*	19	D2
Keadew/*Céideadh*	16	G5
Keady/*An Céide*	18	H3
Kealkill/*An Chaolchoill*	67	A1
Kealvaugh	59	B5
Keeagh/*An Chaothach*	30	H3
Keel/*An Caol*	21	C1
Keelnagore	57	D4
Keeloges	24	G5
Keem	21	B1
Keenagh/*Caonach*		
Co Longford/*An Longfort*	25	D5
Keenagh Co Mayo	14	F5
Keereen	61	D2
Kells Co Kerry	57	D3
Kells/*Ceanannas*		
Co Kilkenny/*Cill Chainigh*	52	G2
Kells/*Na Cealla*		
Co Antrim/*Aontroim*	11	C2
Kells/*Ceanannas*	27	B4
Kelshabeg	45	D3
Kenmare/*Neidín*	58	H4
Kentstown	27	D5
Kerloge	54	E5
Kesh/*An Cheis*		
Co Fermanagh/*Fear Manach*	9	A5
Kesh Co Sligo	16	E5
Keshcarrigan/*Ceis Charraigín*	25	C1
Kilbaha/*Cill Bheathach*	48	F2
Kilbane/*An Choill Bhán*	42	G4
Kilbarry	59	C5
Kilbarry/*Cill Barra*	52	H5
Kilbeacanty	42	E1
Kilbeg	62	G1
Kilbeggan/*Cill Bheagáin*	34	F3
Kilbegnet	24	H5
Kilbeheny/*Coill Bheithne*	51	A5

Kilbenan 32 E1
Kilberry/*Cill Bhearaigh*
Co Kildare/*Cill Dara* 45 A2
Kilberry Co Meath 27 C4
Kilbrack 52 F5
Kilbreedy Co Limerick 50 F4
Kilbreedy Co Limerick 50 E2
Kilbreedy Co Tipperary 51 C2
Kilbrickan/*Cill Bhreacáin* 30 F3
Kilbrickane 43 D5
Kilbricken/*Cill Bhriocáin* 44 F2
Kilbride Co Mayo 23 D2
Kilbride Co Meath 27 B5
Kilbride/*Cill Bhride*
Co Wicklow/*Cill Mhantáin* 46 G3
Kilbride Co Wicklow 36 E5
Kilbrien Co Cork 60 H2
Kilbrien Co Waterford 62 E1
Kilbrin 60 E1
Kilbrittain/*Cill Briotáin* 68 F2
Kilcaimin 31 D4
Kilcappagh 34 H5
Kilcar/*Cinn Charthaigh* 7 D4
Kilcarney 45 D3
Kilcarroll 49 A1
Kilcash 52 F4
Kilcashel 33 B3
Kilcavan 34 G5
Kilchreest/*Cill Chriost* 32 F5
Kilclaran 42 F3
Kilclief 20 G2
Kilcloher 48 F2
Kilclonfert 34 G3
Kilcock/*Cill Choca* 35 C2
Kilcoe 67 A3
Kilcogy/*Cill Chóige* 26 F3
Kilcohan 63 B3
Kilcolgan/*Cill Cholgáin* 32 E5
Kilcolman Co Cork 68 E1
Kilcolman/*Cill Cholmain*
Co Limerick/*Luimneach* 49 C2
Kilcolman Co Waterford 62 E3
Kilcomin 43 C2
Kilcommon/*Cill Chuimín*
Co Tipperary/*Tiobraid Árann* 51 C4
Kilcommon Co Tipperary 43 B5
Kilconierin 32 F4
Kilconly/*Cill Chonla* 31 D1
Kilconnell/*Cill Chonaill* 32 H3
Kilconnor 50 G5
Kilcoo/*Cill Chua* 19 D3
Kilcoole/*Cill Chomhghaill* 46 G1
Kilcor 61 A2
Kilcorkan 41 D2
Kilcormac (Frankford)/*Cill Chormaic* 33 D5
Kilcornan 50 E1
Kilcorney/*Cill Coirne* 59 D2
Kilcotty/*Cill Chota* 54 E3
Kilcredan 61 C4
Kilcrohane/*Cill Chrócháin* 66 G3
Kilcronat 61 B3
Kilcullen/*Cill Chuillin* 45 C5
Kilcummin Co Kerry 58 H2
Kilcummin/*Cill Chuimín*
Co Kerry/*Ciarraí* 47 D5
Kilcurly/*Cill Choirle* 28 E1
Kilcurry/*Cill an Churraigh* 19 B5
Kilcusnaun 49 A5

Kildalkey/*Cill Dealga* 35 B1
Kildangan/*Cill Daingin* 45 A1
Kildanoge 51 C5
Kildare/*Cill Dara* 35 B5
Kildavin/*Cill Damhain* 53 C1
Kildermody 52 G5
Kildorrery/*Cill Dairbhre* 50 H5
Kildress 10 G4
Kilduffahoo 50 H1
Kildurrihy 57 B1
Kilfeakle 51 B3
Kilfearagh 48 G1
Kilfenora/*Cill Fhionnúrach* 40 G2
Kilfinnane/*Cill Fhíonáin* 50 G4
Kilfinny 50 E2
Kilflyn/*Cill Flainn* 48 G4
Kilgarvan/*Cill Gharbhain* 59 A4
Kilglass Co Galway 32 H2
Kilglass/*Cill Ghlais*
Co Roscommon/*Ros Comáin* 33 B1
Kilglass/*Cill Ghlas* Co Sligo/*Sligeach* 15 A3
Kilgobnet/*Cill Ghobnait*
Co Kerry/*Ciarraí* 58 G2
Kilgowan 45 C1
Kilgrogan 50 E2
Kilkea 45 B3
Kilkeasy 52 H3
Kilkee/*Cill Chaoi* 39 D5
Kilkeel/*Cill Chaoil* 20 E5
Kilkelly/*Cill Cheallaigh* 24 E2
Kilkenny/*Cill Chainnigh* 52 G1
Kilkenny West 33 D2
Kilkerran 68 F2
Kilkerrin/*Cill Choirín* 32 G1
Kilkieran/*Cill Chiaráin* 30 E3
Kilkilleen 67 A3
Kilkinlea 49 B4
Kilkishen/*Cill Chisín* 42 E4
Kill 29 C1
Kill/*An Chill* Co Cavan/*An Cabhán* 26 H1
Kill/*An Chill* Co Kildare/*Cill Dara* 35 D4
Kill Co Waterford 62 G1
Killachonna 33 D2
Killaclug 50 H5
Killacolla 50 E4
Killadeas/*Cill Chéile Dé* 17 B1
Killaderry 32 H2
Killadoon/*Coill an Dúin* 21 D4
Killadysert/*Cill an Disirt* 49 C1
Killafeen 42 E2
Killag 64 E3
Killahaly 61 C2
Killala/*Cill Ala* 14 H3
Killallon 27 A4
Killaloe 42 G4
Killaloo/*Cill Dalua* 10 E1
Killamery 52 F3
Killane 35 A3
Killateeaun 22 G5
Killanena 42 F2
Killann/*Cill Anna* 53 C2
Killard 40 E5
Killare 34 E2
Killarga/*Cill Fhearga* 16 F3
Killarney/*Cill Airne* 58 H2
Killarone 30 H2
Killaroo 34 E2
Killashandra/*Cill na Seanrátha* 26 E1

Killashee/*Cill na Sí* 25 C4
Killasser/*Cill Lasrach* 23 D1
Killaun 43 D1
Killavally/*Coill an Bhaile* 22 G4
Killavarilly 61 A2
Killavarrig 60 G3
Killavil/*Cill Fhábhail* 15 D5
Killavoher 32 F1
Killavullen/*Cill an Mhuilinn* 60 G2
Killea Co Donegal 3 A5
Killea Co Leitrim 16 G2
Killea/*Cill Sléibhe*
Co Tipperary/*Tiobrain Árann* 43 C4
Killea Co Waterford 63 B3
Killead/*Cill Éad* 11 C3
Killeagh/*Cill la* 61 C4
Killeany/*Cill Éinne* 39 D1
Killedmund 53 B1
Killeedy 49 C4
Killeen Co Galway 42 E2
Killeen Co Mayo 21 D4
Killeen Co Tipperary 43 C1
Killeen Co Tyrone 10 H5
Killeenaran 31 D5
Killeenasteena 51 C3
Killeenavarra 32 E5
Killeeneenmore 32 E5
Killeenleagh 67 A2
Killeens Cross 60 G4
Killerrig 45 C4
Killeevan 18 E4
Killeglan 33 A2
Killeigh/*Cill Aichidh* 34 F5
Killemadeema 32 G5
Killen/*Cillin* 9 B3
Killenard 44 H1
Killenagh 54 F1
Killenaule/*Cill Náile*
Co Tipperary/*Tioraid Árann* 43 C1
Killenaule/*Cill Náile*
Co Tipperary/*Tioraid Árann* 52 E2
Killeshil 34 G3
Killeshin 45 A4
Killeter/*Coill Iochtair* 9 B4
Killimer 49 A1
Killimor/*Cill Iomair* 33 A5
Killinaboy/*Cill Inine Baoith* 40 H2
Killinardrish/*Cill an Ard-dorais* 60 E4
Killinaspick 52 H4
Killinchy/*Cill Dhuinsí* 12 G5
Killincooly 54 F3
Killiney/*Cill Iníon Léinin*
Co Dublin/*Baile Átha Cliath* 36 G4
Killiney Co Kerry 48 E5
Killinick/*Cill Fhionnóg* 54 E5
Killinierin/*Cill an Iarain* 46 F5
Killinkere/*Cillin Chéir* 27 A2
Killinny 41 D1
Killinthomas 35 A4
Killiskey 46 G1
Killmacahill 61 B5
Killogeary 14 G3
Killogeenaghan 33 D3
Killaghteen 49 C3
Killoe 26 E4
Killoluaig 57 C4
Killomoran 42 E1
Killoneen 34 G4

Killoran/*Cill Odhráin* 32 H4
Killorglin/*Cill Orglan* 58 F2
Killoscobe 32 G2
Killough/*Cill Locha* 20 G3
Killour 22 H5
Killsallaghan 36 F2
Killucan/*Cill Liúcainne* 34 H1
Killukin 25 B2
Killurin Offaly 34 E5
Killurin Wexford/*Cill Liúráin* 53 D4
Killurly 57 C5
Killusty 52 E3
Killybegs Co Antrim 11 B2
Killybegs/*Na Cealla Beaga*
Co Donegal/*Dún na nGall* 8 E4
Killyclogher 9 D4
Killygar 26 E1
Killygordon/*Cúil na gCuiridín* 9 B2
Killykergan/*Coill Uí Chiaragain* 4 F5
Killylea/*Coillidh Léith* 18 G2
Killyleagh/*Cill Ó Laoch* 20 F1
Killyneill 18 G3
Killyon 43 D1
Kilmacanoge/*Cill Mocheanóg* 36 G5
Kilmacow/*Cill Mhic Bhúith* 52 H5
Kilmacrenan/*Cill Mhic Réanáin* 2 G4
Kilmacthomas/*Coill Mhic Thomáisín* 62 F1
Kilmactranny/*Cill Mhic Treana* 16 F5
Kilmaganny/*Cill Mogeanna* 52 G3
Kilmaine/*Cill Mheáin* 31 C1
Kilmainham Wood/*Cill Maighneann* 27 B3
Kilmalady 34 E3
Kilmaley/*Cill Mháille* 40 H4
Kilmalin 36 F5
Kilmallock/*Cill Mocheallóg* 50 G4
Kilmanagh/*Cill Mhanach* 52 F1
Kilmaniheen 49 A4
Kilmead 45 B2
Kilmeadan/*Cill Mhíodháin* 52 H5
Kilmeage/*Cill Maodhog* 35 B4
Kilmeedy/*Cill Mide* 49 D4
Kilmessan/*Cill Mheasáin* 35 C1
Kilmichael/*Cill Mhichil* 59 C5
Kilmihil/*Cill Mhichil* 40 G5
Kilmona 60 G3
Kilmoon 67 A4
Kilmore/*An Chill Mhór*
Co Armagh/*Ard Mhaca* 19 A1
Kilmore Co Cavan 26 F1
Kilmore Co Clare 42 F5
Kilmore Co Down 20 F1
Kilmore Co Mayo 23 C1
Kilmore/*Cill Mhór*
Co Roscommon/*Ros Comáin* 25 B2
Kilmore/*An Chill Mhór*
Co Wexford/*Loch Garman* 64 E3
Kilmore Quay/*Cé na Cille Móire* 64 E3
Kilmore Upper 25 C4
Kilmorna/*Cill Mhaonaigh* 49 A3
Kilmorony 45 A3
Kilmovee 24 F2
Kilmuckridge/*Cill Mhucraise* 54 F2
Kilmurry/*Cill Mhuire* Co Clare/*An Clár* 42 E4
Kilmurry/*Cill Mhuire* Co Clare/*An Clár* 40 F4
Kilmurry/*Cill Mhuire*
Co Cork/*Corcaigh* 59 D5
Kilmurry Co Limerick 50 H2
Kilmurry Co Wicklow 45 C3

Kilmurry McMahon/
Cill Mhuire Mhic Mhathúna 49 B1
Kilmurvy/*Cill Mhuirbhigh* 30 E5
Kilmyshall 53 D1
Kilnacreagh 42 F5
Kilnagross/*Coill na gCros* 25 C1
Kilnahown 32 H4
Kilnaleck/*Cill na Leice* 26 G2
Kilnamanagh/*Cill na Manach* 54 E2
Kilnamartyra/*Cill na Martra* 59 C4
Kilnamona/*Cill na Móna* 40 H3
Kilpatrick 68 F1
Kilpedder 46 G1
Kilquane 57 B1
Kilquiggin 45 D4
Kilraghts/*Cill Reachtais* 4 H4
Kilrane/*Cill Ruáin* 54 F5
Kilrea/*Cill Ria* 4 G5
Kilrean/*Cill Riáin* 8 E2
Kilreekill/*Cill Rícill* 32 H4
Kilroghter 31 C3
Kilronan/*Cill Rónáin* 39 D1
Kilroosky 25 B5
Kilross/*Cill Ros* 51 H3
Kilrush/*Cill Rois* 48 H1
Kilsallagh/*Coil Salach*
Co Galway/*Gaillimh* 24 G5
Kilsallagh/*Coil Salach*
Co Mayo/*Maigh Eo* 22 E3
Kilsaran 28 E2
Kilshanchoe 35 B3
Kilshannig 48 E5
Kilshanny/*Cill Seanaigh* 40 G2
Kilsheelan 52 E4
Kilshinahan 68 E2
Kilskeer/*Cill Scire* 27 A4
Kilskeery/*Cill Scire* 17 B1
Kiltamagh/*Coillte Mach* 23 D2
Kiltarsaghaun 22 G4
Kiltartan 42 E1
Kiltealy/*Cill Téile* 53 C2
Kilteel 35 D4
Kilteely/*Cill Tíle* 50 H2
Kilteevan 25 B5
Kiltegan 45 D3
Kiltiernan/*Cill Tiarnáin*
Co Dublin/*Baile Átha Cliath* 36 G4
Kiltiernan Co Galway 32 E5
Kiltober 34 F3
Kiltoom/*Cill Tuama*
Co Roscommon/*Ros Camáin* 33 B2
Kiltoom Co Westmeath 26 G5
Kiltormer/*Cill Tormóir* 33 A4
Kiltullagh/*Cill Tulach* 32 F4
Kiltyclogher/*Coilte Clochair* 16 G2
Kilvemnon 52 F3
Kilvine 24 E5
Kilwaughter/*Cill Uachtair* 12 E1
Kilwoghan 35 D3
Kilworth/*Cill Uird* 61 A1
Kilworth Camp 61 A1
Kinallen 19 D1
Kinard 49 B2
Kinawley/*Cill Náile* 17 B3
Kincaslough/*Cionn Caslagh* 1 C5
Kincon 14 G4
Kingarrow 8 G1
Kingscourt/*Dún an Rí* 27 B2

Kingsland 24 H2
Kinsmill 10 H4
Kinlough/*Cionn Locha* 16 F1
Kinnacorra 21 D3
Kinnegad/*Cionn Átha Gad* 34 H2
Kinnitty/*Cionn Eitigh* 43 D1
Kinsale/*Cionn tSáile* 68 G1
Kinsalebeg/*Baile an Phoill* 61 D3
Kinsaley 36 G2
Kinvarra /*Cinn Mhara*
Co Galway/*Gaillimh* 30 F3
Kinvarra/*Cinn Mhara*
Co Galway/*Gaillimh* 31 D5
Kircubbin/*Cill Ghobáin* 12 G5
Kirkhills 4 G4
Kirkistown 20 H1
Kishkeam/*Coiscím na Caillí* 59 C1
Knights Town 57 C4
Knock/*An Cnoc* Co Clare/*An Clár* 49 A1
Knock/*An Cnoc* Co Mayo/*Maigh Eo* 23 D3
Knock Co Tipperary 44 E3
Knockacaurhin 40 H3
Knockaderry/*Cnoc an Doire* 49 D3
Knockainy/*Cnoc Áine* 50 G3
Knockalafalla 52 F5
Knockalaghta 24 H4
Knockalough/*Cnoc an Eanaigh* 40 G5
Knockalunkard 40 H3
Knockananna/*Cnoc an Eanaigh* 46 E3
Knockanarra 24 E4
Knockane 59 D5
Knockanevin/*Cnocán Aobhainn* 50 H5
Knockanore 61 C3
Knockanure 49 A3
Knockaroe 44 E3
Knockaun 32 H5
Knockaunarast 61 C1
Knockaunbrack 49 A4
Knockaunnaglashy 58 F2
Knockaunroe 58 E2
Knockayrogeen 57 C1
Knockboy/*An Cnoc Buí* 62 E1
Knockbrack Co Clare 42 F4
Knockbrack/*An Cno Breac*
Co Donegal/*Dún na nGall* 9 B1
Knockbrack Co Kerry 48 G4
Knockbride 27 A1
Knockbridge/*Droichead an Cnoic* 27 D1
Knockbrit/*Cnoc an Bhriotaigh* 51 D3
Knockbrown 68 E2
Knockburden 60 F5
Knockcloghrhim/*Cnoc Clochdhroma* 10 H2
Knockcroghery/*Cnoc an Chrochaire* 33 B1
Knockdarnan 50 F3
Knockdrin 34 G1
Knockdrislagh 60 F2
Knockeenadallane 59 B1
Knockeencreen 49 A5
Knocklofty 51 D4
Knocklong/*Cnoc Loinge* 50 H3
Knockmael 42 E2
Knockmore/*An Cnoc Mór* 23 C1
Knockmourne 61 B2
Knocknaboley 40 G4
Knocknacarry 6 E3
Knocknacurra 68 F1
Knocknagashal/*Cnoc na gCaiseal* 49 A4
Knocknageeha 66 H3

Place	Ref
Knocknagower	42 G3
Knocknagree	59 B2
Knocknahaha	48 G5
Knocknahila	40 F5
Knocknahilan	60 E5
Knocknalina	13 C3
Knocknalower	13 D3
Knocknaskagh	61 B4
Knockraha/*Cnoc Rátha*	60 H4
Knockroe Co Cork	67 A3
Knockroe Co Kerry	58 E4
Knockroe Co Waterford	62 E2
Knocks Co Cork	67 D2
Knocks Co Laois	44 F2
Knockskagh	67 D2
Knockskavane	49 D5
Knocktopher/*Cnoc an Tóchair*	52 H3
Knockvicar	25 A1
Knuttery	60 G2
Kyle	44 H2
Kyleballyhue	45 B4
Kylebrack/*An Choill Bhreac*	32 G5
Kylegarve	51 A1

L

Place	Ref
Labasheeda/*Leaba Shíoda*	49 B1
Laban	32 E5
Lack/*An Leac*	9 B5
Lackagh	35 A5
Lackamore/*An Leac Mhór*	42 H4
Lackan Cross	33 A1
Lackan Co Carlow	45 A5
Lackan Co Roscommon	25 B4
Lackan Co Westmeath	26 F5
Lackan/*An Leacain*	
Co Wicklow/*Cill Mhantáin*	36 E5
Lackareagh	59 D5
Lackbrooder	49 A5
Lacken/*Leacain*	53 B4
Lacken Co Kilkenny	52 G1
Lackendarragh North	60 H2
Lackey	44 E2
Ladysbridge/*Droichead na Scuab*	61 B4
Lady's Island	64 G3
Lagavara	4 H2
Laagganstown	51 C3
Laghey Corner	10 H5
Laghy/*An Lathaigh*	8 G4
Lahardaun/*Leathardán*	22 H1
Lakyle	49 B1
Lambeg/*Lann Bheag*	11 D5
Lamoge	52 G3
Lanesborough/*Béal Átha Liag*	25 C4
Lannaght	42 F2
Laracor	35 B1
Laragh Co Kildare	35 C3
Laragh/*Láithreach* Co Monaghan	18 H5
Laragh/*Láithreach* Co Wicklow	46 F2
Largan Co Mayo	14 E4
Largan Co Rosommon	25 B3
Largan Co Sligo	15 A5
Largy	7 D4
Largydonnell	16 F1
Larne/*Latharna*	12 E1
Latnamard	18 F4
Lattin/*Laitean*	51 A3
Latton	18 F5
Lauragh/*Láithreach*	66 F1

Place	Ref
Laurelvale/*Tamhnaigh Bhealtaine*	19 B2
Laurencetown/*An Baile Mór*	33 A4
Lavagh/*Leamhach*	15 C5
Lawrencetown/*Baile Labhráis*	19 B2
Lady's Island	64 G3
Laytown/*An Inse*	28 F4
Leabgarrow/*An Leadhb Gharbh*	1 B5
Leamlara/*Léim Lára*	61 A3
Leap/*An Léim*	67 C3
Lecarrow/*An Leithcheathrú*	33 B1
Leckaun	16 F3
Leckemy/*Leic Éime*	3 C2
Leenaun/*An Líonán*	22 E5
Legan or Lenamore	26 E5
Leggah	26 E2
Legoniel/*Lag an Aoil*	11 D4
Lehinch/*An Leacht*	40 F3
Leighlinbridge/	
Leithghlinn an Droichid	45 A5
Leitrim Co Clare	40 F5
Leitrim Co Down	20 E3
Leitrim /*Liatrom* Co Leitrim/*Liatrom*	25 B1
Leitrim East	49 A2
Leixlip/*Léim an Bhradáin*	36 E3
Lemanaghan	33 D4
Lemybrien/*Léim Uí Bhriain*	62 F1
Leperstown	63 B3
Lerrig	48 G4
Letterbarra	8 F3
Letterbreen/*Leitir Bhruín*	17 A2
Letterfrack/*Leitir Fraic*	29 D1
Letterkelly	40 F4
Letterkenny/*Leitir Ceanainn*	2 G5
Letterloan	4 E4
Lettermacaward/*Leitir Mhic an Bhaird*	8 E1
Lettermullan/*Leitir Mealláin*	30 E4
Lettermore/*Leitir Móir*	30 E4
Lettershendoney	3 C5
Levally/*An Leathbhaile*	
Co Galway/*Gaillimh*	32 F1
Levally Co Mayo	23 C5
Licketstown	52 H5
Lifford/*Leifear*	9 C2
Limavady/*Léim an Mhadaidh*	3 D4
Limerick/*Luimneach*	50 F1
Limerick Junction/*Gabhal Luimnigh*	51 A3
Linsfort/*Lios Lionn*	3 A3
Lisbane	12 F5
Lisbellaw/*Lios Béal Átha*	17 C2
Lisboduff	18 E5
Lisburn/*Lios na gCearrbhach*	11 D5
Liscananaun	31 D3
Liscannor/*Lios Ceannúir*	40 F3
Liscarney/*Lios Cearnaigh*	22 F4
Liscarroll/*Lios Cearuill*	50 E5
Liscloon/*Lios Claon*	9 D1
Liscrona	48 G1
Lisdargan	57 D1
Lisdoonvarna/*Lios Dúin Bhearna*	40 G2
Lisdowney	44 G4
Lisduff/*An Lios Dubh*	
Co Cavan/*An Cabhán*	27 A3
Lisduff Co Cork	60 G3
Lisduff Co Offaly	33 D5
Lisgarode	43 B3
Lisgoold	61 A3
Lisheen	41 D5
Lisheenaguile	33 A5

Place	Ref
Liskeagh	24 H1
Lislea	19 B4
Lismacaffry	26 F4
Lismire	59 D1
Lismore/*Lios Mór*	61 C2
Lismoyle	33 B1
Lisnadill/*Lios na Daille*	18 H3
Lisnageer/*Lios na gCaor*	18 E5
Lisnagry/*Lios na Graí*	50 G1
Lisnakill Cross	62 H1
Lisnalong	18 F5
Lisnamuck/*Lios na Muc*	10 G2
Lisnarick/*Lios na nDaróg*	17 A1
Lisnaskea/*Lios na Scéithe*	17 C3
Lispatrick	68 G2
Lispole/*Lios Póil*	57 D1
Lisroe	40 H4
Lisronagh/*Lios Ruanach*	52 E4
Lisryan	26 F4
Lissacresig	59 C4
Lissaha	51 D2
Lissalway/*Lios Sealbhaigh*	24 H4
Lissamona	66 H4
Lissanacody	33 A5
Lissananny	24 G3
Lissavard	67 D3
Lisselton/*Lios Eiltin*	48 H3
Lissycasey/*Lios Uí Chathasaigh*	40 H5
Listellick	48 G5
Listerlin	53 A4
Listooder	20 F1
Listowel/*Lios Tuathail*	48 H3
Lisvarrinane/*Lios Fearnáin*	51 A4
Littleton/*An Baile Beag*	51 D1
Lixnaw/*Leic Snámha*	48 G4
Loanends/*Carn Mhéabha*	11 D3
Lobinstown/*Baile Lóibín*	27 C3
Loch Gowna/*Loch Gamhna*	26 F2
Loghill/*Leamhchoill*	
Co Limerick/*Luimneach*	49 B2
Loghill Co Limerick	49 D3
Logleagh	61 B1
Lombardstown/*Baile Limbaird*	60 E2
Londonderry/*Doire*	3 B5
Longford/*An Longfort*	50 F1
Co Longford/*An Longfort*	25 D4
Longford Co Offaly	43 D1
Longwood/*Maigh Dearmahaí*	35 B2
Lorrha/*Lothra*	43 B1
Lorum	53 B1
Loskeran	62 E3
Longhaclerybeg	32 G3
Loughacutteen	51 C4
Loughanaboll	15 B4
Loughanavally	34 F2
Loughanure	1 D5
Loughaunbeg/*An Lochán Beag*	30 G4
Loughbrickland/*Loch Bricleann*	19 C2
Loughduff	26 F2
Lougher	58 E1
Loughgall/*Loch gCál*	19 A1
Loughglinn/*Loch Glinne*	24 G3
Loughguile/*Loch gCaol*	4 H4
Loughinisland/*Loch an Oileáin*	20 F2
Loughmacrory Co Tyrone	10 E4
Loughmoe/*Luachma*	43 D5
Lough Morne/*Loch Morn*	18 G5
Loughrea/*Baile Loch Riach*	32 G5

Loughries 12 G4
Loughshinny 36 G1
Louisburgh/*Cluain Cearbán* 22 E3
Louth/*Lú* 27 D1
Lowertown 66 G3
Lowtown 19 D2
Lucan/*Leamhcán* 36 E3
Lugdoon 15 B3
Luggacurren/*Log an Churraigh* 44 H3
Lukeswell 52 H4
Lullymore 35 B4
Lurgan/Co Mayo 24 E2
Lurgan/*An Lorgain*
Co Armagh/*Ard Mhaca* 19 B1
Lurgan Co Roscommon 24 H2
Lurganare 19 B3
Lurganboy Co Donegal 2 H3
Lurganboy Co Leitrim 16 F2
Lusk/*Lusca* 36 G1
Lyracrumpane/*Ladhar an Chrompáin* 48 H4
Lyradane 60 F3
Lyre/*Ladhar an Chrompáin or An Ladhar*
Co Cork/*Corcaigh* 60 E2
Lyre Co Kerry 49 A5
Lyre Co Waterford 61 B3
Lyrenaglo 61 B1

M

Maam Cross/*An Teach Dóite* 30 F2
Maas 8 E2
Mace 22 G3
Mackan/*Macan* 17 B3
Macosquin/*Maigh Choscáin* 4 F4
Macroney 61 A1
Macroom/*Maigh Chromtha* 59 D4
Madabawn 27 A1
Maddockstown/*Baile Mhadóg* 52 H1
Maganey/*Maigh Geine* 45 B3
Maghaberry 11 C5
Maghera Co Down 20 E3
Maghera/*Machaire Rátha*
Co Londonderry/*Doire* 10 H1
Maghera Cross 42 E3
Magherafelt/*Machaire Fíolta* 11 A2
Magheralin/*Machaire Lainne* 19 C1
Magheramason 3 B5
Magheramorne/*Machaire Morna* 12 F2
Magheraveely/*Machaire Mhílie* 17 D4
Maghery/*An Machaire*
Co Donegal/*Dún na nGall* 8 E1
Maghery Co Armagh 11 A5
Magilligan/*Aird Mhic Giollagain* 3 D3
Maguiresbridge/*Droichead Mhig Uidir* 17 C3
Mahoonagh 49 D3
Mainham 35 C3
Malahide/*Mullach Íde* 36 G2
Malin/*Málainn* 3 B1
Malin Beg/*Málainn Bhig* 7 C3
Malin More 7 B3
Mallaranny/*An Mhala Raithní* 22 E2
Mallow/*Mala* 60 F2
Mallusk/*Maigh Bhloisce* 11 D3
Manorcunningham/
Mainéar Uí Chuinneagáin 2 H5
Manorhamilton/*Cluainín* 16 F2
Manselstown 43 D5
Mansfieldstown 28 E2
Mantua/*An Mointeach* 25 A3

Manulla 23 C3
Marble Arch 17 A3
Mardyke 52 E2
Margymonaghan 3 D3
Markethill/*Cnoc an Mhargaidh* 19 A3
Markhamstown 51 D4
Marlfield 51 D4
Marshalstown/*Baile Mharascail* 53 D2
Martinstown/*Baile Uí Mháirtín* 5 D5
Martinstown Co Limerick 50 G4
Marty 27 B4
Mastergeehy 57 D4
Masterstown 51 C3
Matehy 60 F4
Maulatrahane 67 B3
Maulavanig 67 A1
Maulawaddra 66 G3
Maum/*An Mám* 30 F1
Mauricesmills/*Muilte Mhuiris* 40 H3
Mayglass 54 E5
Maynooth/*Maigh Naud* 35 D3
Mayo/*Maigh Eo* 23 C3
Mayobridge/*Droichead Mhaigh Eo* 19 C4
Mazetown 11 D5
McGregor's Corner 5 D5
McLaughlins Corner 4 G5
Meanus/*Méanas* 50 F2
Meelick 33 B5
Meelin/*An Mhaoilinn* 49 D5
Meenaclady/*Mín an Chladaigh* 1 D3
Meenacross 7 C3
Meenacross 8 E1
Meenaneary 7 D3
Meenbannad 1 C5
Meenbannivane 49 A5
Meenglass 9 A2
Meenlaragh/*Mín Larach* 1 D3
Meennaraheeny 49 B5
Meigh 19 B4
Mellifont 28 E4
Menlough/*Mionlach*
Co Galway/*Gaillimh* 32 G2
Menlough/*Mionlach*
Co Galway/*Gaillimh* 31 C4
Middlequarter 61 D1
Middletown/*Coillidh Chanannáin* 18 G3
Midfield/*An Trian Láir* 23 D2
Midleton/*Mainistir na Corann* 61 A4
Milehouse/*Teach an Mhíle* 53 D2
Milemill 45 C1
Milestone/*Cloch an Mhile* 51 B1
Milford/*Áth an Mhuilinn*
Co Armagh/*Ard Mhacha* 18 H2
Milford/*Átha an Mhuilinn*
Co Cork/*Corcaigh* 50 E4
Mill Brook 17 D4
Mill Town/*Baile an Mhuilinn* 11 C3
Millbank 11 D3
Millbrook/*Sruthán an Mhuilinn* 12 E1
Millford/*Baile na nGallóglach* 2 G4
Millisle/*Oilean an Mhuilinn* 12 H4
Millstreet/*Sráid an Mhuilinn*
Co Cork/*Corcaigh* 61 A1
Millstreet /*Sráid an Mhuilinn*
Co Cork/*Corcaigh* 59 C2
Millstreet Co Waterford 61 D1
Milltown Co Armagh 19 A2
Milltown/*Baile an Mhuilinn*

Co Cavan/*An Cabhán* 17 C5
Milltown Co Donegal 8 F4
Milltown Co Donegal 2 G3
Milltown Co Dublin 36 G1
Milltown Co Galway 32 G1
Milltown Co Galway 24 E5
Milltown/*Baile an Mhuilinn*
Co Kerry/*Ciarraí* 57 C1
Milltown/*Baile an Mhuilinn*
Co Kerry/*Ciarraí* 58 G1
Milltown Co Kildare 35 B5
Milltown Co Kilkenny 52 H4
Milltown Co Londonderry 4 E3
Milltown Co Londonderry 4 F4
Milltown Co Westmeath 34 F1
Milltown Malbay/*Sráid na Cathrach* 40 F4
Milltownpass/
Belach Bhaile an Mhuilinn 34 G2
Minane Bridge/
Droichead an Mhionnáin 68 H1
Minerstown/*Baile na Mianadóirí* 20 F3
Minorstown 52 E4
Mitchelstown/*Baile Mhistéala* 51 A5
Moanmore Co Clare 48 H1
Moanmore Co Tipperary 50 H3
Moat Farrell 26 E4
Moate/*An Móta* 33 D3
Model Village (Cork) 60 E4
Modelligo 61 D2
Modreeny 43 B3
Mogeely/*Maigh Dhíle* 61 B4
Mohil 44 H5
Mohill/*Maothail* 25 C2
Moira/*Maigh Rath* 11 C5
Moll's Gap 58 G4
Monagear 54 E2
Monaghan/*Muineachán* 18 F3
Monagoun 61 B2
Monaincha Bog 43 D3
Monalour 61 C1
Monamolin/*Muine Moling* 54 F2
Monamraher/*Móin na mBráthar* 62 E3
Monard Co Tipperary 51 A3
Monard Co Waterford 61 C1
Monaseed/*Móin na Saighead* 46 E5
Monaster/*An Mhainistir* 50 F2
Monasteraden/*Mainistir Réadáin* 24 G2
Monasterevin/*Mainistir Eimhín* 35 A5
Monea/*Maigh Niadh* 17 A2
Moneen Co Clare 48 F2
Moneen Co Galway 31 D2
Moneenroe 44 H4
Monettia Bog 34 F5
Moneycashel 16 H3
Moneycusker 59 C5
Moneydig/*Muine Dige* 4 F5
Moneygall/*Muine Gall* 43 C3
Moneyglass/*An Muine Glas* 11 B2
Money More Co Donegal 2 E5
Moneymore/*Muine Mór* 10 H3
Moneyneany/*Món na nIonadh* 10 G2
Moneyslane 19 D3
Moneyreagh/*Monadh Riabhach* 12 E5
Monilea/*An Muine Liath* 34 G1
Monivea/*Muine Mhéa* 32 F3
Monkstown Co Antrim 12 E3
Monkstown/*Baile na Mhanach*
Co Cork/*Corcaigh* 60 H5

Montpelier 42 G5
Mooncoin/*Móin Choinn* 52 H5
Moone/*Maoin* 45 B2
Moord 61 D4
Moortown 11 A4
Moorfields/*Páirc an tSléibhe* 11 C2
Morenane 50 E3
Mornington/*Baile Uí Mhornáin* 28 F4
Moroe/*Maigh Rua* 50 H1
Mortlestown 50 G4
Moskeagh 60 E5
Mosney Camp 28 F5
Moss-side/*Mas Saíde* 4 H3
Mossley/*Maslaí* 12 E3
Mothel 52 F5
Mount Bellew Bridge/*An Creagán* 32 G2
Mount Nugent/*Droichead Uí Dhálaigh* 26 G3
Mount Stewart 12 G5
Mount Talbot/*Mun Talbóid* 33 A1
Mount Temple/*An Grianan*
Co Westmeath/*An Iarmhí* 33 D2
Mount Temple Co Sligo 15 D1
Mount Uniacke/*Cúil Ó gCorra* 61 B3
Mountallen 16 G5
Mountbolus/*Cnocán Bhólais* 34 E5
Mountcatherine 60 H3
Mountcharles/*Moin Searlas* 8 F4
Mountcollins/*Cnoc Uí Choileáin* 49 B5
Mountfield/*Achadh Ard* 10 E4
Mountjoy/*Muinseo* 9 D4
Mountmellick/*Mointeach Mílic* 44 G1
Mountnorris/*Achadh na Cranncha* 19 A3
Mountrath/*Maighean Rátha* 44 F2
Mountshannon/*Baile Uí Bheoláin* 42 H3
Moveen 48 G1
Moville/*Bun an Phobail* 3 D3
Moy Co Galway 41 D1
Moy/*An Maigh*
Co Tyrone/*Tír Eoghain* 18 H1
Moyard/*Maigh Ard* 29 C1
Moyarget 4 H3
Moyasta/*Maigh Sheasta* 48 H1
Moycarky 51 D1
Moycullen/*Maigh Cuilinn* 31 C3
Moydow/*Maigh Dumha* 25 D5
Moygashel/*Maigh gCaisil* 10 H5
Moyglass/*Maigh Ghlas* 51 D2
Moygawnagh 14 G4
Moyle 45 B4
Moylisha 45 D5
Moylough or Newtown Bellew/*Maigh Locha*
Co Galway/*Gaillimh* 32 G2
Moylough Co Sligo 24 F1
Moymore 42 E4
Moynalty/*Maigh nEalth* 27 B3
Moynalvy 35 C2
Moyne Co Wicklow 46 E3
Moyne Co Longford 26 E2
Moyne/*An Mhaighean*
Co Roscommon/*Ros Comáin* 24 G3
Moyne Co Tipperary 43 D5
Moyrahan 13 C3
Moyreen 49 B2
Moyrus 29 D3
Moys 3 D5
Moyvally/*Maigh Bhealaigh* 35 B2
Moyvane (Newtown Sandes)/
Maigh Mheain 49 A3

Moyvore/*Maigh Mhórdha* 34 E1
Moyvoughly/*Maigh Bhachla* 33 D2
Mountmelleray 61 C1
Muckamore/*Maigh Chomair* 11 C3
Mucklon 35 B3
Muckross 58 H3
Muckrush 31 C3
Muff/*Magh* 3 B4
Muff Glen/*Glas-Staill* 3 C5
Muinganear 49 A5
Muingaphuca 58 F2
Muingwee 49 A4
Muingydowda 57 C4
Mulhuddart/*Mullach Eadrad* 36 E3
Mullafarry 14 G4
Mullagh/*An Mullach*
Co Cavan/*An Cabhán* 27 A3
Mullagh/*Mullach* Co Clare/*An Clár* 40 F4
Mullagh Co Galway 32 H5
Mullagh Co Mayo 22 E4
Mullagh Co Meath 35 D2
Mullaghbane 19 A5
Mullaghboy 12 F1
Mullaghglass 19 B3
Mullaghmacormick 25 C3
Mullaghmore/*An Mullach Mór* 16 E1
Mullaghroe 24 G1
Mullan Head 4 G5
Mullan Co Londonderry 4 F4
Mullan/*An Muileann*
Co Monaghan/*Muineachán* 18 F2
Mullany's Cross 15 B5
Mullen 24 G3
Mullenaboree 60 G2
Mullennaglogh 52 F3
Mullennakill 53 A3
Mullinacuff/*Muileann Mhic Dhuibh* 45 D4
Mullinahone/*Muileann na hUamhan* 52 F2
Mullinavat/*Muileann an Bhata* 52 H4
Mullingar/*An Muileann gCearr* 34 F1
Multyfarnham/*Muilte Farannáin* 26 G5
Mungret/*Mungairit* 50 F1
Murher 49 A3
Murntown/*Baile Mhúráin* 54 E5
Murreagh/*An Mhulríoch* 57 B1
Murrisk/*Muraisc* 22 F3
Murroogh 40 G1
Mweennalaa 48 H5
Myross 67 C3
Myshall/*Miseal* 45 C5

N

Naas/*An Nás* 35 C4
Nad 60 E2
Nahana 34 H5
Naran 8 E2
Narraghmore/*An Fhorrach Mhór* 45 B1
Naul/*An Aill* 28 F5
Navan/*An Uaimh* 27 C5
Neale/*An Éill* 30 H1
Nealstown 44 E2
Nedanone 58 E5
Nenagh/*An tAonach* 43 A4
New Birmingham/*Gleann an Ghuail* 52 E1
New Buildings/*An Baile Nua* 3 B5
New Chapel Cross 57 D5
New Inn/*An Dromainn*
Co Cavan/*An Cabhán* 26 H2

New Inn/*An Cnoc Breac*
Co Galway/*Gaillimh* 32 G4
New Inn Co Laois 44 H1
New Kildimo 50 E1
New Ross/*Ros Mhic Thriúin* 53 B4
New Twopothouse Village/
Tigh Nua an Dá Phota 60 F1
Newbawn/*An Bábhún Nua* 53 C4
Newbliss/*Cúil Darach* 18 E4
Newbridge/*An Droichead Nua*
Co Galway/*Gaillimh* 32 H1
Newbridge Co Limerick 49 D2
Newcastle/*An Caisleán Nua*
Co Down/*An Dún* 20 E3
Newcastle/*An Caisleán Nua*
Baile Átha Cliath/Co Dublin 36 E4
Newcastle Co Galway 32 F3
Newcastle Co Tipperary 51 D5
Newcastle/*An Caisleán Nua* Co Wicklow 46 G1
Newcastle West/*An Caisleán Nua* 49 C3
Newcestown 67 D1
Newchapel 51 D4
Newferry 11 A2
Newinn/*Loch Ceann* 51 C3
Newmarket/*Áth Trasna*
Co Cork/*Corcaigh* 59 D1
Newmarket Co Kilkenny 52 H3
Newmarket on Fergus/*Cora Chaitlín* 41 D5
Newmills Co Cork 67 D3
Newmills/*An Muileann Úr*
Co Donegal/*Dún na nGall* 9 A1
Newmills/*An Muileann Nua*
Co Tyrone/*Tír Eoghain* 10 H5
Newport/*Baile Uí Fhiacháin*
Co Mayo/*Maigh Eo* 22 F2
Newport/*An Port Nua*
Co Tipperary/*Tiobraid Árann* 42 H5
Newry/*An tlúr* 19 B4
Newtown Co Galway 32 G4
Newtown Co Kildare 35 C3
Newtown Co Kilkenny 52 F1
Newtown Co Laois 45 A4
Newtown Co Limerick 50 G3
Newtown Co Mayo 22 H3
Newtown Co Meath 27 D3
Newtown Co Offaly 33 B5
Newtown Co Roscommon 33 A3
Newtown Co Roscommon 24 H4
Newtown Co Tipperary 51 A3
Newtown Co Tipperary 43 A3
Newtown Co Tipperary 43 D3
Newtown Co Waterford 62 E2
Newtown Co Waterford 62 G1
Newtown Co Waterford 61 D3
Newtown Co Wexford 64 E3
Newtown Co Wexford 63 D4
Newtown Cashel/*Baile Nua an Chaisil* 33 C1
Newtown Cloghans/*An Baile Ur* 14 H5
Newtown Cunningham
/*An Baile Nua Chuinneagain* 3 A5
Newtown Forbes/*An Lois Breac* 25 C4
Newtown Gore/*An Dúcharraig* 17 B5
Newtown-Crommelin/
Baile Nua Chromlain 5 D5
Newtownabbey/*Baile na Mainstreach* 12 E3
Newtownadam 51 C4
Newtownards/*Baile Nua na hArda* 12 G4
Newtownbutler/*An Baile Nua* 17 C4

Newtownhamilton/*Baile Úr* 19 A4
Newtownlow 34 F3
Newtownlynch 31 D5
Newtown Mt. Kennedy/
Baile an Chinnéidigh 46 G1
Newtownshandrum/
Baile Nua Sheandroma 50 E4
Newtownstewart/*An Baile Nua* 9 D3
Nicholstown 53 A5
Ninemilehouse/*Tigh na Naoi Míle* 52 F3
Nobber/*An Obair* 27 C3
Nohaval/*Nuach a Bháil* 68 H1
North Ring 68 E2
Northlands/*An Táchairt Thuaidh* 27 B1
Noughaval Co Clare 41 D4
Nurney/*An Urnaí*
Co Carlow/*Ceatharlach* 45 B5
Nurney Co Kildare 45 B1
Nutts Corner/*Coirnéal Nutt* 11 C4

O

Oaghley 48 H3
Oatfield 42 F5
O'Briens Bridge/*Droichead Uí Bhriain* 42 G5
O'Callaghansmills 42 F4
Oghill 33 A4
Ogonnelloe/*Tuath Ó gConáile* 42 G3
Oilgate/*Maolán na nGabhar* 54 E3
Old Head 68 G2
Old Kilcullen 45 C1
Old Kildimo 50 E1
Old Ross 53 B4
Old Town Co Laois 44 G3
Old Town/*An Seanbhaile*
Co Roscommon/*Ros Comáin* 33 B4
Old Town Co Wexford 53 C2
Oldcastle/*An Seanchaisleán* 26 H3
Oldgrange 51 D5
Oldleagh 45 A3
Oldleighlin/*Seanleithghlinn* 45 A5
Oldtown Co Dublin 36 F1
Oldtown Co Roscommon 33 C3
Omagh/*An Ómaigh* 9 D4
Omeath/*Ó Méith* 19 C5
Onaght/*Eoghanacht* 30 E5
Oola/*Úlla* 51 A2
Oranmore/*Órán Mór* 31 D4
Oristown 27 B4
Orritor/*Na Coracha Beaga* 10 G4
Oughtdarra 40 F1
Oughter 34 E4
Oughterard/*Uachtar Ard* 30 H2
Oulart/*An tAbhallort* 54 E2
Outeragh 51 C4
Ovens/*Na hUamhanna* 60 F5
Owenbeg/*An Abhainn Bheag* 15 A3
Owenbristy 32 E5
Owning/*Ónainn* 52 G4

P

Palace/*An Phailís* 53 B3
Palatine 45 B4
Palatine Street 50 H2
Pallas Co Galway 32 H3
Pallas Co Laois 44 G2
Pallas Green/*An tSeanphailís* 50 H2
Pallas Green (New)/*Pailís Ghréine* 50 H2
Pallasboy 34 G3

Pallaskenry/*Pailís Chaonraí* 50 E1
Pallis 46 F5
Palmerstown/*Baile Phámar* 36 E3
Park Co Londonderry 10 E1
Park Co Wexford 64 E3
Park Co Mayo 23 C2
Parkacunna 60 H1
Parkbane 68 E1
Parkbridge 45 D5
Parkgate 11 D3
Parkmore/*An Phairc Mhór* 31 D5
Parknasilla 58 E5
Parteen 42 F5
Partry/*Partraí* 22 H4
Passage 32 H1
Passage East/*An Pasáiste* 63 B3
Passage West/*An Pasáiste* 60 H5
Patrickswell/*Tobar Phádraig* 50 F2
Paulstown/*Baile Phóil* 53 A1
Peak 32 G4
Peterswell/*Tobar Pheadair* 42 F1
Pettigo/*Paiteagó* 9 A5
Pharis/*Fáras* 4 H4
Piercetown Co Cork 60 G4
Piercetown Co Wexford 54 E5
Pike 43 B1
Pike Corner 35 C1
Pike of Rush Hall/*An Paidhc* 44 E3
Piltown/*Baile an Phoill* 52 G4
Pluck 2 H5
Plumbridge/*Droichead an Phlum* 9 D2
Pollagh Co Galway 31 D5
Pollagh/*Pollach*
Co Offaly/*Uíbh Fhailí* 33 D4
Pollatlugga 32 H4
Pollatomish/*Poll an Tómais* 13 D3
Pollboy 33 A4
Pollshask 24 G5
Pomeroy/*Pomeroy* 10 F4
Pontoon 23 C1
Port 28 F3
Port Laoise 44 G2
Portacloy 13 D2
Portadown/*Port an Dúnáin* 19 A1
Portaferry/*Port an Pheire* 20 H1
Portaleen 3 C1
Portarlington/*Cúil an tSúdaire* 34 H5
Portavogie/*Port an Bhogaigh* 20 H1
Portballintrae/*Port Bhaile an Trá* 4 G2
Portglenone/*Port Chluain Eoghain* 11 A1
Portland 43 A1
Portlaw/*Port Lách* 52 G5
Portmagee/*An Caladh* 57 B4
Portmarnock/*Port Mearnóg* 36 G2
Portmuck 12 F1
Portnablahy/*Port na Bláiche* 2 F3
Portnashangan 26 G5
Portnoo/*Port Nua* 7 D2
Portraine/*Port Reachrainn* 36 G1
Portroe/*An Port Rua* 42 H3
Portrush/*Port Rois* 4 F3
Portsalon/*Port an tSalainn* 2 H2
Portstewart/*Port Stíobhaird* 4 F3
Portumna/*Port Omna* 43 A1
Pottore 16 H5
Porturlin 13 D2
Poulanargid 59 D5
Poulnamucky 51 C4

Power's Cross/*Crois an Phaoraigh* 42 H1
Poyntz Pass/*Pas an Phointe* 19 B3
Priest Town 61 D1
Priesthaggard 53 B5
Prosperous/*An Chorrchoill* 35 C4
Puckaun/*Pocán* 43 A3

Q

Quarrytown 11 C1
Querrin/*An Cuibhreann* 48 H1
Quigley's Point/*Rinn Uí Choigligh* 3 C3
Quilty/*Coillte* 40 F4
Quin/*Cuinche* 42 E4

R

Radestown 44 H5
Raffrey/*Rafraidh* 20 F1
Raghly 15 C2
Rahaghy 26 H4
Rahara 33 A1
Rahan/*Raithean* 34 E4
Raharney/*Ráth Fhearna* 35 A1
Raheen Co Carlow 45 D4
Raheen Co Kerry 59 A2
Raheen Co Tipperary 51 C4
Raheen Co Westmeath 34 E2
Raheen/*An Ráithin*
Co Wexford/*Loch Garman* 53 C4
Raheenagh 49 C4
Raheenlusk 54 F2
Raholp 20 G2
Rake Street 14 F5
Ramsgrange/*An Ghráinseach* 53 B5
Ranamackan 32 H5
Randalstown/*Baile Raghnaill* 11 B2
Rapemills 43 C1
Raphoe/*Ráth Bhoth* 9 B1
Rascalstreet 59 C1
Rasharkin/*Ros Earcáin* 4 G5
Rashedoge 2 G5
Rath 43 D1
Rathcormack/*Ráth Chormaic* 61 A2
Rathangan/*Ráth Iomgháin* 35 A5
Rathanny 48 H5
Rathaspick 26 F5
Rathbrit 51 D3
Rathcabban/*Ráth Cabáin* 43 B1
Rathcarran/*Rath Chairn* 27 B5
Rathcoffey 35 C3
Rathconor 25 A4
Rathconrath/*Ráth Conarta* 34 F1
Rathcool Co Cork 59 D2
Rathcoole/*Rath Cúil*
Co Dublin/*Baile Átha Cliath* 36 E4
Rathcore/*Ráth Cuair* 35 B2
Rathcormack 15 D2
Rathcrony 40 H4
Rathdangan/*Ráth Daingin* 45 D3
Rathdowney/*Ráth Domhnaigh* 44 E4
Rathdrum/*Ráth Droma* 46 F3
Rathduff 26 E5
Ratheenroe 66 H3
Rathernan 35 B4
Rathfeigh/*Ráth Faiche* 28 E5
Rathfilode 60 H3
Rathfriland/*Ráth Fraoileann* 19 D3
Rathfylane 53 C3
Rathgarry 44 H4

Rathgormuck/Ráth Ó gCormaic 52 F5
Rathgranagher 23 C5
Rathkea 51 A3
Rathkeale/Ráth Caola 49 D2
Rathkeevin 51 D4
Rathkenny/Ráth Cheannaigh 27 C4
Rathkeva 24 H3
Rathkineely 24 H3
Rathlackan 14 G3
Rathlee/Ráth Lao 15 A3
Rathlyon 45 C4
Rathmaiden 62 F1
Rathmelton/Ráth Mealtain 2 H4
Rathmore/An Ráth Mhór
Co Kerry/Ciarraí 59 B2
Rathmore/An Ráth Mhór
Co Kildare/Cill Dara 35 D5
Rathmore Co Meath 27 B5
Rathmoylan Co Waterford 63 B4
Rathmoylan Co Meath 35 B2
Rathmullan/Ráth Maoláin 2 H4
Rathnamagh 14 G4
Rathnew/Ráth Naoi 46 G2
Rathnure/Ráth an Iúir 53 C3
Rathoma 14 G4
Rathorgan 61 A3
Rathowen/Ráth Eoghainn 26 F5
Rathroeen 14 H4
Rathruane 66 H3
Rathtoe 45 C4
Rathvilly/Ráth Bhile 45 C3
Rathwire 34 H1
Ratoath/Ráth Tó 36 E1
Ratooragh 66 G3
Ravensdale/Gleann na bhFiach 19 B5
Ravernet/Ráth Bhearnait 11 D5
Ray/An Ráith 2 H4
Readypenny 28 E2
Reaghstown 27 D2
Reananerree 59 B4
Reanaclogheen/Ré na gCloichín 62 E3
Reanascreena/Rae na Scríne 67 C2
Rear Cross/Crois na Rae 51 A1
Recess/Sraith Salach 30 E2
Reclain 10 F5
Redcastle 3 C3
Redcross/Chrois Dhearg 46 G3
Redgate 54 E3
Redhills/An Cnoc Rua 17 D5
Redwood 43 B1
Renvyle 21 C5
Rerrin/Raerainn 66 F2
Revallagh 4 G3
Rhode/Ród 34 H3
Richill/Log an Choire 19 A2
Riesk 61 A3
Ring/An Rinn 64 G3
Ringaskiddy/Rinn an Scidígh 60 H5
Ringsend/Droichead an Carraige 4 E4
Ringstown 44 F2
Ringville/An Rinn 62 E3
Rinnafarset 1 C4
Rinneen Co Clare 40 F3
Rinneen Co Cork 67 B3
Rinville 31 D4
Riverchapel 54 F1
Riverstick/Áth an Mhaide 68 G1
Riverstown Co Cork 60 H4

Riverstown/Baile Idir dhá Abhainn
Co Sligo/Sligeach 16 E4
Riverstown/Baile Uí Lachnáin
Co Tipperary/Tiobraid Árann 43 C1
Robertstown/Baile Riobaird 35 B4
Robinstown/Baile Roibín
Co Meath/An Mhí 27 C5
Robinstown Co Wexford 53 D5
Rochestown Co Kilkenny 52 H4
Rochestown Co Kilkenny 53 A5
Rochestown Co Tipperary 51 C5
Rochfortbridge/
Droichead Chaisléan Loiste 34 G2
Rockchapel/Séipéal na Carraige 49 C5
Rockcorry/Buíochar 18 F5
Rockhill 50 F3
Rockmills 60 H1
Rockstown 46 G3
Rodeen 25 B2
Roevehagh 32 E5
Rooaun 33 B5
Roonah Quay 21 D3
Roosky Co Mayo 24 F1
Roosky/Rúscaigh
Co Roscommon/Ros Comáin 25 C3
Rooty Cross 33 B3
Rosapenna 2 G3
Rosbercon 53 A4
Roscat 45 C4
Roscommon/Ros Comáin 25 A5
Roscrea/Ros Cré 43 D2
Rosegreen/Faiche Ró 51 D3
Rosemount 34 E2
Rosenallis/Ros Fhionnghlaise 44 F1
Rosmuck/Ros Muc 30 F3
Rosmult 51 C1
Rosnakill/Ros na Cille 2 H3
Rossbeg/Ros Beag 7 D2
Ross Behy 58 E2
Ross Carbery/Ros Ó gCairbre 67 C3
Ross Port/Ross Dumhach 13 D3
Ross West 22 H2
Ross/An Ros Co Meath/An Mhí 26 G3
Rossadrehid/Ross an Droichead 51 B4
Rossanean 58 H1
Rossaveel/Rós an Mhíl 30 F4
Rossbrin 66 H3
Rosscahill/Ros Cathail 30 H3
Rosses Point/An Ros 15 D2
Rossinver/Ros Inbhir 16 G2
Rosslare/Ros Láir 54 E5
Rosslare Harbour/Calafort Ros Láir 54 F5
Rosslea/Ros Liath 18 E3
Rossmackowen 66 F2
Rossmore Co Tipperary 51 C1
Rossmore Co Cork 67 D2
Rossmore/An Ros Mór
Co Cork/Corcaigh 59 C5
Rossmore Co Laois 45 A4
Rossmore Co Monaghan 18 F3
Rossnowlagh/Ros Neamhlach 8 F5
Rostellan/Ros Tialláin 61 A5
Rostrevor/Ros Treabhair 19 C5
Rosturk 22 E2
Roughfort 11 D3
Roundfort 23 C5
Roundstone/Cloch na Rón 29 D2
Roundwood/An Tóchar 46 F1

Rousky 10 E3
Roxhill 11 B2
Ruan/An Ruán 41 D3
Rubane/Rú Bán 12 H5
Rush/An Ros 36 G1
Rusheen 59 D4
Rusheeny 30 G2
Ryehill 32 F3
Rylane 60 E3

S

Saggart 36 E4
Saint Johnstown/Baile Suingean 9 C1
Saint Mullins 53 B3
Saintfield/Tamhnaigh Naomh 20 F1
Saleen 61 A5
Sallins/Na Solláin 35 C4
Sallybrook 60 H4
Sallypark 43 B4
Salthill/Bóthar na Trá 31 C4
Saltmills/Muillean an tSáile 63 C3
Sandholes/Clais an Ghainimh 10 G4
Sandyford/Áth an Ghainimh 36 F4
Santry/Seantrabh 36 F2
Saul 20 G2
Scardaun Co Mayo 23 D5
Scradaun Co Roscommon 33 A1
Scarriff/An Scairbh 42 G3
Scartaglin/Scairteach an Ghlinne 59 A1
Scarva/Scarbhach 19 B2
Scotch Corner 18 G4
Scotch Street/Sráid na hAlbanach 19 A1
Scotshouse/Teach an Scotaigh 17 D5
Scotstown/Baile an Scotaigh 18 E3
Scrahan 48 F5
Scrahanfadda 59 A2
Scramoge/Scramóg 25 B4
Scrarour 60 H1
Screen/An Scrín 54 E3
Screggan/An Screagán 34 E4
Scriggan 3 D5
Scurlockstown 27 B4
Seaforde/Baile Forda 20 E2
Seapatrick 19 C2
Seskin 52 E4
Seskinore/Seisceann Odher 9 D5
Shanacrane 67 B1
Shanagarry/An Seangharraí 61 B5
Shanaglish 42 E2
Shanagolden/Seanghualainn 49 C2
Shanahoe/Seanchua 44 F3
Shanballard 32 G3
Shanbally/An Seanbhaile
Co Cork/Corcaigh 60 H5
Shanbally Co Galway 32 G1
Shanballyedmond 51 A1
Shanballymore/An Seanbhaile Mór 60 G1
Shangarry 32 H5
Shankill/Seanchill 36 G4
Shanlaragh/Seanlárach 67 C1
Shannakea/Seanachae 49 C1
Shannon/Sionainn 42 E5
Shannon Harbour/
Caladh na Sionainne 33 C5
Shannonbridge/
Droichead na Sionainne 33 B4
Shanraghy 45 A3
Shanrahan 51 B5

Shanrath 49 D4
Shantonagh/*Seantonnach* 18 G5
Shanavogh 40 G4
Sharavogue/*Searbhóg* 43 C2
Shercock/*Searcóg* 27 B1
Sheskin 14 E4
Shevry 43 B5
Shillelagh/*Síol Ealaigh* 45 D5
Shinrone/*Suí an Róin* 43 C2
Shrigley 20 S1
Shrone 48 H2
Shronell 51 A3
Shronowen/*Srón Abhann* 48 H2
Shrule/*Sruthair* 31 C1
Sillahertane 67 B1
Silverbridge/*Béal Átha an Airgid* 19 A5
Silver Stream 18 F3
Silvermines/*Béal Átha Gabhann* 43 A4
Sion Mills/*Muileann an tSiáin* 9 C2
Six Crosses 48 H3
Six Road Ends 12 G4
Sixmilebridge
/*Droichead Abhann Ó gCearnaigh* 42 E5
Sixmilecross/*Na Coracha Móra* 10 E5
Skahanagh 67 A1
Skahanagh North 60 H3
Skahanagh South 60 H3
Skeagh Co Cork 67 A3
Skeagh Co Westmeath 34 E1
Skehanagh Co Galway 32 F2
Skehanagh Co Galway 42 E1
Skeehen 51 A5
Skerries/*Na Sceirí* 28 G5
Skibbereen/*An Sciobairín* 67 A3
Skreen Co Meath 27 D5
Skreen/*An Scrín* Co Sligo/*Sligeach* 15 C3
Skull/*An Scoil* 66 H3
Slade 63 C4
Slane/*Baile Shláine* 27 D4
Slieveroe/*Sliabh Rua* 53 A5
Sligo/*Sligeach* 15 D3
Smarmore 27 D3
Smerwick 57 B1
Smithborough/*Na Mullaí* 18 E3
Smithstown 44 H4
Sneem/*An tSnaidhm* 58 E5
Sooey 16 E4
Spa/*An Spá* 48 F5
Spancelhill 41 D3
Spanish Point Co Clare 40 F4
Spanish Point Co Cork 66 G4
Sperrin 10 F2
Spiddle/*An Spidéal* 30 H4
Spink 44 H3
Spittaltown 34 E3
Spring Town 3 B5
Sraghmore 46 F1
Srah 13 C4
Srahanboy 44 E2
Sraheens 21 D2
Sraheens/*Na Sraithíní* 23 C2
Srahmore/*An Srath Mór* 13 D4
Srah/*An tSraith* 22 H4
Sruh 61 C1
St Margaret's 36 F2
Stabannan 28 E2
Stackallan/*Stigh Colláin* 27 C4
Stacummer 3 A2

Staffordstown/*Baile Stafard* 11 B3
Stamullin 28 F5
Staplestown 35 C3
Stepaside 36 F4
Stewartstown/*An Chraobh* 10 H4
Stillorgan 36 G4
Stone Bridge 18 E4
Stonepark 50 G2
Stonyford Co Antrim 11 D4
Stonyford/*Áth Stúin*
Co Kilkenny/*Cill Chainnigh* 52 H2
Stormont 12 E4
Strabane/*An Strath Bán* 9 C2
Stradbally/*An tSráidbhaile*
Co Waterford/*Port Láirge* 62 F2
Stradbally Co Kerry 47 D5
Stradbally/*An tSráidbhaile*
Co Laois/*Laois* 44 H2
Strade 23 C2
Stradone/*Sraith an Domhain* 26 H1
Straffan/*Teach Srafáin* 35 D4
Strahart/*Sraith Airt* 53 D1
Straid 11 B2
Straid/*An tSraid* 12 E2
Strand/*An Trá* 49 C4
Strandhill/*An Leathros* 15 D3
Strangford/*Baile Loch Cuan* 20 G2
Stranocum/*Sraith Nócam* 4 H3
Stranorlar/*Srath an Urláir* 9 A2
Stratford/*Áth na Sráide* 45 C2
Straw 10 G2
Streamstown Co Galway 29 C1
Streamstown/*Baile an tSruthain*
Co Westmeath/*An Iarmhí* 34 E2
Street/*An tSráid* 26 F4
Strokestown/*Béal na mBuillí* 25 B3
Stroove 3 D2
Stuake 60 E3
Summer Cove 68 G1
Summerhill/*Cnoc an Linsigh* 35 C2
Suncroft/*Crochta na Gréine* 45 B1
Swan 44 H3
Swanlinbar/*An Muilcann Iarainn* 17 A4
Swatragh/*An Suaitreach* 10 H1
Swinford/*Béal Átha na Muice* 23 D1
Swords/*Sord* 36 F2

T

Taghmaconnell 33 A3
Taghmon/*Teach Munna* 53 D5
Taghshinny 34 E1
Tagoat/*Teach Gót* 54 F5
Tahilla 58 F5
Tallaght/*Tamhlacht* 36 E4
Tallanstown/*Baile an Tallúnaigh* 27 D2
Tallow/*Tulach an Iarainn* 61 B2
Tallowbridge 61 C2
Tamlaght/*Tamhlacht*
Co Fermanagh/*Fear Manach* 17 B2
Tamlaght O'Crilly 11 A1
Tamnamore/*An Tamhnach Mhór* 10 H5
Tandragee/*Tóin re Gaoith* 19 B2
Tang/*An Teanga* 33 D1
Tankardstown 50 F4
Tara Co Meath 35 D1
Tara Co Offaly 34 E3
Tarbert/*Tairbeart* 49 A2
Tarmon/*An Tearmann* 49 A1

Tassagh/*An Tasach* 18 H3
Taur 59 C1
Tawnyinah 24 E2
Tawnylea 16 F4
Tawny/*An Tamhnaigh* 2 G3
Tedagh 66 H2
Tedavnet/*Tigh Damhnata* 18 F3
Teelin 7 C4
Teemore 17 B4
Teer 47 D5
Teeravane 57 B1
Teerelton/*Tír Eiltín* 59 D5
Teermaclane/*Tír Mhic Calláin* 41 D4
Teevurcher/*Taobh Urchair* 27 B2
Templeboy/*Teampall Baoith* 15 B3
Templecrum 52 G4
Templederry/*Teampall Doire* 43 B5
Templeetney 52 E4
Templemartin/*Teampall Mártan* 60 E5
Templemore/*An Teampall Mór* 43 C4
Templeoran 34 G3
Templepark 43 C3
Templepatrick/*Teampall Phádraig* 11 D3
Templeshanbo/*Teampall Seanbhoth* 53 C2
Templetouhy/*Teampall Tuaithe* 43 D4
Templetown 63 C3
Templeusque 60 H4
Tempo/*An tIompú Deiseal* 17 C2
Termon 2 G4
Termonbarry 25 C4
Termonfeckin/*Tearmann Feichin* 28 F3
Terryglass/*Tír Dhá Ghlas* 43 A1
Tevrin 34 H1
The Bush Co Tyrone 10 H5
The Bush Co Louth 28 F1
The Butts 45 A5
The Cross/*An Chrois* 3 B5
The Curragh/*An Currach* 35 B5
The Diamond/*An Diamant*
Co Antrim/*Aontrim* 11 C4
The Diamond Co Tyrone 11 A4
The Downs/*Na Dúnta* 34 H1
The Drones 4 H4
The Dry Arch 4 H3
The Five Roads 36 F1
The Harrow 54 E2
The Heath 44 H1
The Leap 53 C4
The Loup/*An Lúb* 11 A3
The Pigeons/*Na Colúir* 33 D1
The Pike Co Tipperary 43 B2
The Pike Co Waterford 62 F2
The Rock/*An Charraig* 10 G4
The Rosses/*Na Rosa* 1 C5
The Rower/*An Robhar* 53 B3
The Sheddings 11 D1
The Spa/*An Spá* 20 E2
The Sweep 52 G4
The Temple/*An Teampall* 12 E5
The Vee 51 C5
Thomastown/*Baile Mhic Andáin*
Co Kilkenny/*Cill Chainnigh* 52 H2
Thomastown Co Limerick 50 H4
Thomastown Co Meath 27 B3
Thomastown Co Tipperary 51 B3
Thornton 45 C1
Threecastles 44 G5
Three Mile House 18 F4

Three Wells	46	F3
Thurles/*Durlas*	51	D1
Tibohine/*Tigh Baoithán*	24	G2
Tiduff	48	E3
Tikincor	52	E4
Timahoe Co Kildare	35	B3
Timahoe/*Tigh Mochua* Co Laois/*Laois*	44	H2
Timoleague/*Tigh Molaige*	68	E2
Timolin	45	B2
Tinahely/*Tigh na hÉille*	46	E4
Tinmuck	34	E3
Tinnakilla	53	D4
Tipperary/*Tiobraid Árann*	51	A3
Tirkane/*Tír Chiana*	10	H1
Tirnaneill	18	F3
Tirneevin	42	E1
Toames	59	D5
Tober Co Cavan	16	G4
Tober Co Offaly	34	E3
Toberbeg	45	C2
Tobercurry/*Tobar an Choire*	15	C5
Toberelatan	32	F5
Tobermore/*An Tobar Mór*	10	H2
Tobernadarry	31	C1
Toberscanavan	15	D4
Toem/*Tuaim*	51	A2
Togher Co Cork	67	C1
Togher Co Louth	28	F3
Togher Co Meath	35	B2
Togher Co Offaly	34	H3
Togherbane	48	F4
Tomhaggard/*Teach Moshagard*	64	F3
Tonabrocky	31	C4
Tonlegee	22	G4
Tonyduff/*An Tonnaigh Dhubh*	27	A1
Toom/*Tuaim*	67	C1
Toomaghera	40	G2
Toomard/*Tuaim Ard*	32	G1
Toombeola	29	D2
Toome/*Droichead Thuama*	11	A3
Toomyvara/*Tuaim Uí Mheára*	43	B4
Tonregee	21	D1
Toor/*An Tuar*	43	A5
Tooraneena	61	D1
Tooraree	49	B2
Tooreen/*Tuairín*	60	G2
Tooreencahill	59	B1
Tooreendermot	49	C5
Toorgarriff	60	G2
Toorlestraun	15	B5
Toormakeady/*Tuar Mhic Éadaigh*	22	G5
Toormore/*An Tuar Mór*	66	G3
Toornafulla	49	C4
Torque	34	G3
Towergare	62	H1
Trabolgan	61	A5
Tracton	68	H1
Trafrask	66	G1
Tralee/*Trá Lí*	48	G5
Tramore/*Trá Mór*	62	H1
Trasternagh	32	F2
Trawlebane	67	A2
Trean	22	G5
Treantagh/*Na Treantachta*	2	F5
Trien/*An Trian*	24	G4
Trillick/*Trileac*	17	C1
Trim/*Baile Átha Troim*	35	C1
Trust	32	H3
Tuam/*Tuaim*	32	E1
Tuamgraney/*Tuaim Gréine*	42	G3
Tubber/*An Tobar*	42	E2
Tubbrid Co Kilkenny	44	F5
Tubbrid Co Tipperary	51	C5
Tulla/*An Tulach* Co Clare/*An Clár*	42	E3
Tulla Co Clare	41	D1
Tullagh	59	B5
Tullaghaboy	40	G4
Tullaghan/*An Tulachán*	16	E1
Tullagher/*Tulachar*	53	A3
Tullaghought	52	G4
Tullaherin	52	H2
Tullamore Co Kerry	48	H3
Tullamore/*Tulach Mhór* Co Offaly/*Uíbh Fhailí*	34	F4
Tullaree	48	E5
Tullaroan/*Tulach Ruáin*	52	F1
Tullassa	40	H4
Tullig Co Clare	48	F1
Tullig Co Kerry	48	H4
Tullig Co Kerry	58	F2
Tullow/*An Tulch*	45	C4
Tullyallen/*Tulaigh Álainn*	28	E4
Tullycanna	53	D5
Tullycoly	16	F4
Tully Cross	21	D5
Tullyhogue/*Tulaigh Óg*	10	H4
Tullylease	49	D5
Tullyroar Corner	18	H1
Tullyvin/*Tulaigh Bhinn*	18	E5
Tulrohaun/*Tulach Shrutháin*	24	E4
Tulsk/*Tuilsce*	25	A3
Tuosist/*Tuath Ó Siosta*	58	F5
Turin	34	H1
Turlough Co Clare	40	H1
Turlough/*Turlach* Co Mayo/*Maigh Eo*	23	C2
Turloughmore/*An Turlach Mór*	32	E3
Turnaspidogy	59	B5
Turnpike Cross	60	G1
Turreen	25	C5
Twomileborris/*Buiríos Léith*	51	D1
Two Mile House	35	C5
Tylas	35	D1
Tynagh/*Tíne*	32	H5
Tynan/*Tuíneán*	18	G2
Tyrella	20	F3
Tyrrellspass/*Belach an Tirialaigh*	34	F3

U

Unionhall/*Bréantrá*	67	B3
Upperchurch/*An Teampall Uachtarach*	43	B5
Upperlands/*Áth an Phortáin*	10	H1
Upton/*Garraí Thancaird*	68	F1
Urhin	66	E2
Urlaur/*Urlár*	24	F2
Urlingford/*Áth na nUrlainn*	44	E5

V

Vallymount/*An Chrois*	45	D1
Ventry/*Ceann Trá*	57	B1
Vicarstown/*Baile an Bhoicáire*	45	A1
Victoria Bridge/*Droichead Victoria*	9	C2
Villierstown/*An Baile Nua*	61	D2
Virginia/*Achadh an Iúir*	27	A3

W

Walterstown	27	D5
Ward/*An Barda*	36	F2
Waringsford	19	D2
Waringstown/*Baile an Bhairínigh*	19	C1
Warrenpoint/*An Pointe*	19	C5
Watch House	35	D5
Watch House Village	45	D5
Waterfall/*Tobar an Iarla*	60	G5
Waterford/*Port Láirge*	52	H5
Watergrasshill/*Cnocán na Biolraí*	60	H3
Waterloo	60	F4
Waterville/*An Coireán*	57	C5
Welchtown	8	H2
Wellingtonbridge/*Droichead Eoin*	53	C5
Wells	54	F2
Westport/*Cathair na Mart*	22	G3
Westport Quay	22	F3
Westtown	62	H2
West Town/*Baile Thiar*	1	D2
Wexford/*Loch Garman*	54	E4
Wheelam	35	B5
White Gate	58	F1
White's Cross/*Crois an Fhaoitigh*	60	G4
Whiteabbey/*An Mhainistir Fhionn*	12	E3
Whitechurch/*An Teampall Geal* Co Cork/*Corcaigh*	60	G3
Whitechurch Co Wexford	53	A5
Whitecross/*Corr Leacht*	19	A3
Whitegate/*An Geata Bán* Co Clare/*An Clár*	42	H3
Whitegate/*An Geata Bán* Co Cork/*Corcaigh*	61	A5
Whitehall/*An Baile Nua* Co Roscommon/*Ros Comáin*	25	C4
Whitehall Co Westmeath	26	G5
Whitehead/*An Cionn Bán*	12	F2
Whiterock	12	G5
Whites Town	28	G1
Whitesides Corner/*An Phrochlais*	11	B2
Wicklow/*Cill Mhantáin*	46	H2
Wilkinstown/*Baile Uilcín*	27	C4
Willbrook	40	H3
Williamstown/*Baile Liam* Co Galway/*Gaillimh*	24	F4
Williamstown/*Baile Liam* Co Westmeath/*An Iarmhí*	33	C2
Windgap/*Bearne na Gaoithe*	52	F3
Wolfhill/*Cnocán na Mactíre*	44	H3
Woodburn/*Sruth na Coille*	12	E3
Woodenbridge	46	F4
Woodford/*An Chráig*	42	H1
Woodlawn/*Móta*	32	G3
Woodstown	63	B3

Y

Yellow Furze	27	D4
Youghal/*Eochaill* Co Cork/*Corcaigh*	61	C4
Youghal Co Tipperary	42	H3